CHICKEN SOUP FOR THE LATINO SOUL

CHICKEN SOUP FOR THE LATINO SOUL

Celebrating la Comunidad Latina

Jack Canfield
Mark Victor Hansen
Susan Sánchez-Casal

Health Communications, Inc.
Deerfield Beach, Florida

www.hcibooks.com
www.chickensoup.com

We would like to acknowledge the many publishers and individuals who granted us permission to reprint the cited material. (Note: The stories that are in the public domain or that were written by Jack Canfield, Mark Victor Hansen or Susan Sánchez-Casal are not included in this listing.)

University Avenue. Reprinted by permission of Arte Publico Press and Pat Mora. © 1985 Pat Mora.

Enchiladas: Metaphor for Life! Reprinted by permission of Elizabeth Renee Fajardo. © 2003 Elizabeth Renee Fajardo.

The Healing. Reprinted by permission of Dahlma C. Llanos. © 1999 Dahlma C. Llanos.

What's Up with Dads and Pork-Chop Sandwiches? Reprinted by permission of Angela Christina Cervantes. © 2003 Angela Christina Cervantes.

(Continued on page 335)

Library of Congress Cataloging-in-Publication Data

Chicken soup for the Latino soul : celebrating la comunidad Latina / [compiled by] Jack Canfield, Mark Victor Hansen, Susan C. Sánchez.
   p. cm.
   ISBN-13: 978-0-7573-0311-1 (trade pbk.)
   ISBN-10: 0-7573-0311-0 (trade pbk.)
   1. Hispanic Americans—Social life and customs—Anecdotes.
2. Hispanic Americans—Social conditions—Anecdotes. 3. Hispanic Americans—Biography—Anecdotes. I. Canfield, Jack, 1944- II. Hansen, Mark Victor. III. Sánchez, Susan C.

E184.S75C485 2005
305.868'073—dc22

2005050201

Publisher: Health Communications, Inc.
   3201 S.W. 15th Street
   Deerfield Beach, FL 33442-8190

Cover design by Kevin Stawieray
Inside formatting by Dawn Von Strolley Grove

This book is dedicated, with
love and respect, to the
more than forty million
Latinos and Latinas of the United States.
¡Pa'lante, siempre!

Contents

3. LIFE'S LESSONS/*LECCIONES QUE DA LA VIDA*

4. LATINO IDENTITY/*LA IDENTIDAD LATINA*

5. CHALLENGES/*LOS DESAFÍOS*

6. OUR LANGUAGES/*NUESTRAS LENGUAS*

7. REAL HEROES/*HEROES VERDADEROS*

8. THE SPIRITUAL AND THE SUPERNATURAL/*LO ESPIRITUAL Y LO REAL MÁGICO*

Acknowledgments

We wish to express our deepest gratitude to the following people who helped make this book possible:

Our families, who have been chicken soup for our souls!

Jack's family, Inga, Travis, Riley, Christopher, Oran and Kyle, for all their love and support.

Mark's family, Patty, Elisabeth and Melanie, for once again sharing and lovingly supporting us in creating yet another book.

Susan's family, Craig, Ryan, Colin, Max Fernando and Jessica, *por su amor, cariño y apoyo constante.*

Our publisher, Peter Vegso, for his vision and commitment to bringing *Chicken Soup for the Soul* to the world.

Patty Aubery and Russ Kalmaski, for supporting us on this journey, with love, laughter and endless creativity.

D'ette Corona, for her enthusiasm, diligent work, constant support and guidance in helping us produce this book.

Barbara Lomonaco, for her generosity, expert story evaluation and general support.

Patty Hansen, for her thorough and competent handling of the legal and licensing aspects of the *Chicken Soup for the Soul* books. You are magnificent at the challenge!

Laurie Hartman, for being a precious guardian of the *Chicken Soup* brand.

Robert Berardi, for creating smart and creative cartoons for the book.

Kim Kirberger, for her crucial support and encouragement during the inception of *Latino Soul,* and for helping Susan get the project off the ground. Thank you for your gift of generosity.

Colin Mortensen-Sánchez, for opening the door to Susan's coauthorship of *Latino Soul,* for his steady and creative counsel, and for breathing inspiration and confidence into the project throughout the four years of its production. And for the love.

Very special thanks to Marilu Travis, for volunteering endless hours to assist us in soliciting stories and researching contact information, and for her loving and positive attitude, *y por su solidaridad y apoyo diarios.* You have blessed *Latino Soul* with your generosity, and we will be forever grateful.

Craig Kollegger, for creating and maintaining the *Latino Soul* Web site, and for countless hours of technical, logistical and loving support. And for making dinner and cleaning up the dishes while his wife worked on *Latino Soul.*

Michael Sánchez, for his diligent assistance in producing batches of stories for the book.

Michele Sánchez, for her love, exuberance and second-mothering of Susan's children throughout the four years of the book's production.

Ryan Mortensen-Sánchez and Amie Macdonald, for supporting Susan's vision for the project from the start.

Veronica Romero, Teresa Esparza, Robin Yerian, Jesse Ianniello, Lauren Edelstein, Jody Emme, Debbie Lefever, Michelle Adams, Dee Dee Romanello, Shanna Vieyra, Lisa Williams, Gina Romanello, Brittany Shaw, Dena Jacobson, Tanya Jones and Mary McKay, who support Jack's and Mark's businesses with skill and love.

Sandra Bark, for editing our final readers' manual. Thank you for your diligent work.

Special thanks to Elisabeth Rinaldi for her magnificent editing of the manuscript, and to Bret Witter, Allison Janse and Kathy Grant, the editorial staff at Health Communications, Inc., for their devotion to excellence.

Terry Burke, Lori Golden, Kelly Maragni, Tom Galvin, Sean Geary, Patricia McConnell, Ariana Daner, Kim Weiss, Paola Fernandez-Rana, the sales, marketing and PR departments at Health Communications, Inc., for doing such an incredible job supporting our books.

Tom Sand, Claude Choquette and Luc Jutras, who manage year after year to get our books translated into thirty-six languages around the world.

The art department at Health Communications, Inc., for their talent, creativity and unrelenting patience in producing book covers and inside designs that capture the essence of *Chicken Soup*: Larissa Hise Henoch, Lawna Patterson Oldfield, Andrea Perrine Brower, Anthony Clausi, Kevin Stawieray and Dawn Von Strolley Grove.

All the *Chicken Soup for the Soul* coauthors, who make it such a joy to be part of this *Chicken Soup* family.

Our expert panel of readers who helped us make the final selections and offered invaluable suggestions on how to improve the book: Marie Delgado Travis, Caroline Sánchez, Michele Capriotti, Elizabeth García, Al Carlos Hernández, Cristina Cornejo, Antonio Farias, Amie A. Macdonald, Darwin Ortiz, Heather Kirk, Irene Morales Del Valle, Jim Ridgell, Jody Feagan, John Laguna, Kathy Cano Murillo, Leticia Gómez, Aileen Colón, Liz Fortini, Lupe Ruiz Flores, Maria López-Bernstein, Martha David Laguna, Norma Oquendo, Jack Himelblau, Jessica L. Corn, Verónica Bucio, Julio Vázquez and Janie Torres.

To those whose names we may have inadvertently omitted, please accept our apologies and sincere gratitude for your contribution to *Latino Soul*.

To everyone who submitted their heartfelt stories,

poems and quotes for possible inclusion in this book, *reciban nuestro profundo agradecimiento y saludos afectuosos.* While we were not able to use everything you sent in, we value deeply the stories you shared with us and the support and interest you have shown for *Chicken Soup for the Latino Soul.*

And, above all, our warmest thanks to the talented authors whose stories have brought *Latino Soul* to life, and whose experiences and insights encourage us to live each day with courage, solidarity, humor and love.

Introduction

It has been an honor for me to coauthor *Chicken Soup for the Latino Soul*, which I hope will make a meaningful contribution to Latino communities across the nation. I have worked for four years on *Latino Soul* and have nurtured every piece of writing in the book. I have had the pleasure of working with a diverse group of Latino/a authors whose talent and spirit have inspired me throughout the process, and whose stories are the heart and soul of *Latino Soul*. While any reader of this series will be drawn to the powerful stories told in these pages, *Latino Soul* will have special meaning for Latinos/as, who will find stories and poems that reflect in significant ways many of the challenges we face, the joys we share, the hurdles we jump, the wisdom of our elders, the laughter that unites us, the losses we endure, the lessons we learn, the people who hold our families together, and the faith, hope and relationships that keep us sane and moving forward.

My goal in writing, collecting, and editing stories and poems for *Chicken Soup for the Latino Soul* was to make available to readers a book that presents universally human themes from within Latino perspectives and experiences. The experiences narrated in this collection include the history of Latino immigrants whose sacrifice and hard work have contributed decisively to the growth and prosperity of this nation, and who have paved the way for new generations of Latinos in the United States; the sense of connection to our ancestral homelands, or the longing for that connection; the complexity of Latino identity; the search for spiritual connection with our loved ones who have passed away, and the importance of caring for the dying, and remembering and celebrating the dead; the challenge and advantage of bilingualism, the struggle to preserve the Spanish language in adverse conditions, and the often comical consequences of living in two languages (Spanglish); the inspiration drawn from Latino cultural traditions and spiritual beliefs; Latino faith in the power of community; the central place of family in our cultures, and the fierce loyalty of children to their parents, grandparents and siblings; the vital importance of mothers and grandmothers (*las abuelitas*) in providing and caring for us and in teaching us life's lessons; the supreme value of food in our cultures, and the way that Latinos love, learn and strengthen cultural bonds in the kitchen; the belief in the supernatural, and the stories of inexplicable events and magical powers that are often tied to tales of faith, miraculous healing, Indian and African traditions and spiritual renewal.

It has been my great pleasure over the last four years to receive an outpouring of love and support from Latino/a people all over the United States who have thanked me for making this contribution to our communities. But it is I who want to thank each and every person who has made contact with me. Thank you, *de todo corazón*, for your kind words and constant support, and for giving me the inspiration and confidence to keep going. Thank you for having waited patiently for the release of this book.

I am thrilled to present this collection of compelling stories *en celebración de la comunidad latina*. My hope is that

Latino Soul will give all of us an opportunity to honor the diversity, dignity and beauty of Latino life in the United States. *¡Que disfruten!*

Susan Sánchez-Casal

Share with Us

We would like to invite you to send us stories you would like to see published in future editions of *Chicken Soup for the Soul*.

We would also love to hear your reactions to the stories in this book. Please let us know what your favorite stories are and how they affected you.

Please send submissions to:

Chicken Soup for the Soul
P.O. Box 30880
Santa Barbara, CA 93130
fax: 805-563-2945

You can also visit the *Chicken Soup for the Soul* site at:

www.chickensoup.com

We hope you enjoy reading this book as much as we enjoyed compiling, editing and writing it.

1

OUR LIVING HERITAGE/*NUESTRO PASADO PRESENTE*

To be a Latina is to know the depth, power and beauty of my cultura (culture). It is to celebrate my antepasados (ancestors), and at the same time, to live in the present. To be Latina is to be centered, grounded, empowered and blessed. To be Latina is to understand the divine in me, the eternal in me and the unique soul-rooted essence of me. To be Latina is to say, "Sí se puede" (Yes, we can), and "¿Y por qué no?" (Why not?). To be Latina is to acknowledge grace and to move forward with commitment. To be Latina . . . to be Latina . . . to be Latina . . . to be Latina is my joy, my most precious gift.

Denise Chávez

University Avenue

We are the first
of our people to walk this path.
We move cautiously,
unfamiliar with the sounds,
guides for those who follow.
Our people prepared us
with gifts from the land,
fire, herbs and song.

Yerbabuena soothes us into morning,
rhythms hum in our blood,
abrazos linger round our bodies,
cuentos whisper lessons *en español.*

We do not travel alone.
Our people burn deep within us.

Pat Mora

Enchiladas: A Metaphor for Life!

El amor entra por la cocina.

Latino Proverb

My *familia* is from Colorado. During my first year of college, I returned home for a family celebration: my grandparents' fiftieth wedding anniversary. The whole Fajardo clan was busy with preparations for this auspicious occasion. While helping to make what seemed like a million enchiladas, I stood at the kitchen counter and looked over at my great-aunt Lucía.

She was a beautiful woman, about seventy years old at the time. The youngest of eight siblings (born a decade after my grandmother), she usually took over the role of head cook for all family celebrations. Her reasoning was that she was younger and had more stamina. I suspect it was because she could roll enchiladas faster than any human being alive. It was a God-given gift. I admired her greatly and was always amazed at her dedication to every detail of our fiestas: baking all the bread from scratch, making *tamales* days ahead, cooking green chili to die for and preparing enchilada sauce that, to this day, makes me weep with joy.

That day, I really looked at her for the first time in my life. She was always so busy with the *comida* or organizing the last details of preparing the food that she never had time to talk about herself. I was newly puzzled by her self-imposed exile at the kitchen stove, and it occurred to me that my *tía* had been cooking for us for all of our lives. She had no grandchildren of her own. All three of her sons had died tragically, and her remaining daughter was childless. I knew in my heart that this must have been a terrible burden for her to bear, but I never heard her complain. I never heard her once mention the hardships she had witnessed when she was a child. Nor had I ever heard her speak of the humiliation she had endured because she was from a poor Chicano family. I knew from others in the family that my *abuelos* and my other old ones had seen great misfortune and pain.

I gathered my nerve and stared at her a long time before I asked her about her life. I recall stammering as I asked her how she always seemed so happy when she had lost so much. I think that I even told her that most people would not have been able to go on after losing so many children.

What she said to me that day changed my whole outlook on life. She looked at me and, wiping her hand on her apron, smiled.

"M'ija," she said softly, "I look at my life like making enchiladas."

I laughed when I heard her say this, but she went on:

You see, my niece, you start out with the corn tortilla; that is the foundation of the enchilada, the family. Then you dip the tortilla in warm oil; that makes the tortilla soft and pliable to work with. I like to think of the oil as sacred; it is an anointing of the familia with all that is precious in life. It is similar to going to church and having the priest put sacred oil on your forehead. The family is being blessed.

Next you fill the corn tortilla with cheese and onions. The queso is sweet and rich, made from the milk of life. It is symbolic of the joy and richness of this world. But how can you appreciate the queso without the onion? The onion may make us weep, yet it also makes us realize that there is a reason the cheese tastes so sweet. That reason is because there is a contrast to the queso, a balance to the joy . . . sorrow is not necessarily bad. It is an important part of learning to appreciate this life.

Then the enchiladas are covered with the most delicious sauce in the world—a sauce so red and rich in color it reminds me of the blood of the Cristo, a sacrifice of love. Still to this day my mouth waters when I smell enchilada sauce cooking on the stove.

The most important ingredient in the sauce is agua. Water is the vital source of all we know and are. It feeds the rivers that make the great oceans. Water rains from the skies to nourish the fertile earth so that the grains, grasses, flowers and trees may grow. Water comforts us when we hear the sound of it flowing over mountain cliffs. Water quenches our thirst and bathes our tired bodies. We are baptized with water when we are born, and all the rest of our days spent on this Earth are intertwined with water. Water is the spirit of the sauce.

The enchilada sauce also has garlic, salt, chili powder and oil. These are the things that add the spice and zest to life, just as they do to the sauce. Making the sauce is a lot like making your own life: You get to choose the combination of ingredients, and you get to decide just how spicy and salty you like it.

When everything is put together, you have the "whole enchilada." You must look at the enchiladas you have made and be happy with them; after all, you are the one who has to eat them. No use whining about maybe this or maybe that; there is joy and sorrow and laughter and tears. Every enchilada is a story in itself. Every time I dip, fill, roll and pinch an enchilada, I think of some part of my life that has gone by or some part that is still to be. M'ija, you have got to pinch a lot of enchiladas in this life! Make that experience a good one, and you will become una viejita like me.

I couldn't believe that my auntie, who had never spoken more than two words about her philosophy on life, had just explained the universe to me. I wiped my hands on my apron and began to laugh.

"Thank you," I said, between tears and smiles. "I will never forget what you just told me!"

And I never have.

Renee Fajardo

The Healing

Cada mal tiene su cura.

Latino Proverb

It happened hundreds of miles away on my grand-mother's porch. I went there to recuperate from the surgery that had taken away my uterus, ovaries and so many years of monthly battles with my body that I thought of it more as an adversary than part of my being. I had read all about the depression and mood swings and reduced libido that would follow, but no one mentioned the emotional barrenness that had descended upon me and left me helpless. I did what I had always done when I felt lost: I went home to be healed by the sun and the sea and my grandmother's hands.

There was the plane and then there were her arms taking me in and letting me rest my head and heavy heart. The first day, she threw away the pills and prescriptions in my bag. She called her friend Yeya from across the road, and Cecilia from over the rise and Aurelia from the *botánica.* They consulted with each other, and together they decided on my new *remedios*. Every day *abuela* went into her garden and collected herbs. Then it began—the endless baths in *lengua de perro* to reduce the swelling and calm the nerves, gallons of *genjibre* tea to calm the vomiting, *higuera* to fight infection and *flor de virgen* to lift the sadness.

But the most important part of my recovery had nothing to do with herbs. The most important *remedio*, it turned out, was community. "I don't care what the *doctorcitos* said. That girl living alone up there in the cold . . . no wonder she got sick. She needs warmth on the inside and on the outside." And all the ladies agreed.

A cot was set out for me on the porch, and every day, as my grandmother went about her chores, her white-haired friends hobbled up the hill and across the road. After they had washed the breakfast dishes, they would twist their hair into buns, put on their gold earrings and come to sit with me. They brought secret ointments warmed by the sun and applied the balm all over my body. As I lay there too tired and pained to care, I surrendered myself to their hands—wrinkled hands that missed holding babies and soothing toddlers. They brought me their love in the folds of those wrinkles and kneaded it into my body. And while their hands worked, they gave me the gift of their stories that lived under their nails, between their fingers, in their hair. They told me of their lives and the lives of others— everyone in the town. They shared their dreams with me and their disappointments. They celebrated their joys and whispered their failures.

I looked at them with their limp aprons and their cracked feet in oversized men's slippers. I watched their mouths and listened to the words floating out through ill-fitting dentures or swollen gums. The days grew into weeks, and still I listened. They filled my days and my emptiness with their teeming lives. My grandmother told them I was writing down their stories, and they smiled behind cupped hands and brought me more, trusting that I would be gentle with their tales. They brought them in their pockets, their teacups, their photo albums, their treasure boxes. They brought them in lockets and broken picture frames and yellowed newspapers. They must have rummaged in the bottom of their drawers, under the beds, between the old dresses, in the back of the wardrobes. They brought me huge, leather-bound Bibles and yellowed christening gowns and pressed flowers. They brought me the pieces of their lives and bade me make them a quilt of words. When the world was moving too fast for them, they asked me to stop time.

It took a community to heal me, a community of old women bringing me the many stages of their lives. And now that those ladies are long gone, all that is left of their world is their stories. They told me stories I had never heard and stories each of them knew by heart. As they spoke, they suddenly turned into a group of young girls playing in the creek, young women sending their men to war, mothers-of-the-bride letting go of their no-longer-little girls, old women sitting before their husbands' coffins wondering what life held in store in the empty days ahead. Their stories made me realize that my life, just like theirs, would be lived in stages, and that this was only one of them. Their stories were gifts from their hearts, *remedios* that helped me recognize my own humanity in theirs, gave me strength, and restored my mind and heart.

The strength and hope I heard in the stories of these *ancianitas* inspired me to be a writer, so that I could share their lives and their wisdom with others, long after they were gone. I am forever grateful.

Dahlma Llanos Figueroa

What's Up with Dads and Pork-Chop Sandwiches?

Dime con quién andas y diré quién eres.

Latino Proverb

Mr. Delgado spreads two slices of white bread with mayonnaise. He looks over at his pork chop hissing in the frying pan and rubs his hands together like a fruit fly eyeing an overripe peach. His daughter, Elizabeth, and I sit at their kitchen table and watch him slice up an onion and hum a love song to his pork chop. We've watched him make pork-chop sandwiches for the past twenty-five years. He always hums "Sólo tú," a Mexican *corrido* that would leave the toughest macho crying in his tequila, but Mr. Delgado is grinning from ear to ear at the pork chop turning crispy brown.

When the pork chop is "browner than me," as he likes to say, he'll gently place it on the bread he's prepared with mayonnaise, a lettuce leaf, a reel of onion and *mmmmmm*, the sandwich is good to go. Mr. Delgado sits down with us and smiles. Always smiles.

"Heaven," he says between bites and closed eyelids. This is all he needs, he says, and winks at me.

"*Mi familia,* good friends like your father, *m'ija,* and a good job where I can afford pork-chop sandwiches whenever I want."

Heaven.

Before Elizabeth and I can make our escape from the table, Mr. Delgado tells us, for the hundredth time, how he met my dad years ago in the '70s when "Mexican-Americans were Chicanos and not confused Hispanics," and if it wasn't for the almighty pork-chop sandwich and a "crazy Chicano march in *Califas,*" they never would have become such close friends. I don't really mind hearing the story over and over; in fact, I think it gets better every time Mr. Delgado tells it. He's always adding extra details never revealed before. Upon hearing a new or exaggerated bit, Elizabeth and I raise our eyebrows at each other. Once, Mr. Delgado added a love interest to the story, and another time a wild low-rider car chase, and later a confrontation with the ghost of Che Guevara.

My father's version always stays the same, ending with the same proud revelation:

"So you see, *m'ija,* I saved that damn Chicano's life."

Both men are from the same Kansas town, but didn't meet until they went to a Chicano civil-rights rally in California back in the '70s. At the rally, when an organizer asked if there were any Chicanos from Kansas present, both my father and Mr. Delgado raised their fists.

When Mr. Delgado tells the story, he says he didn't like my dad at first. He said my dad seemed like one of those goody-two-shoes, Catholic altar-boy types always trying to make peace, always trying to help out. My father had trimmed jet-black hair, black-rimmed glasses, and baggy khakis. He wore a crisp and clean white-collared shirt with a scapula of *La Virgen* around his neck. Mr. Delgado had a mop of curly black hair. He wore old jeans and leather sandals and some sort of fringed leather vest over a white undershirt stained with *salsa verde*.

After a four-hour march filled with speeches, singing and Aztec chants under a hot California sun, Mr. Delgado soon learned to appreciate my goody-two-shoes "Catholic boy" father. Hungry, thirsty, without a dime in his pocket—the night before he had spent all his bus and food money on a tattoo and too many *cervezas*—Mr. Delgado searched for my father to ask for a ride back to Wichita. About to give up his search for my father and hitchhike back to Kansas, my dad spotted him and waved him over. My dad pulled out two bottles of Coca-Cola and a thick pork-chop sandwich from a brown lunch sack and shared it with him.

Mr. Delgado says my father became like his right arm at that precise moment. (Elizabeth and I always giggle at that.) Mr. Delgado and my father returned from California with Che Guevara patches, Aztec war god tattoos on their backs and, more important, as *compadres*.

Compadres are inseparable once they meet. It becomes stronger than your last name and as casual as your first. If my father says, "Yeah, my *compadre* and I are going to look at that property tomorrow," everyone knows he is talking about Mr. Delgado. *Compadres* or *comadres* are the people you'd trust to watch your children. They are that close.

I love the relationship the two men have. Both complain about their backs, plan Fourth of July festivities during Christmas Mass and gripe that the priest puts them to sleep. On their days off, they gather at the driveway and shake their heads at my parked Chevy Corsica. My father and Mr. Delgado have tried to teach me how to change a flat tire for the last ten years.

"I've got AAA!" I wave my auto card at them. "I don't need to learn how."

My father crosses himself and asks the Holy Trinity and

not AAA to bless me. Always sensing my father's concern, Mr. Delgado squats down near my right front tire and assures me he's going to show me again just in case AAA doesn't answer my call.

"I hate stupid tires! I can't ever get those darn lug nuts off," I answer back. "If I get a flat, I'll just wait for someone to stop and help."

My father crosses himself in the name of the Father, the Son and the Holy Spirit. The next day he buys me a new set of tires from Sears.

My father and Mr. Delgado have a friendship based on losing sleep over both their daughters' driving habits and the Chicano movement.

Elizabeth and I like to tease our fathers about their "rebellious Chicano past," the two of them trekking across Kansas, Colorado and California for *La Causa*. Sometimes, together on the front porch, we will all thumb through photo albums where our fathers are leather-brown young men with goatees and baggy khakis. For every photo, there is a lecture about bilingual education, fair housing and resistance to total cultural assimilation. Elizabeth and I once counted over twenty photos of our fathers with their fingers gathered in a fist punched high against the Kansas sky—high and hard enough for God to feel and look down in wonderment. "There are Chicanos in Kansas?"

¡Sí, Señora! Mexicans, like my *abuelo*, who traveled from Jalisco to Kansas at the age of fourteen to work on the rail-roads. Mexicans, like my grandparents, who stayed and raised proud Mexican-Americans in Kansas towns like Hutchinson, Garden City, Newton, Wichita and Topeka. Kansas Chicanos, like our fathers, who were the first in their families to graduate from college and who brought home to their daughters books about César Chávez, Delores Huerta and Frida Kahlo. The same Chicanos

whose brown fingers, now released from the fist, show me how to check my oil and put air in my tires. The same brown fingers that like to tear off a piece of pork chop while it's cooking in the skillet, and the same brown fingers that cross themselves when I tell them I'm considering another career change. Now they cross themselves with brown-callused fingers, but they still pray for their daughters, and they still pray for *la raza*.

If you ask my dad how he and Mr. Delgado became *compadres*, he will say it was the Chicano movement. If you ask Mr. Delgado, he will say it was the pork-chop sandwich.

Either way, both men are right, and we are all the better for it!

Angela Cervantes

The Blessing

It is a custom in many Hispanic Catholic homes to ask your parents or grandparents for a blessing (bendición) when you see them for the first time that day or when you are departing. In response, they would bless you by saying, "May God bless you" ("Que el Señor te bendiga") . . .

Carmen Alvarado

I grew up in a poor neighborhood in Philadelphia, and, when I was a child, I didn't care at all for the custom of asking for my mother's blessing. It seemed too old-fashioned and sort of meaningless in those days. The few times I did ask, I did it just to please her.

I felt ashamed because the mothers of Anglo kids never required their children to ask for a blessing when they left the house. A simple "See ya later!" was more than enough. In those days, the Anglo way seemed like a more "manly" good-bye, and I didn't want to be laughed at by my friends or have them think I was less of a "guy" than they were.

When I was a child, I couldn't put my feelings into words, but I knew that somehow the act of asking for *bendición* made me feel stained or dirty. As the years passed, I buried the memory of that shame. I hid it deep in my soul like a dark and bitter thorn that would prick my conscience every so often.

With the passage of time, life's experiences have given me a different perspective on things. After my mother's death in 1978, I began to miss that beautiful Puerto Rican custom of asking for and receiving your mother's blessing. My mother's death woke me up, as I was devastated to suddenly realize that I would never have that opportunity again.

I returned to Puerto Rico in 1987 to visit my grandmother, Doña Carmelina Eustaquia Rivera de Font. We were talking about things, nothing of any real importance, when suddenly my nose began to itch. I was instantly overcome by a sneeze so strong it seemed to rock the entire neighborhood of Santa Teresita, Santurce, where my grandmother lived.

My grandmother eyed me silently with feigned gravity and pronounced, "Bless you . . . ! And may the germ that made you sneeze, die!"

Her response caught me off guard. I looked at her, and we both burst out laughing. I realized how wonderful it felt to have received that verbal display of affection from the mother of my mother, and I was struck by the tenderness and beauty of relationships that exist between mothers, grandmothers and sons.

When it was time for me to leave, I stopped at the doorway and said, "*Abuela* . . . give me your blessing."

"*Que Dios te bendiga, m'ijo,*" my grandmother said.

I breathed in deeply, and the secret thorn buried deep in my soul disappeared. I felt lighter and purified.

My grandmother died in 1994, but the memory of the

sweet blessing she gave me that day is still with me. Today, at times when I least expect it, I yearn to ask for and receive *bendición* from the elders in my family. A few weeks ago, I had a long and pleasant telephone conversation with my uncle Agapito who lives in Río Piedras, Puerto Rico. We talked about all kinds of things, like family, politics and music. But before we said our goodbyes, I said, "Uncle, give me your blessing . . ."

Aurelio Deane Font

NO RODEO®

NO RODEO © *Robert Berardi. Used by permission.*

Where Rosaries Ride the Wind

I come from a world
Where rosaries ride the wind
From rearview mirrors,
And men visit in back alleys
Crouching
Like earth women giving birth,
And crucifixes hang above beds
In rooms where bodies glisten
From the heat of want,
Boys wear their mother's names tattooed
Over their hearts,
And grandmothers commune with saints.
I come from a world
Where church doors never close,
And prayers and candles sell
In liquor stores
Alongside cigarettes and gum,
And radios blast their love songs
Late into the night
Long after the moon has gone.

Maria Ercilla

Titi Flori's Pasteles-Maker Machine

Donde una puerta se cierra, otra se abre.

Latino Proverb

Having grown up *puertorriqueño en Nueva York,* I remember with great fondness having *pasteles* during the Christmas holidays. *Pasteles* is the quintessential Puerto Rican dish consisting of a rectangular-shaped patty (depending on who's folding) made of *masa,* ground green bananas and *yautia* or yucca, and tender, spiced morsels of pork. The patty is then wrapped inside paper—or banana leaves for the die-hard traditionalist—and boiled in salted water.

The starchy paste, the *masa,* is traditionally hand-grated with an instrument called the *guayo.* Getting the *masa* right is the most elusive element of the dish, but essential for the proper *pastel.* Don't get *puertorriqueños de Nueva York* started on the right way to make *la masa,* and don't dare mention that you use the *food proceso* to make it, or you will surely evoke a harmonic chorus of *"ayyyyy nooooo, estás loco!"* (it's not the same). You see, making *la masa* for the *pasteles* has become for New York Puerto Ricans the Rubicon that divides the true *puertorriqueño* from the Nuyorican. Those who are seduced by modern technology are looked upon with suspicion by their culturally "pure" brothers and sisters.

My daughter was three years old and had yet to taste her first *pastel* when my parents came from Puerto Rico to visit their old neighborhood in Williamsburg, Brooklyn. In honor of the occasion, my sister-in-law decided to make *pasteles* so that my mother could teach us the secrets of how to make this dish *al estilo de* Doña Ana. My mother is an acclaimed *pasteles*-maker, and you will never find her secret tips, even in the most authentic cookbooks.

I took my daughter to Williamsburg to visit her *abuela* and to spend some time with the family. The highlight of the evening was Titi Flori, my sister-in-law, who was showing off her newly acquired *Pasteles*-Maker machine. It was a hand-crafted contraption put together with a little ingenuity and lots of nuts and bolts. It consisted of a metal box that held a motor and an attached metal disc. The disc was shaped like an old LP and perforated with holes to form a surface that looked like a circular *guayo*. Bolted to the box was what looked like an upside-down pot with a hole in the middle, and sticking out the side was a downward sloping chute. In theory, one would put the bananas in the hole and then turn on the motor, which would then rotate the circular *guayo* and grate the bananas. The formed *masa* would then be steadily pushed down the chute where it would collect in an aluminum tray. ¡*Y mira!* Instant *masa*.

We marveled at this machine! Even *abuela* Ana, who initially had eyed the machine suspiciously, conceded after a taste test that *la masa* was PR-FDA approved. It seemed that we had finally found the perfect melding of tradition and modern convenience. The consistency of the *masa* would not be compromised, thanks to the circular *guayo*, but the time to produce it would be cut to a fraction, given the high-powered motor. And best of all, your fingernails would still be intact! In addition, the machine was made by a local *botánica* owner, so the blessings of the Orishas came with the warranty. It was too good to be true.

Titi Flori began her labor of love, which was made less strenuous by her wonderful machine. Things were going at a brisk pace and it seemed we would be folding the *masa* in no time, when suddenly a strained sound came from the machine. The motor grumbled, and the *masa* stopped flowing from the chute. Titi turned it off and scratched her head, grimacing, "What was that noise?" She scooped up the excess *masa* and removed the circular *guayo*. "Maybe the *masa* got into the motor, but it looks clean to me . . ."

The men stopped watching the football game to take their turn diagnosing what was wrong with *"la máquina, esa." "Es que necesita un tornillo aquí, mira se salió,"* said Tío Ralphie. *"No, eso tiene que ver con el motor,* you put too many bananas in at one time," said Tío Danny. *"Muchacho, tú estás loco, esa porquería no sirve. Al tipo ese de la botánica le gusta vender cuanta madre que haya,"* bellowed Abuelo Víctor. It was a mystery that defied three generations of self-proclaimed expert mechanics. All the back-engineering and beer-fueled bickering did not get anyone closer to reviving the machine.

"With all of these bananas to *guayar,* we will be here forever," Titi Flori said. "I would take the machine back to the *botánica,* but it must be closed by now." We were all starting to face the sad fact that there might not be any *pasteles* that day.

In the midst of all this, Abuela Ana was serene and almost Buddha-like. She was no stranger to adversity—having successfully raised four children in a NYC housing project—and her calm attitude would be the envy of any

Zen Master. She took my daughter's hand and gently pulled her to a quiet corner.

"M'ijita, te voy a demostrar cómo guayar los guineos para formar la masa," Abuela Ana told her. My daughter was to learn the fine art of *pasteles*-making the old-fashioned way. Thank God she was too young to be concerned about her nails!

"Let's begin with the different kinds of bananas and starchy vegetables that go into making *la masa*," the master postured, "and then I will show you how to work the *guayo.*" She held it out to her, saying, "Feel how rough this side is."

For the next several hours, my mother lovingly and patiently taught my daughter about *pasteles*-making. As the lessons progressed, all the women shared their stories about how they learned to make *pasteles*, and as the men's help was enlisted, they too shared stories about helping to make this great dish. Several hours, countless stories, much laughter and many folded *pasteles* later, the job was done, and everyone sat down to watch *Sábado Gigante.* It was time for me to get back home with my daughter.

We made our rounds of good-byes *y bendiciones,* and as I drove home that night I thought about the evening and smiled. Maybe making *pasteles* should be labor-intensive. Maybe that's the point. It's a hands-on job, and anyone who wants to eat is invited to *guayar!*

Laughter, love and stories are the secret herbs and spices of this meal, and they cannot be bought, manufactured or engineered. What we learned that day was that making *pasteles* is an opportunity for family, friends and neighbors to share in the creation of community and love. *¡Buen provecho!*

Joe Colón

NO RODEO®

NO RODEO © *Robert Berardi. Used by permission.*

Salsa Lessons

. . . I create and celebrate our típico Caribbean dance. I take pride in my heritage, bringing the richness of our culture to everything I do.

María Torres

Growing up, Saturday was cleaning day. Protest did no good, so, reluctantly, my brother and I would drag our feet into the kitchen where my mother would tell us what we had to do.

My mother did all the heavy cleaning, and we usually had something simple to do. I would dust all the furniture and make the beds. My brother would vacuum and throw out the trash.

Just before we got started, Mother, who has always had a knack for making even the most mundane chore fun, would turn on the record player. No matter how tired we were, once the music came on, we came alive. With salsa blaring from the record player, cleaning somehow became easier.

My mother would dance with the broom, the mop, or a

pillow; anything could be a dancing partner. My brother and I would laugh, and eventually we would all end up dancing. The beat of the bongo drums in salsa music has a way of crawling into your soul, and once you're hooked, there's no turning back.

I have always loved music and was eager to learn to dance. Mami began teaching me steps. She instructed me how to keep my upper body steady while swaying my hips and moving my feet to the beat. My mother knew most of the words to the songs, and she would sing while twirling me around the room. We would do conga lines, and dance in and out of all the rooms in our little house. Every time a good song came on, we would drop what we were doing and begin dancing. It wasn't uncommon for my dad to come home for lunch and find his wife and children dancing, and the housecleaning still not done.

At first, my brother wasn't too enthusiastic about learning to dance. He would roll his eyes, pretending he wasn't interested, but my mom never got discouraged. She would ignore his sulking and entice him to join us. As he got a little older and realized that girls like boys who can dance, his interest grew. Although salsa is very different from other forms of dancing, learning to dance gave us the ability to pick up steps to the music of our generation.

The habit of putting on music whenever I have to do chores at home has never left me. Any time I have to get busy, you'll hear salsa blaring from the speakers installed all over my house. I also dance with sofa cushions and imaginary partners while my children laugh at their nutty mom. I taught my sons how to dance this way, and now my five-year-old daughter and I share in weekly dance sessions.

Thinking back on those Saturday mornings, I realize that we were learning more than just how to dance. We learned that while life isn't always easy or fun, we have the ability to make the most out of every situation. The important thing is the attitude we choose to have when dealing with the circumstances we find ourselves in.

Music kept my mother sane those first few years in the United States. It helped her deal with her sadness. It helped her forget how broke we were and how uncertain the future was. I'm sure the music took her back home to Guantánamo, to the *carnavales* and a carefree time in her life.

Salsa takes me straight to my Caribbean roots. The words to the songs talk of the island where I was born. Salsa helps me stay connected to a place and a way of life I have always been curious to know more about. When I'm dancing salsa, the drums beat steadily with my heart, and for a moment this Cuban girl is back in Guantánamo.

María Luisa Salcines

Papa's Best Lesson

It was my grandfather who first taught me to be proud of being Latina. My grandfather told his children and all his grandchildren many wonderful stories about our history and our heritage. He told us that we were the descendants of one of the greatest, oldest and most beautiful cultures in the world. He said honoring our heritage meant that we had to educate ourselves, do the best we could whether it was in school or at work, and that we had to not only respect and care for our families, but also respect and care for ourselves. . . . I will always be grateful to my family for those lessons on how to be a proud and strong Latina.

Linda Chávez-Thompson

From kindergarten through high-school graduation, I went to a Catholic convent school, Ursuline Academy, in the old border town known as Laredo, Texas. My parents were not wealthy, but they sacrificed many things to keep me in a parochial school.

Many of my friends were Anglos, but the majority of them were Latinas like myself. We played, sang and studied together, had slumber parties, picnics and sock hops in those carefree days of the fifties. We grew up eating tacos, enchiladas and tamales, but we couldn't resist burgers, Cokes and apple pie either.

We were raised in a city where the great Rio Grande divides Mexico and the United States, but we loved to cross the bridge that gave us the flavor of both. Sometimes I felt torn between the two, tangled together like badly cast fishing lines. For example, my parents spoke Spanish to me at home, reminding me often: "Never forget where you came from, your roots, your culture, your language and Mexico, the land where your grandparents were born." But at school we were fined a quarter if we were caught speaking Spanish! That confused and upset me. I surrendered many quarters to the nuns because I was always speaking what came naturally. But eventually, after being punished so many times for speaking Spanish, I began to see our native language as something to be ashamed of.

I have fair skin and honey-colored eyes. My grandfather used to call me *Blanca Nieves* (Snow White)! Once, the pep squad went to an out-of-town football game, and afterwards we stopped at a burger place for a bite to eat. It took forever for someone to wait on us, and when someone finally came, it was the manager telling us to leave the restaurant because they did not serve Mexicans there. Talk about discrimination! Then he had the nerve to look at me, the Mexican Snow White, and say, "Oh, but *you* can stay."

We stormed out, but not before I confronted him and asked, "What makes you think you're superior to us?"

He just pointed at his sign that said they had a right to refuse service to anyone.

The next day, with tears running down my face, I told my father how I felt about our experience at the restaurant. His emerald green eyes betrayed his anger, and tears welled up in them like hot lava. He asked me, "Are you ashamed of your race?" I replied that people were beginning to make me feel like we were of a lower class because of the color of our skin, because we spoke Spanish or because of our accented English. I told him that I liked being called Snow White, and that I was beginning to resent being labeled Chicana, Mexican or Latina. I had come to believe that it was better to be Anglo than Latina, since Anglos aren't fined for speaking their language, and all the heroes and heroines that I saw in the movies or read about in the history books were definitely Anglos with blonde hair and blue or green eyes.

That night my father made a promise that changed my life. He promised to take us to Mexico City on a vacation where we could learn more about the beauty, history, art, culture and people of our ancestral country.

What a delightful time we spent—visiting our relatives, going to museums and palaces, learning the names of mountains. At the museums, my father made me read each historical caption and all the facts about the great heroes of Mexican history, the generals, soldiers and troops from the revolution. The evenings were filled with fiestas in Garibaldi Plaza with mariachis dressed in their beautiful *charro* costumes. We saw the gorgeous *folklórico* dancers and singers at the *Palacio de Bellas Artes,* and we climbed the famous pyramids at Teotihuacán. I was intrigued and inspired by the majestic architecture of the buildings of Mexico City, especially the Basilica of Our Lady of Guadalupe.

But most of all, I was impressed by the kindness and charm of the people we met and the way they welcomed us back to our ancestral land.

Since that memorable journey, I have been so proud to tell people who ask me that I am a Latina, Chicana or Mexican-American, whichever name they decide to use. I am no longer insulted. I speak up for *both* of my countries, and I speak the two languages every day.

I will always be grateful to my *papá* for the wonderful lesson he taught me during those visits to Mexico, where I was enlightened to see beyond color or accents, labels or stereotypes.

Today, I don't mind being called *Blanca Nieves,* but I am 100 percent proud to be Latina.

Olga Valle-Herr

Grandma's Recipe

Obey and honor your parents, respect and obey the gods, be honest, tell the truth, and don't eat too quickly.

Aztec Teaching

I remember Grandma's cooking—the way the scent of fresh tamales delighted my nose and enticed my salivary glands. She blessed the pot, always blessed the pot before they steamed. "They taste better with God's blessing," she would say. I always wanted the recipe for her mouth-watering tamales, but she always asked me to wait.

"There's time," she would say.

I remember Grandma's tamales. . . . Her hands kneading the *masa* dutifully, and how, with the gentle stroke of the back of a spoon, she would spread the dough on the corn husks, stroking patiently, like an artist delicately applying colors on canvas.

"Living life is like neatly spread dough on corn husks. If you're not patient and you spread the dough too thick and too quickly, you'll get lumpy tamales that quickly fall apart. Don't be in too much of a hurry to grow up," she would say. "Spread your time evenly and enjoy each day." My stomach rumbled and my mouth watered, anticipating the first tender chew of fresh steamed *masa* with beans and *chile*. She'd say a little prayer before the first bite, always before the first bite. "They taste better when you've thanked God for bringing you another meal," she would say. And then, finally, we would eat.

When I left my hometown, my grandma held a crinkled paper in her hand. She extended her arm, her wrinkled, leathery hand shaking uncontrollably as she reached for my palm. "You've always wanted the recipe," my grandma smiled with tears in her eyes.

I was very sad to leave my beloved grandmother behind, but I was so happy that she left me the recipe for her tamales, thinking that by following it I could rekindle my relationship with her, although we would be hundreds of miles away.

I didn't read the piece of paper until I got home later that evening. When I opened it, I realized that my grandmother had given me much more than a recipe for tamales. On the page, along with the tamale recipe, was my grandmother's recipe for life: *Bless your meals, be patient and give thanks each day.*

Jacqueline Méndez

Abolengo

Remember, my son,
when you perceive
the disdain of others . . .
that you are a descendant
of the valiant *Conquistador*
who carried the Holy Cross
of our Redeemer
across the oceans.
Who with faith in the Lord
and in the name of his Monarch,
ordered his ship burned,
so as not to look back,
and shape your destiny
in a mythical New World.

Son, keep well in mind,
that you bear the regent blood
of the Chieftain and his island bride,
gentle, yet gigantic spirits,
patient, generous beings,
who suffered disillusionment,
disease and hard work

—endless and without pity—
to bequeath to you an opulent land.

Don't forget, my treasure,
that through your veins
runs the sweat
of the mighty slave,
his sculptural black body
forged in sun and splendor . . .
A man who, with pride,
even enchained,
raised callused hands
in fisted, existential cry
and challenged
his cruel destiny . . .
final and essential element
of your rich ancestry.

Don't bemoan your fate, Son
—don't throw it to the void!—
when your grandfathers
—so many times great—
suffered dearly in your place
to leave you an inheritance beyond price,
garnered century by century
with pain, sacrifice
and noble deed incessant.
Because of this,
yours is a duty sacred,
to lift your head,
and with body held proud,
to be—finally—
in their honor and stead—
happy.

Marie Delgado Travis

2

THE LOVE OF FAMILY/*EL AMOR DE LA FAMILIA*

Familia is the very center of Latino culture . . . It is the strongest thing about us and the most universal.

Gregory Nava

Mama Can't Read

Last night, sitting with a group of friends who share my love for words, someone wondered what my mother would think if she read a silly thing I had written.

"My mother doesn't read or write," I told them. I saw their shocked expressions.

I've never been ashamed of my mother's illiteracy. Never. They could assume it was some kind of culturally deprived circumstance or a measure of my family's lack of intelligence. I knew better. I tried to explain.

"She's not ignorant or lacking," I said. Then I caught myself. Why should I explain? Yes, I wish she could have had the chance to read, but that's the way it's always been. In spite of the hardship not reading has been for her, what was missing ended up bringing us closer. Some of my most cherished memories are of sitting in the kitchen and reading the newspaper to my mother. How could they possibly understand this special link, my personal bond to my mother?

"How awful it must be to not be able to read," one woman commented.

I glanced around the roundtable of educated faces and

saw disbelief and pity in their eyes. I didn't want to glorify my mother's lack of education or be insensitive to it, but I resented having to defend my mother's illiteracy. Then I thought about my own love of books. As a child, I escaped my hopelessly poor surroundings through the magic of reading. From the depths of our struggling existence, reading was my ticket out.

But what about Mama?

I wondered if Mama's life could have been different. If I should have at least asked how she felt about it or offered to teach her. I was filled with guilt and sadness, and I longed to be with her, feel her arms around me.

I remember waking up early and reading portions of the newspaper to Mama in the kitchen. She'd always have a cup of steaming *atole* for me. I felt closer whenever I read to her: Her interest or excitement was mine. Her eyes lit up in various shades, depending on the subject. If it was a killing or scandal, her eyes got wide as silver dollars. She'd raise her hands to her cheeks and cry, *"Ay, Dios mío!"* She'd want to hear every detail twice. If I read news of something especially nice, her eyes would melt into tears of happiness, *"Ay, qué suave, m'ijo."* She hung on every word, savored every line. I became her eyes, her window to the world.

Mama's favorite part of the newspaper was the obituary section. After the main news, she'd always press me for it. It was a game I played. Save the best for last. "Who died?" she'd ask anxiously. To an outsider, it might seem like a depressing way to view life, but to me, and especially to her, there was something about the obits section that brought great anticipation.

My own anticipation came from watching her reaction. I must admit, I'd get caught up in the drama, too. As I read, my mood would change, and my tone would soften, almost to a whisper. I'd solemnly read the list of deaths, pausing briefly for effect. If there was one even slightly familiar, I was to go over and over it until we understood exactly where the connection was. My mother's heart would race, she'd shake her hands, wipe her brow and talk about how we knew this person. If it was someone very close, or worse, family, then she'd grab for her apron to wipe away the tears of sadness and shock.

Eventually, I grew up and moved away. I wrote letters to Mama whenever possible. Sometimes I'd write a short story about our family and send it to one of my sisters with instructions to read it to her. I knew she'd cry because my stories were gentle slices of our family, reminders of our lives. I pictured exactly how she would hear them, the words winding their way into her heart.

"Look, Mama, this is about us, *our* stories," I'd write. Her face would light up, tears in her eyes.

"Read it again, *m'ija*," she'd beg my sister. "I want to hear it again."

Last week, I drove home to visit her in the early morning. She no longer stands over the table patting *masa* for tortillas, as she'd like to do, to please me. Her hands are wracked with arthritis, barely able to hand me the cup of *atole* as I sit down and unfold the newspaper. Her figure, once proud and upright, is now slumped, and she uses a walker to move slowly across the kitchen. It hurts to see her this way. I wish I could buy something to rejuvenate her tired body, to keep her with me.

Our days are slipping away.

I stop, look lovingly at her and ask, "Mama, did you ever feel bad because you couldn't read?"

She stares at me, then scolds, "Don't be silly. I have you to read to me." Then, with that familiar twinkle in her eyes that magically erases all doubt, she asks, *"A ver, m'ijo,* tell me who died."

Charles A. Mariano

I Graduate Barkely

To make a great dream come true, the first requirement is a great capacity to dream; the second is persistence.

César Chávez

After slowly sipping my grandmother's *caldo*, I sat on the flower-printed sofa under a sea of thick blankets. My body ached and my nostrils cried from the stench of *vaporú* that covered my chest. I glanced at the old square clock and realized that the mailman would soon make his daily stop. I wondered if today he would deliver the letter that would determine my fate.

My grandmother had just entered the bathroom when I slipped on my *chanclas* and bolted out the front door toward the silver box. Somehow in the midst of the rain, there was a ray of light that illuminated the big package. My joyful screams were silenced when my grandmother appeared.

"*¿Estás loca?* For why are you outside?"

"Grandma, I got in! I did it! I got into UC Berkeley!"

As I ran inside to call my dad, my grandma gave me one of her famous huffs and "you're pushing your limits" looks. "Dad, I got in! I'm going to Berkeley!" "That's good, *m'ija*, but don't you want to go to UC Davis? Be close to your family? Berkeley's so far. I have to get back to work. We'll talk tonight."

That evening my grandmother lingered around our house and waited for my father and me to talk. My father didn't say much because he knew that my heart was set, and there was no use trying to battle the stubborn blood that boldly pumps through our family. On the other hand, my grandmother wouldn't stop telling me what a bad choice I was making. She said that Berkeley was too expensive, the Bay Area was too crazy, there were good community colleges nearby, I would be alone in a city, and that basically I was a horrible daughter for even thinking of abandoning my "helpless" divorced father and younger brother.

I'm not going to lie: My grandmother's words left bruises, but I understood her point of view. My grandma came from a generation where women kept the house spotless, never ordered take-out and only left their family-home when it was time to start a family of their own. Ironically, my grandmother was rebellious, and it is *her* mischievous tales that have fueled my determination to break life's barriers.

When my great-grandmother passed away, my grandma moved in with her *tía*, who made her work as a servant. In addition to maintaining the ranch, my grandma would accompany her *tía* on short journeys throughout the *campo* to sell produce. During that time, my grandmother straddled horses, kept a knife hidden in her boot for safety and became known as *"María la loca"* by the *campesinos*. Searching for something more in life, my grandma ran away and headed north because she heard that women had more freedom in the United States.

Eventually, she settled on the border of California and Mexico where she worked two jobs to save money for her dream of a better life. While living in Mexicali, she met a man who impressed her with his charm and told her that he would provide for her. After some time, the two married, and my grandmother's focus turned to her new family. However, my grandfather basically placed my grandmother into another servile position, ruling her every move. My grandfather's controlling and abusive ways finally ceased when he passed away after having a heart attack, leaving my pregnant grandmother with gambling debts and little money. Despite the countless obstacles, my grandmother remained strong, raised her seven children and advocated for her family, making sure they would take full advantage of life's opportunities.

Her story has always motivated me to persevere, and, as a result, I moved to Berkeley in the fall of 1996. In the beginning, being away from my family and adjusting to my new life was extremely difficult. I could really feel the distance take hold. On the occasional weekends home, I felt like a visitor when I stared at the blank walls of my old room. My relationships with each of my family members, mostly with my grandmother, had changed. Our conversations were brief, and my grandmother's refusal to really look me in the eyes made me hear her unspoken words of disapproval.

As my undergraduate career continued to unfold, my grandmother and I slowly reconnected when I asked for her help. She shared her secret recipes with me, picked out the perfect houseplant for my new apartment and assisted with my Spanish homework. Little by little, she would show her support with her goody bags (which usually consisted of fruit, Top-Ramen and *pan dulce*) and by slipping a dollar or two into my pocket when she gave me her good-bye blessing.

Four years flew by and before I knew it, graduation was right around the corner. I asked my grandmother to be my honored guest and accompany me in the walk across the Greek Theater. Despite her fears of huge crowds, she agreed to remain by my side during the entire program.

That evening she wore her best outfit, pinned a fresh flower from her garden to her blouse and placed a small amount of pink blush on her cheeks to signal the special occasion. My eyes overflowed with tears, and at that moment I knew that I had truly made her proud.

As the volunteer motioned our row to stand, my grandmother gently squeezed my right hand. "*M'ija,*" she said softly, "I make it only to grade three, but today I graduate *Barkely.*"

Regina Ramos

Brothers

Puedes ser solamente una persona para el mundo, pero para alguna persona tú eres el mundo.

Gabriel García Márquez

Last night, my brother and I got into a dumb argument over the phone. I hate fighting with him. We don't argue that often, but when we do, I take it to heart and feel terrible until it gets sorted out. My stomach gets knotted up, and I worry that our relationship will never be the same. It's a stupid fear, but I get it every time.

Danny is twelve years older than me. He's a police officer. He's shy around strangers, but open around family. That's something we share. We tend to laugh at the same things, and we both hate being the center of attention. He's the person I bounce things off of, the person I go to when something bothers me. And if something good happens, he's usually the first person I call. He's one of those people in your life who makes you feel safe when you're with him. I can't put my finger on it, but I feel more secure and confident knowing that he's nearby.

It wasn't always like that. Danny and I didn't grow up together. I never even knew he existed until our father died when I was sixteen. Danny's name was listed in the obituary under "surviving children." At that point in my life, I knew I had one older brother, Rainy. I thought that was it as far as siblings went. So who the heck was Daniel? My mom filled me in, in her matter-of-fact way: Danny is much older than me, he has a different mom, he has two little daughters, he's a very nice guy and he's a cop. And then my mother—never one to sugarcoat things—simply said, "Your father never took a lot of interest in Danny, kind of like how he was with you."

Danny and I met at our father's funeral, a big Mexican affair with mariachis and men in cowboy boots. It was an odd feeling. Rainy looked like my mom. I looked like a cross between my mom and my dad. But Danny looked exactly like our father. It was uncanny. He was younger, of course, but the shape of the face and the body were the same. And he had sad eyes. All Cordova men have sad eyes; my mom once said we looked like cows about to be slaughtered.

We didn't see each other for many years after that. A twelve-year age gap is huge when you're a teenager. But then, years later, when I was twenty-eight, my brother Rainy died. Danny came to the funeral, looking more like our dad than ever with a few more years behind him. He had a trim goatee and a blue sport coat and a gold bracelet on his right wrist. We talked, and he said it wasn't right that we kept "meeting each other at funerals. We're brothers."

After that, we made an effort to get to know each other. I worked a late shift on a newspaper copy desk and would call him on my lunch hour, usually nine in the evening. He always made time for me, even with a wife and two kids and working as a narc. He would call me when he was pulling overtime or had slow moments in the police car. Sometimes he would call on one of his dead late shifts: "Just talk to me. I need to stay awake. Say anything."

Often, we would talk about the way we grew up. Our father never had much of a role in my life. Instead, he was a shadowy figure who would drift in and out a couple of times a year, a man with thick eyeglasses who was drenched in the aroma of cheap filter-tipped cigars. There was never really an emotional connection there. I didn't talk about it with anyone before. Neither did Danny. He told me that I was the only one he felt comfortable discussing it with because I was the only one who understood. At times, it was odd. We were brothers who knew these deep, intimate feelings the other one shared, but I couldn't tell you Danny's favorite baseball team. I didn't know how well he spoke Spanish or the name of the girl he took to the prom. He didn't know that I loved pop music or that I once gave Sheena Easton a bouquet of carnations as a pledge of my undying love.

But we cobbled a relationship out of what we did know, and it grew. We began to see each other more and more. Now, we talk several times a week. We go watch the Diamondbacks together and borrow each other's movies. He took me to buy my first suit. I wrote his latest resume. He has the keys to my house, and I have the keys to his. We can make each other angry, and we can make each other laugh.

There are other things. I've gone through some hard times with my health. I call him, afraid of what the future holds, and he makes me feel better. He has had some personal trials; he told me once that he was glad to have a little brother he could lean on.

We know each other's friends. People who have met me recently don't know we didn't grow up together; it seems like a moot point now. If our schedules get extra busy, we still talk several times a week, even if it's just, "Hey, what the hell are you doing? What's going on?"

Sometimes, it's odd to think we didn't grow up together. People say you can't choose your family, but in a way we did. He said he thinks part of it is because we're Latino. We're naturally drawn to our families and put a high value on that relationship in our culture. Once, one of my bosses said he liked to see us together because he had never seen two brothers who were closer. That felt good.

That's why it's so hard for me when I argue with him. Deep inside, I think I'm afraid he'll walk away from me, like my dad did, and that we will lose that closeness. I've never been able to tell him that, but he surprised me last night when we were quarreling on the phone.

"You know, I'm not going anywhere," he said, cooling down quickly, like always. "No matter what you do or say, you're always going to be my brother. Nothing can change the way I feel about you. We're blood. We're *brothers*."

They say you can't choose your family, and that's true. But even if I could, I would choose Danny.

Randy Cordova

The Promise

The family is one of nature's masterpieces.

George Santayana

There was a great deal of blood on the floor, and she just kept bleeding. Lamaze class never mentioned anything like this. Doc was cool as ice. A small-town obstetrician, he didn't care much for chitchat. Oh, he was friendly enough, just not in the way we, expatriates from New York City, had envisioned a rural doctor to be.

This delivery was different, even for Doc. I could tell by the way he kept talking. There was no sense of panic that anyone listening in could hear, but the nurses, who had been by his side for more than twenty years, well, they were practically hysterical at the sound of Doc's mono-tone voice just going on and on about how everything was all right.

Everything was not all right. I looked down at my wife, strapped into a torturous birthing position. All color had drained from her lips, lips I thought I knew so well after all these years. I cursed myself. After all, it was I who had begged to have a child. She looked at me with noncommittal eyes. These were not the eyes I saw flashing intense pain and a plea for help at me earlier, as our baby refused to come out, forcing her through eleven hours of labor.

With one final gasp and a terrifying scream that made me think the baby would come flying out of my wife's mouth, our daughter came into the world. Whenever I wonder why she's such a loud child, I think back to what she must have heard and gone through as she fought her mom, trying to ignore the eviction notice on her warm, quiet womb.

"Everything is going to be okay," the nurses kept telling me as I stood by my wife's side. Thinking it best not to lie to her as well, I told her jokes:

"Do eleven toes run in your side of the family?"

She forced a smile, trying to get me to calm down, seeing the near panic on my face; I was unable, as usual, to hide my emotions from her.

"Hey, be patient. They haven't taken the other one out yet. Didn't I tell you we were having twins?"

This wasn't far from the truth. A part of her placenta had remained inside, preventing her womb from sealing up properly, making for a spectacular mess. I had seen the placenta come out, and it seemed almost as big as our baby.

And what a baby she was. She didn't scream, but immediately she started making a stuttering sound. She arrived a month early, but showed no signs of being a preemie. Bluish-purple and covered with a fine white membrane that reminded me for some reason of chicken fat, she looked my way for the longest time before turning back to the nurse who was cleaning her and trying to record her size with a tape measure, only to have to gently take it away from Lina, who had managed to close her little fingers around it.

"We have to take her to the OR," said Doc. He finally stood

up from the stool between my wife's legs and addressed us both, a faint smile crossing his face, which made me very nervous. I reached down and kissed Lizy, tears streaming down my face. I thought I had seen her in her finest hour during the birth of our daughter, showing courage and strength I hadn't imagined any human possessed.

I smiled as hard as I could. Her eyes came to life, eyes I had fallen so in love with years earlier and which lately I had begun to take for granted as we settled into the monotony of marriage. A soft glow returned to her for a moment as she reached up to caress my cheek, wiping the tears away and saying, "Don't worry, sweetie. Go have a long talk with our daughter."

As they wheeled her through the doors of the OR, I stood there paralyzed, the clean antiseptic smell of the place making me nauseous. I wanted more time with her. Just another minute to tell her the thousands of things I never got around to somehow, but I managed to yell out "I love you!" before she completely passed through the swinging doors. A nurse caught my arm and walked me over to the birthing room, where another nurse handed me my daughter, bundled up but stretching her neck and head back to get a better look at the world about her. Precious child. The nurse walked us to my wife's room, encouraging me as she continued to guide me by the arm until I couldn't hold it in any longer and broke down crying.

My daughter looked at me with intense black eyes—her mother's eyes—as I sat down in the room to wait. Wait. I laid Lina down in the hospital bassinet and sat on the bed next to her, leaning close as we talked in private for the first time in eight months. It was then I made her a promise—a promise to be kind and gentle to her, a promise to be strong like she was after having gone through so much to get here. We talked about her mom, and how she would be right back, and how there was no need to worry. This time, as I heard myself say it, I actually believed the words, and I watched and listened to my baby making her stuttering sounds, gripping my index finger tightly.

I made the same promise to her mother years ago. She looked long and hard at me after I proposed, leaving me there on the cool terra cotta floor of the rooftop bistro, waiting. She cocked her head ever so slightly, squinting hard, something she did when she was thinking with her heart, a heart that was patient and methodical from a life lived with disappointment.

"How will you treat me?" she asked quietly. It could have been her mom or grandmother asking as it seemed that the men ran out on all the women in her family.

"With kindness and gentle hands," I said.

It was enough for the moment.

Time stopped hounding me in that little hospital room as I held my daughter, rocking her back and forth as she yawned, closed her eyes and fell asleep, with one hand holding on to my finger.

The door opened and Doc walked in, smiling. I tried to get up, but he motioned me down.

"She's fine. Recovering well and should be back up in an hour. The bleeding has stopped, and it's just a matter of letting her regain her strength for a few days before she can go home."

I thanked him with such enthusiasm that the man blushed. He turned, hesitating a moment at the door as if he had forgotten to say something, but instead an enormous smile took over his face as he wished us a good night.

I felt a sudden release and draining of energy, as if my body would crumble, thinking of my family and how hard I would work to keep the promise that held up my world.

Antonio Farias

El Niño Bendito de la Grandmom

"*Calmarse, calmarse,*" my brother Matthew whispers to his dinner plate as he rocks back and forth, dropping his fork to clutch at his ear.

Mama stands and spoons more green beans onto his plate before she heads to the kitchen.

"Come *ahora*, Matty. Eat your supper, Baby."

Daddy leans over to put the fork back in Matty's hand, giving him a reassuring pat on his back. I watch Matty push his food around before he manages to fork some meatloaf into his mouth. He rocks slower now, stopping to look around the room briefly as Mama sits back down and hands him a warm dinner roll from the basket in her hand.

Something about Mama's simple gesture, seeing her bring Matty food, reminds me of being little and wondering about my older brother and his funny tics. Convinced that Matty was seeing or hearing something special the rest of us weren't allowed to experience, I used to follow my older brother's wandering eyes, determined to see the invisible mysteries that always seemed to take his attention away from the everyday.

Mama's own mother, Grandmama María, always gentle with Matty and understanding of his funny ways, explained autism to me after my first day of kindergarten. Some of the older boys had teased Matty on the bus, calling him names and sucking their thumbs as they pointed at him. I asked Grandmama María why the boys did that to him, why they treated my brother like he was stupid, *un tonto*.

Grandmama explained in her warm, liquid accent how Matty's specialness made him a child of God, our family's own *niño bendito*, able to see all of the angels and saints that surround and watch over us every day.

"*Calmarse*," she used to whisper to Matty at night when nightmares would haunt him, making him squirm and wriggle until his bed became a prison. Smoothing his sheets and stroking his forehead with her rough but cool hands, she would sing to Matty softly, holding him in a gentle hug that sent all the nighttime demons away.

"You are special, *una muchacha inteligente*, Gloria," Grandmama would say to me as I got older and began to bring home report cards with As and Bs.

"Your gifts are your own. Use them to take you to great places, to take you closer to God and what you want from life. Someday, Matty may need you, his little sister. As long as you are strong, you will be strong enough for both of you. *Nuestro Dios sabe esto*. I know this as well. "

Grandmama always sent me off to school with these warm thoughts, speaking slowly so I would understand her slang-style Spanish, patiently unveiling the precious bit of wisdom until it was mine to keep. Her words felt rich and valuable, like the beautiful shells she kept on her shelf, brought back with her from the warm Puerto Rican tides near her home of Santurce.

Refusing to talk much about the life of poverty she had left behind in Puerto Rico, Grandmama María would instead share stories about the amazing colors the sky used to take against the sand on warm, sensual nights when she was a child. Though many parts of her history were a secret to us, we all knew that in 1939, while living with a distant cousin in the Bronx, María had, on instinct, marched into the busiest-looking building she saw when she left the apartment that morning. By the end of the day, María had gotten a job making bras for thirty-five cents an hour.

Grandmama's stories, her special flavor of Latina wisdom and her profound love for life, made her sudden heart attack and passing last year more difficult than my family thought possible. Mama wasn't able to stop crying for a week, and Papa walked around the house quietly, looking up often as if expecting to see María sitting at the table or by the window doing her cross-stitch.

Although twenty years old, Matty was excused from the funeral, both Mama and Papa believing that the trauma would confuse and overload him. I still wish he had been there with me, holding my hand, being my big brother. We could have said good-bye to Grandmama María together. I think he would have liked that.

Doctors say that autistics often repeat words they've once heard, that phrases get trapped in their psyche, to be repeated randomly throughout a lifetime. These days, when Matty repeats Grandmama María's words, when he chants her phrase of tenderness—*calmarse, calmarse*—consoling himself from things only he can see, maybe, as others say, he is only repeating what he's heard. Perhaps he's confirming modern medical theory by parroting phrases that got stuck and now continue to spin in a mind that holds its own secrets.

But I believe he is doing other things:
Like speaking to Grandmama María.
Hoping to feel her cool hands on his forehead again.

Asking her to smooth his twisted sheets.
Remembering our angelic Grandmama María as only
 a *niño bendito* can.
Spreading her love.

         Sylvia M. DeSantis

The Bear

The other day on the radio, I heard a male talk-show host discussing the "awful" plight of Latinas: Their families don't expect them to achieve and don't have goals for their girls to do well in school and go on to college. He believed that all Latino families wanted their girls to start families and be good mothers, aspiring to nothing else. I had to smile—he was right in some ways, but he was also so wrong. He did not understand what our families want for us and why. He did not understand the strength and courage our culture provides for us and how. He did, how-ever, lead me down memory lane to the day when I dis-covered what he did not know. . . .

She came into my room, gingerly holding a package in her hands, and sat on my bed, shedding quiet tears as I made my way around to her. Walking slowly to where she sat, I kept wondering, *What can I say? What can I do?* All the time I was thinking, *If I am not strong now, I'll never make it. This is my moment of truth. I need to be strong for both of us right now, or I will never get out of here. I will never have a chance to explore my potential.*

For the past four years, since my dad had left, I had been looking after my little sister and my mom. She had suddenly been thrust into the role of breadwinner, and I into the role of caretaker. I had cooked, cleaned, babysat, baked goodies for bake sales, helped my little sister with homework and attended school functions. My mother would have preferred that I stay home with her and continue to support her in these roles, but I had made a firm decision to get a college education, and there was no turning back.

Holding back my own tears, I sat down beside her and put my arms around her shoulders. I told her everything would be fine, and that I would always be her daughter. I would still take care of her, but I needed to do this. She said, "I know. I love you, and I'm so proud of you. I know that going to college has been a dream of yours for years. I am going to miss you, but I want you to know that I love you, no matter what, and I understand why you have to go. I am so proud of you."

At that moment, my mom tenderly handed me the package she held so delicately in her hands. I took the gift and opened it slowly, wondering what else she had gotten me after the towels, linens, calculator and dictionary. It was a raggedy, forlorn-looking Paddington Bear. The bear came with an oversized yellow hat, a blue overcoat and a tag that read, *Please Look After This Bear.* I burst into tears. My mother looked at me tenderly and said, "Please, look after this bear, take good care of it, and if the bear ever needs anything, let me know." We both knew she was talking about me. We both knew she wanted me to take good care of myself as I ventured forth into unknown territory, as I took steps to become my own person—not by getting married as my mom had done, but by going to the university, as no one else in our family had ever done.

The bear would become a symbol of our bond, of our

love and of our growth as mother and daughter. She would frequently call and ask me how "the bear" was doing. I kept the bear on my bed as a constant reminder of the love of a mother who did not understand all that was happening in her daughter's life, but who, in her own way, was trying to be supportive of her ambitious daughter's dreams.

As a Latina, I grew up in a world of very different expectations. I was expected to be the stereotype the radio talk-show host was speaking about: I was supposed to be a good wife and mother someday, the keeper of family traditions, the holder of the beliefs and values that were an integral part of our family heritage and culture. I was expected to learn how to cook and to support my husband's efforts to care for the family. No one expected me to want something else for myself.

I, on the other hand, had different expectations. I had dreams that went beyond what my family, my community and my culture had in mind for their daughters. I wanted to get a college education and have a career.

Reconciling dreams with cultural and familial expectations can be very difficult. When we decide to pursue a different path, it is a break with tradition, belief and values. Our culture does not always expect women to go out and seek their place in the world. It can be especially hard for our mothers because they may see our breaking the mold as a comparison of a life not lived, opportunities not taken, dreams not fulfilled. We, as Latinas, need to be careful that we do not reject the way of life our mothers chose—and instead, honor and respect them for the women they chose to be, for the foundation they laid for us to build our dreams upon.

Yes, it took me a while to appreciate all my mom has done for me and the sacrifices she has made, but I know she had the courage to do what she did because she, like me, is a strong Latina—a Latina who has taken all that is good about her life and her culture and channeled that energy into loving and supporting her family.

I still have my Paddington Bear gracing my bedroom. It is a constant reminder to me of a mother's love that has given me roots and given me wings. Roots that anchored me throughout all of life's challenges. Wings that allowed me to soar and to freely dream of becoming the woman I could become.

My mother's support taught me that *our cultural legacy gives us the courage to become the individuals we were meant to be and to inspire others to do the same.*

The man talking on the radio that day about the "poor Latinas"? He obviously never met me or my mother!

Zulmara Cline

Beyond the Grave

I can clearly remember the happy weekends my family and I spent at my *abuelita* Susana's apartment in the South Bronx. We are a big Dominican family and loved getting together in my grandmother's home. As soon as you walked in, you would be enveloped in the delicious smells coming from the kitchen. You could practically taste the rice, beans and *pernil* in the air. If one of her five grandchildren had a birthday, there'd be a freshly baked cake with icing and sprinkles on the dining-room table. If it was Easter Sunday, you could count on getting a huge Easter basket filled with toys, plush teddy bears and lots of candy. As an eight-year-old child, going to her home was magical. She was a great cook and homemaker, but an even greater human being.

She had a calm and welcoming demeanor that could put anyone at ease. She was warm and nurturing, always caring for others, but not enough for herself. We don't know when she was diagnosed with lung cancer, but when we found out it was too late. She died the same year she told the family of her illness. By then, all we could do was comfort her and each other and enjoy what little time we had left together. She died in the hospital on December 26, 1989, five days after her sixty-second birthday.

We all missed her dearly. Family and close friends crammed into her apartment for a *velorio*, to pray for her and mourn her loss. That was the first and only time I ever saw my father cry. Tex didn't grieve aloud as everyone else. Silent tears streamed down his face, but I knew inside he was raging with grief. I understood that she had died, but, at such a young age, I couldn't fully grasp the impact of a loved one's death.

A couple of months after her death, I became very sick with a respiratory illness that just wouldn't go away. My mother was worried and prayed for my health.

One night she dreamt of my grandmother. In her dream, my grandmother rang the doorbell of our apartment. My mother opened the door in surprise.

"Susana, what are you doing here? You're not supposed to be here. You're dead."

"I didn't come to see you," Susana said. "I'm here to see Yahaira."

She went past my mother, entered my bedroom and closed the door behind her.

The next day I approached my mom in the living room.

"Mami, can I have a candle?"

"Why do you want a candle, Yary?" My mother frowned.

"It's for Abuelita Susana. I want to pray for her."

My mother remembered her dream from the night before and agreed to buy me the candle. Within the week, my respiratory illness had disappeared.

Since then I have maintained my "special bond" with my *abuelita*. Every once in a while, I make sure to light a candle in her name and pray. When I reach out to her in my time of need, I feel her presence and her love. It's been fifteen years since her death, and still, it comforts me to know that she can hear me and feel my love for her.

My mother retells this story every time the family gets together. For us, it's proof that family, love and faith know no limits. Love has no boundaries and can be felt across distance and time. Even from beyond the grave.

Yahaira Lawrence

Dad, the Rock Star of Tamale Makers

Muchos cocineros dañan la comida.

Mexican Saying

The week after Thanksgiving marks the beginning of tamale season. No sooner than the last piece of pumpkin pie is lifted from the tin, the questions begin for my dad, the tamale maestro.

"Uncle, can I come help you make tamales this year?" asks one of my perky cousins. "I really want to learn how so I can take over the tradition."

Yeah, right. As if it were that easy. Dad's tamales are ultimate perfection in flavor, consistency and presentation. They are the Carlos Santana of our Christmas buffet. For decades, my dad has been shredding, mixing, soaking, stirring, smearing and rolling ingredients to produce more than twenty dozen tamales within a three-day period. After all these years, I have enough crazy stories to rival a George Lopez stand-up routine. Here is one of my favorites.

In the movies, the tamale maker of *la familia* is always a kind, gentle and ultracheery matriarch who, with the help of all the women in the family, works her magic in the kitchen while sharing long, endearing stories. There are always happy little children around for that "awwww" effect.

So sweet.

Okay, reality check. Making enough tamales within a few days to feed a small army is enough to turn the sweetest of Nanas into a raging control freak. From straining the chiles to dropping the ball of *masa* in a glass of water and praying that it floats, the entire process is grueling and stressful.

I know because I've witnessed my dad go through it year after year. His temper gets short when too many nosy busybodies, like my cousins and I, pop into the kitchen to "help." Don't they know they are just heating up the room and slowing down his one-man mass-production line? The trouble is, no one can move fast enough to keep up with him. He doesn't play around. He takes this task more seriously than working the slots at the casino.

Dad dreads the experience as much as we savor the end result. Every December he threatens to boycott the act altogether, but with our constant nagging, his playful pride won't let him. He knows he rocks. He knows Christmas dinner would not be the same without his culinary contribution.

One year, he was in one of the worst moods I've ever seen. It was the one time when we truly accepted the idea that there wouldn't be any of his tamales for the holidays. Despite his official "I'm tired, I'm not doing it this year" speech, all our family whined and begged like sorry babies until he threw his hands up in the air and gave in. The entire week he complained and cussed. He tossed the bags of *hojas* on the counter with fierce anger and commanded all of us to stay the "blank" out of his way so he could get this "blank" over with.

Our response?

"Okay, but can you please make me a special mild batch, Dad?" I asked. "You know I don't like them too hot."

Next my mom piped in.

"Okay, honey," she said to Dad, "but don't forget to add more salt. Last year they needed more salt."

Next my little daughter, Maya.

"Grandpa, can I come watch?" she asked innocently.

Poor Dad! Not an ounce of respect!

Finally, Christmas day came, and we all piled into Nana's little house. We were starving. We waited all year for this moment. Where were those tamales?

My dad, looking as cool and debonair as Donald Trump, entered the cramped dining quarters holding the platter of his famous red chile treasures. He placed them on the table and looked at all of us with a long, thin smile. I thought I saw one eyebrow pop up. *Hmmm.* That look didn't register. Oh, well. He signaled for us to dig in. Talk about a tamale mosh pit! The twenty of us practically competed to see who could remove their husk first.

Almost simultaneously, we got to the good part and began to chomp.

"Are these the mild ones?" I asked, as I stuffed the first hunk in my *boca grande*.

Silence came over the room.

"Whoa," my cousin stated seriously, with his mouth full.

"*UUUnnnnncle!*" screamed my other cousin. I noticed her eyes were filled with tears. Ewwww. My tongue felt like it was on fire. At that moment, I knew what that sneaky smile was all about.

"Dad!!!" I chimed in my high-pitched voice. "These aren't mild! These are HOT! Extra, *EXTRA* hot!"

It was his revenge. We wanted our tamales. He gave us our tamales. He made an "exclusive" recipe that year: suicide hot (to match his mood at the time). I've never seen him laugh so hard as he watched us panic and climb over one another in Nana's tiny house to get drinks of anything icy cold.

We all have a newfound respect for my dad's tamales now—not only within the family, but also around the country. Last year, *Better Homes and Gardens* did a feature story on my dad and his tamales. To prepare for the photo shoot, a few of us finally got to see him make them from start to finish. He took time to explain every little detail, and demonstrated how to plop and roll the *masa* into the husk. And just like in the movies, all of us were gathered in the kitchen making tamales as he told us endearing stories about how he and my uncle Joe (also a tamale master) used to work at a tamale factory as kids. My little kids, DeAngelo and Maya, were there for the "Awww" factor. Again! Just like in the movies!

Making tamales is as important to him as it is to us. This year, Dad had to go on dialysis, and we're not sure if he will have the energy to keep up the tradition. We want him to hand over the kitchen and take a rest. He deserves it. He has served us well and set the standard. Thanks to his step-by-step lessons, we are honored to attempt to take over the duty. Hot chiles and all.

Kathy Cano Murillo

NO RODEO®

NO RODEO © *Robert Berardi. Used by permission.*

In the Blood

The brown-eyed child
and the white-haired grandfather
dance in the silent afternoon.
They snap their fingers
to a rhythm only those
who love can hear.

Pat Mora

Our Wonderful "Tragedy"

Nada es verdad ni nada es mentira, todo depende del cristal con que se mira.

Latino Proverb

Four years before I was born, my mom gave birth to a baby boy with Down syndrome. In 1958, children with Down syndrome were a rare breed and were often kept hidden and out of the public eye because they brought shame to their families. Little was known about this condition, but Mom and Dad took it in stride and were determined to make the best of the situation. The fragile little baby was nicknamed *Chispo*, Spanish for "tiny bit." He was only three pounds when he entered the world. Doctors didn't give Chispo much of a chance—a year at the most. After a few months in the hospital, my parents brought their physically challenged child home, determined to give Chispo the best year they could provide.

A year turned into two, and my mom had another child, a healthy baby girl. And two years after that, I came along. Chispo was now four and still couldn't walk on his own, but that didn't stop him from using me as his personal human teddy bear. We spent a great deal of time in my playpen where he would prop me up, lay me down, toss me around and, when mom wasn't looking, he would insert foreign objects up my nostrils and into my ears. I'm told that with the aid of his walker, he would drag me around the house. Maybe because I got tired of being his personal mop, I opted for walking sooner than usual—they tell me I took my first steps when I turned eight months old. The little boy in the walker taught me how to walk, and from then on we became a dynamic duo who drove my parents insane. Chispo finally started walking on his own when he was six, just in time to torment our younger brother, who had come along two years after me.

As my siblings and I grew older, we grew closer. There are five of us: Irene, Chispo, Maggie, Carlos and Miguel. My parents treated all of us the same; there were no extra points for higher intelligence, athletic ability, mental retardation or physical handicap. Four of us shared the first two of the above, but Chispo—the only one lacking those same two qualities—was by far the leader of the pack. During the years we attended the same school, we all lived in Chispo's shadow. Even when he didn't attend our school, he managed to somehow become the physical education teacher's assistant. Every kid from first to ninth grade knew Chispo and thought he was way cool. When we tried to cash in on his popularity, kids wouldn't believe that we were related. We would argue the point until the phys ed. teacher confirmed that we were indeed related—something I will treasure for as long as I live.

At one point, doctors predicted that Chispo wouldn't live past the age of eighteen. At the time, I was ten and figured that I had four years to prepare. Well, Chispo's eighteenth birthday came and went. Today he's forty-five—alive and kicking. My parents are now up in age, and their health is failing a bit. My little brother and I live far away in California, and my sisters have their own families to attend to, but every day when Mom and Dad wake up, there's an angel from heaven at their bedside encouraging them to go on. The "tragedy" that my parents brought into the world on February 2, 1958, grew up to become their most trusted and loyal companion.

My family has never felt an ounce of shame or regret about Chispo's condition. We've always believed he's an angel God sent to teach everyone who came in contact with him a lesson on how to live life. He's good, pure and honest, incapable of causing harm. He has affected the lives of many with his unconditional love, which flows freely and doesn't discriminate. Ironically, Chispo, who many in our world might judge as less than "normal," has taught us the dignity, nobility and virtue of being fully human. For as long as we live, we will proudly carry his example and his legacy in our hearts.

Carlos R. Bermúdez

Tita

Margarita Solis de Hernández is my grandmother. I was unable to say *abuelita* when I was small, so I named her Tita. Today if you wanted to meet my *tita*, you would have to visit a nursing home in Torrance, California. There is a beautiful patio with a fountain in the center of the building where a very kind nurse named Rosa wheels her out for fresh air.

You would see a frail, ninety-pound woman with cotton-white hair, wrinkled skin and no teeth. She no longer recognizes her loved ones and doesn't even know where she is. However, to those of us who have had the privilege of knowing her, we see an elegant lady who has lived her ninety-seven years with passion.

When I look at Tita, I see a beautiful woman who had a glorious love affair with a very handsome man, Alberto Solis. He worked in music and later became a pilot for Howard Hughes.

As Tita sleeps peacefully in her hospital bed, I see a sophisticated lady who has traveled all around the world. After the untimely death of my grandfather, Tita and her sister Julie went to places most people only dream of visiting. Hawaii, Japan, China, Russia, France, Italy, Germany and England were among their many destinations. Tita had a Bette Davis style and loved her four o'clock "*copitas*," which was either a shot of gold tequila or a Beefeater martini straight-up with extra olives (on the side as not to disperse any content from the glass).

As the nurses and attendees walk in and out of Tita's room, I want to stop each one of them and tell her story. "This is not just any little old lady. This is my *tita!*"

I shout it silently from my heart as I watch the kindly hospital staff patiently tend to her. "She met Pancho Villa for heaven's sake! She's seen the world! Do you know who this woman is?"

Even now, everybody falls in love with Tita. She blows kisses and tells the people who feed and bathe her that she loves them. Although her mind and body are deteriorating, Tita's spirit is alive and well. Her eyes still sparkle with love. Sometimes I can even see that light of mischievousness that once gleamed when she'd play canasta, spin the roulette wheel or bargain with the vendors as we shopped in Juárez. "*Pero Señor . . . somos mexicanos . . .*" she would say, with a sly smile and that funny little glint in her eye. That expression would always get us a great price!

As I look down the hallway of the nursing home, it occurs to me that each of these rooms has a "Tita." Every frail, hunched-over body with cotton-white hair has a unique story filled with love, loss, pain, happiness and adventure. Most of them survived the Depression and experienced World War II. They were around before TV, studied in one-room schoolhouses, and, if you asked them, they could tell you about a time when you could see a picture show and buy a hamburger and a Coke, all for about a quarter.

Today, Tita is very much like a new baby. She is fed pureed food, wears diapers and looks with wonder around the room as if she sees angels floating around the ceiling. Sometimes as she looks, she points and calls out to her loved ones who have passed on. She sees little girls in white dresses playing with their dolls, family members and friends. She smiles, laughs and even speaks to them with love.

One day, my uncle and I witnessed Tita's "visitation" by family members together. "Oh, Cindy," he said with tender sadness. "Our little Tita is hallucinating."

I smiled back at him, and as the tears filled my eyes, I quietly said, "Just because we can't see them, Uncle Dickie, doesn't mean they're not there." I think they will continue to visit her until they're ready to welcome her home.

Cindy Lou Jordan

Oysters and Zarzuelas

Abuela Rufa,
my great-grandmother,
cigar-smoking,
bossy,
I-wear-the-pants-in-the-family
kind of woman,
used to set her chair
out back
on the porch,
Sunday afternoons
under the old avocado tree,
balmy breezes off Key West
flirting with her,
pail full of oysters
between her legs.
One by one,
she'd pry them open
with her ivory-hard nails,
a spritz of lime
and Tabasco,
and down they'd go.

READER/CUSTOMER CARE SURVEY

REFG

We care about your opinions! Please take a moment to fill out our online Reader Survey at **http://survey.hcibooks.com**.
As a **"THANK YOU"** you will receive a **VALUABLE INSTANT COUPON** towards future book purchases
as well as a **SPECIAL GIFT** available only online! Or, you may mail this card back to us.

(PLEASE PRINT IN ALL CAPS)

First Name _____ MI. _____ Last Name _____

Address _____

State _____ Zip _____ City _____ Email _____

1. Gender
- ☐ Female ☐ Male

2. Age
- ☐ 8 or younger
- ☐ 9-12 ☐ 13-16
- ☐ 17-20 ☐ 21-30
- ☐ 31+

3. Did you receive this book as a gift?
- ☐ Yes ☐ No

4. Annual Household Income
- ☐ under $25,000
- ☐ $25,000 - $34,999
- ☐ $35,000 - $49,999
- ☐ $50,000 - $74,999
- ☐ over $75,000

5. What are the ages of the children living in your house?
- ☐ 0 - 14 ☐ 15+

6. Marital Status
- ☐ Single
- ☐ Married
- ☐ Divorced
- ☐ Widowed

7. How did you find out about the book?
(please choose one)
- ☐ Recommendation
- ☐ Store Display
- ☐ Online
- ☐ Catalog/Mailing
- ☐ Interview/Review

8. Where do you usually buy books?
(please choose one)
- ☐ Bookstore
- ☐ Online
- ☐ Book Club/Mail Order
- ☐ Price Club (Sam's Club, Costco's, etc.)
- ☐ Retail Store (Target, Wal-Mart, etc.)

9. What subject do you enjoy reading about the most?
(please choose one)
- ☐ Parenting/Family
- ☐ Relationships
- ☐ Recovery/Addictions
- ☐ Health/Nutrition
- ☐ Christianity
- ☐ Spirituality/Inspiration
- ☐ Business Self-help
- ☐ Women's Issues
- ☐ Sports

10. What attracts you most to a book?
(please choose one)
- ☐ Title
- ☐ Cover Design
- ☐ Author
- ☐ Content

TAPE IN MIDDLE; DO NOT STAPLE

BUSINESS REPLY MAIL
FIRST-CLASS MAIL PERMIT NO 45 DEERFIELD BEACH, FL

POSTAGE WILL BE PAID BY ADDRESSEE

Chicken Soup for the Soul®
3201 SW 15th Street
Deerfield Beach FL 33442-9875

FOLD HERE

Do you have your own Chicken Soup story
that you would like to send us?
Please submit at: **www.chickensoup.com**

Comments

I don't know
if oysters are aphrodisiacs,
but by the time she'd reach
the bottom of the pail,
she'd be in love with the world,
singing *zarzuelas*
from her childhood days,
inviting everyone to join her
on the porch
in the shade,
where she'd kiss the children,
hug the women,
and share *una copita de jerez*
with the men,
shouting for all to hear,
"I've never found a pearl,
but I've learned about hope."

Maria Ercilla

The Cuban Kitchen Dance

Love is a lot like dancing—you just surrender to the music.

Anonymous

The unforgiving heat waves rolled off the stove as the aroma of creamy Cuban café perfumed the whole house, floating into the bedrooms and bathrooms and out the backyard into the Miami Beach air.

An earthy steam rose from a pot of *potaje* (stew) as it bubbled and hissed, while the Queen of Salsa, Celia Cruz, belted out her tunes from a little kitchen counter radio.

There was Mami, center stage, swirling and swaying rhythmically on the kitchen floor as if she were the star of her own Broadway show. Her wisps of auburn hair followed her every move. When she moved to the left, her hair whipped to the left, as if on command. When she moved to the right, it shifted in that direction with the same precision.

Mami always did this. It was a daily kitchen routine. She would break into dance while toasting bread, washing dishes or beating eggs to concoct some sweet Cuban flan. She would spend the day cooking or cleaning while my sister, Cary, and I were at school and my dad was exterminating bugs at local Miami Beach hotels.

That day was a typical lunch hour for my mom except that I happened to be home. It was Saturday. I was standing in the corner, a ten-year-old boy with coffee-hued curly hair, giggling at the sight of his wacky mother dancing with an invisible partner. And then it happened. The kitchen floor became the dance floor, and Mami suddenly pulled me on center stage, to, ugh, *bailar.*

Oh, my gosh, I thought to myself. *¡Qué pena! Why me? Why not Cary? Where's Papi? Can any of our American neighbors see us through the windows?*

I didn't know how to dance, but that didn't stop Mami from forcing my two left feet to move. She whipped me around on the kitchen floor the way she whipped fluffy meringue. She twirled me like a strand of pasta!

I tried to escape, but to no avail. Her arms locked me in place. Celia Cruz did her thing on the radio, and Mami did hers in the kitchen, with me in tow.

The music played, and Mami began to strut her stuff.

"Ahora Yonito, a la izquierda, a la derecha, adelante y para atrás," my mom announced, calling me by my family nickname, telling me to move to the left, then right, back and forth.

I tried to follow her lead, but I couldn't capture the beat. I wanted to breakdance or just break away, period.

"Mami, no quiero hacerlo," I complained. "My friends at school don't dance to this stuff!"

Her response? *"Ahora Yonny, a la izquierda, a la derecha, adelante y para atrás! Anda!"*

She wasn't listening, maybe because la Celia was singing at the top of her lungs in the background, or maybe because Mami was gonna teach me how to dance no matter what.

I was frustrated. So was my mom. I kept stepping on her feet instead of the beige kitchen tile.

Dancing felt awkward. My skinny legs couldn't keep up with her curvaceous flowing strides. My legs were like two sticks that wouldn't bend. I felt like a right-handed person suddenly forced to write with his left hand.

Seeing my frustration, my mom stopped and told me to listen to the beat pounding from the radio. She held my hands and said to clap whenever I heard the beat.

CLAP! CLAP! CLAP CLAP! CLAP! CLAP CLAP!

For a while, it sounded like a round of applause thundering in the kitchen.

But then, something happened. Mr. Two Left Feet began to catch on. After I clapped to the rapid gunfire of beats, my mom told me to move to them.

Swing back, CLAP!

Step forward, CLAP!

To the left, CLAP!

To the right, CLAP!

My hands were clapping, and my feet were stomping, and I found myself swaying and swirling with Mami. The Cuban kitchen dance!

The spurts of Latin beats flowed from the radio into my heart, legs and arms. Some beats were *rápido*. Others were *lento*. Either way, I caught on to the burst of beats and to the rhythms crackling from the tiny kitchen counter radio.

We danced on and on to Celia, then to other timeless Cuban favorites.

My mom led the way that day, but, eventually, I began to lead her. I twirled her all over the kitchen, then the *comedor*, as beads of sweat lined our faces, and our hearts thudded to the beats. It was dance fever!

Memories of the Cuban kitchen dance were stirred recently when I bought my first home in Boston, Massachusetts, about 1,500 miles away from Mami's *cocina*/dance floor. And funny enough, my new kitchen resembles Mami's, with a bright beige tiled floor, wooden kitchen cabinets and a little kitchen radio that sits on my Formica counter.

On weekends, as I prepare my lunch, I catch myself dancing with an invisible partner to the sounds of Gloria Estefan or Shakira, moving to the left, shaking it to the right, *adelante y para atrás!*

I close my eyes, listen to the beat and imagine that I am ten years old all over again, dancing with Mami in our Cuban kitchen.

Johnny Diaz

NO RODEO®

NO RODEO © *Robert Berardi. Used by permission.*

NO RODEO, *Robert Berardi,* ©2005, *reprinted by permission of Robert Berardi.*

Mother's Shoes

I implore you to see with a child's eyes, to hear with a child's ears, and to feel with a child's heart.

Antonio Novello

My mind struggles to remember a time, many years ago, when I was just a child. I was four years of age, and the memory is not complete or vivid, more like a puzzle with pieces missing, a movie fast-forwarded in certain places.

It's a cloudy, overcast day. There is a parade in town, and it's really crowded. I'm standing next to my mother, holding her hand and trying to see the parade through all the people in front of me, but I'm so small I mostly see the backs of their legs. Realizing this, my mother pushes me gently out onto the curb to sit with my siblings. From here the view is better, though a little scary because everything looms overhead. Now the chance of being stepped on by a horse or something larger seems real.

People are laughing and clapping all around me, and everyone seems so happy.

I'm sitting on the curb, watching the clowns go by in their silly hats and red noses. I see their large funny shoes and their colorful clothes, but as much as I like them, I can't help being afraid when one of them stoops down to hand me a balloon. I turn to look for my mother, feeling the urge to run back to her, but my older brother wraps his arm around me and soon we are giggling again.

The music from the marching band fills my head, and I am laughing with my brothers and sisters as a group of little dogs dances for us. Some boys on bikes do tricks, ringing their bells and honking their horns as they go by.

I'm very happy and excited by everything going on around me, but I find myself looking back every once in a while to where my mother stands. I can't see her face because of all the people, but I recognize her worn, scuffed shoes. They have been in the same place since she pushed me out onto the curb. Every time something comes by that scares me, I look back for my mother's shoes, knowing she will be there waiting for me to run and hide in her arms if I become too afraid.

It seems that all too soon the parade is over, but we are still sitting on the curb, confetti and ticker tape all around us. My sisters are excitedly talking about their favorite part of the parade, each trying to outdo the other. My older brother sits next to me, holding my hand as I lean against him. I'm getting sleepy, and I want to go home. I turn to look for my mother's shoes, but this time they aren't where they were before. Afraid, I cry out and feel my brother squeeze my hand.

"*Mira*," he whispers, pointing the other way.

I turn to see my mother standing there, smiling at us. She looks so beautiful. She's holding a box, and from it comes the sound of peeps and scratching. She lowers the box so we can look into it, and baby chicks look up at us.

Each of them is dyed a bright pink, green or yellow. There are five chicks in all, one for each of us.

"*Feliz Día de Pascuas,*" my mother says.

We all jump up and down, clapping our hands and laughing because we are so happy.

We sit on the curb playing with the baby chicks for a while and coming up with names for them.

Finally, my mother hands the box to my brother and gently picks me up. I lay my head on her shoulder as we start for home, and soon I am fast asleep, dreaming of funny clowns and pink baby chicks.

Irma Y. Andrade

3

LIFE'S LESSONS/ *LECCIONES QUE DA LA VIDA*

Lo que en los libros no está, la vida te enseñará.

Latino Proverb

Things I Learned from My Mother

The stars are constantly shining, but often we do not see them until the dark hours.

Anonymous

When I was sixteen, my best friend and I went to the neighborhood Woolworth, crammed ourselves into a tiny, curtained cubicle and, after paying a quarter, mugged wildly while a camera took four consecutive snapshots of us. The resulting pictures, a strip of black-and-white photographs of inferior quality, made us laugh for hours. Much later, when Marilyn and I were examining the pictures for what seemed to be the hundredth time, she said something that made me question whether the pictures were as amusing as I first imagined.

"You remind me of your mother in these pictures," Marilyn remarked.

I went home and threw the pictures into the trash.

Back then, there was nothing that could insult me more than being compared to my mother. The truth was, and it hurts me to admit it, I was ashamed of her. And so, throughout my teen years, I did everything possible to prove that I was the antithesis of what I perceived her to be.

I had not always felt negatively about Mami. As a little girl, I was nicknamed "*El Chiclet*" because one of our neighbors observed that I stuck to my mother much like a piece of gum stubbornly adheres to the bottom of a shoe. Whether my mother was shopping, washing clothes or catching a TV show at our neighbor's apartment, I was there with her. I was so attached to her, in fact, that I often spent hours perched on a stool watching her iron the men's shirts she took in to earn a few extra dollars. I would be mesmerized by the fluid movements of her hands as she spread each shirt flat, smoothed it with her palms and rhythmically ironed the wrinkles away.

Most times, Mami hummed or sang as she worked her way through dozens of shirts, but on occasion, if I begged long enough, she would tell me a story. Mami would entertain me with stories about Juan Bobo, the famous Puerto Rican simpleton, or her own versions of fairy tales. My favorite was one about a damsel who rode on the back of a mythical creature to rescue her true love. Mami loved board games and could play Parcheesi or Chinese checkers for hours. She always beat me at Chinese checkers. I asked her once why she never let me win. She said that when I finally learned to play well enough to win on my own, I would appreciate it all the more. To this day, I can't recall if that ever happened.

I don't remember exactly when my feelings for my mother changed. I do know, however, that by the time I was in high school, Mami and I spent most of our time bickering. I resented everything about her, even those things she had no control over. I was embarrassed by her appearance because she was short and overweight. I was ashamed of her pitiable lack of education and broken

English. I was mortified whenever she went through other people's garbage and salvaged things like toasters and irons so she could fix them and have a "new" appliance. The things I resented most of all, however, were Mami's rules. At eighteen, I still had a midnight curfew, and I was never allowed to sleep over at any friend's house. I fought her on every rule she imposed. Our home was a battlefield because she would not give in to me, just like she'd never let me win at Chinese checkers.

I moved out of my house eight months after I graduated from high school. In the years that followed, my mother and I lived in relative, distant peace. We talked on the phone occasionally; we saw each other even less. I never revealed anything about my life to her that would cause conflict between us. We both liked it that way.

It was not until I had my first child that my relationship with my mother began to change. My sister's daughter, my mother's only other grandchild, was already ten, and Mami was thrilled to have a new grandson to play with. We started visiting each other more often, and I discovered that Mami instinctively knew how to grandparent. She gently guided me when I asked for advice, but she never interfered.

Shortly after my son celebrated his second birthday, Mami was diagnosed with acute leukemia and was hospitalized for eight months. Weakened by chemotherapy and now confined to a wheelchair, Mami was no longer able to live alone. My husband and I offered to bring her to live with us.

While my sister and I were sorting through Mami's possessions in anticipation of her move into my home, I discovered the sepia-toned strip of pictures that Marilyn and I had taken at Woolworth. Somehow, Mami had rescued them from the trash and saved them in her photo album. As I grinned at the silly snapshots, I still could not see the resemblance between Mami and me that had been so obvious to my friend.

If I were ever to categorize the periods of my life that have given me the most grief and the most joy, I would have to say that the time my mother lived with us would count as both. During those years, my husband and I sacrificed our privacy and built our lives around my mother's comfort and care. We took her to all of her doctor's appointments, drove her to chemotherapy sessions and shopped for special foods. I monitored her medications and learned to inject her with insulin to control the diabetes she developed from the chemotherapy drugs. And yet, I have many wonderful memories of that time as well.

I can remember Mami's excitement when my son, Nick, and I gave her a wheelchair tour of the Bronx Zoo, and she spotted a baby giraffe. I can still recollect her exhilaration when we took her to visit her family in Puerto Rico. And best of all, I can still recall the bickering between Mami and Nick when they played Chinese checkers. She complained that he cheated, and he whined, not surprisingly, that she never let him win.

Two years after coming to live with us, Mami passed away, leaving me with an unbridgeable chasm of grief that, in some ways, I still carry with me today. Every once in a while, I pull out my mother's old album and stare at that yellowed strip of photographs that my friend and I took so many years ago.

The young girl in those photos who was ashamed of her mother has grown up. Today I search to find a similarity with the woman who taught herself to read and write, who had to iron men's shirts to make ends meet, and who was the best darned small-appliance repairman on La Salle Street.

Sylvia Rosa-Casanova

Learning to Fly

*What matters in life is not what happens to you,
but what you remember and how you remember
it.*

Gabriel García Márquez

I never really knew my father, even though I grew up in his presence. His love affair with booze kept him occupied most of the time, but when there were glimpses of affection, they were magical.

My father could make a completely aerodynamic aircraft out of a piece of paper like I had never seen anyone do. Every opportunity I had, I asked him to build me one of those planes. He took what seemed like hours—folding and tearing and licking and scrutinizing. The end result was a plane that, if launched under a stiff wind, could travel a whole block.

My father knew about my fascination with his planes, yet he never took the time to teach me how to make one. Perhaps it was because he knew that his planes were the price of admission into my heart until his next appointment with the bottle. If I knew how to make one, he would no longer have the currency. Or perhaps I never really wanted to learn. Those special moments with him were so rare.

As I got older, I lost interest in his planes, and we kept growing apart until eventually we rarely spoke.

Today, I make paper airplanes for my own two sons—not nearly as well as my father—but I see and feel the same magic and enthusiasm in them that I felt during the special times with my father.

I wish he were here to see what a great pilot he was, in spite of everything.

I miss you, *Papi.*

Steve Peralta

Every First Friday

*La experiencia no es el más amable de los mae-
stros, pero sin duda el más sabio.*

Latino Proverb

I looked out the window and couldn't see a thing. I had to scrape off the frost with my fingernails in order to glimpse the gusting wind and thrusting snow. No one would dare venture out on such a cold winter night unless they had no other choice: My mother was one of those people. Mama was on her way to her job cleaning offices in downtown Chicago. Under her scarf and hat, I could see her tired eyes. Standing next to her was my younger brother, César. He was also covered from head to toe in winter wear, but his eyes sparkled.

On the first Friday of the month, Mama was allowed to bring her children to work. I was about twelve years old at the time; my brother was ten. She worked Monday through Saturday from 11 P.M. to 6 A.M. She had to take three buses to get downtown. On every first Friday, César was right there with her. I, on the other hand, was always too busy. If it wasn't baseball practice, basketball tryouts or some movie, I'd come up with another excuse. I couldn't see myself staying awake all night cleaning offices. César and Mama would beg me to go along, but after a while they stopped asking, knowing I'd say no. It was different for my brother. César would come home and excitedly tell me how he had helped Mom vacuum the carpets, dust, and throw out the trash. But the highlight of his night was always playing hide-and-seek with the other workers' children.

My mother's coworkers were all immigrants, mostly Polish and Mexican women. Many were from our neighborhood, and they, too, would take their sons and daughters to clean offices on those first Fridays. Most of them labored this horrendous shift so they could send their children to Catholic schools. My mother was no exception.

My parents came to this country from Mexico and at first did not speak English, so the only jobs they could find were manual labor. Remarkably, through it all, my mother never complained about being too tired or too busy. She cooked us breakfast every morning, was always there for us after school and made sure we were safely in bed before she left for work.

How cozy it must be for lawyers and dentists to show off their offices to their children. It's much different taking your child on three buses on a cold Friday night to help you clean them. But my mother was willing to do it. She wanted our company, but more important, she wanted to show us how she paid the bills. But I never once saw for myself how Mama earned her livelihood.

When I was a senior in high school, I asked my brother why he had loved going to those offices so much. Did he actually like dusting and vacuuming? His answer wasn't at all what I expected. He said the reason he went was not that he liked picking up after other people, but because he loved spending time with Mom. He said he felt sad each night when she left for work; he was always wishing she didn't have to go. So for at least one evening a month, he had the chance to be right there with her. I felt ashamed, wondering why I hadn't seen it that way. To me, it was a chore, something I was too good for. I had the luxury of saying no; my mother didn't. And my brother had actually *chosen* to do it.

Ironically, after graduating from college with a degree in accounting, César found a job in the very same building my mother had cleaned years before. On his first day, César wore a suit; he was now a businessman. My mother straightened his tie, kissed him on the cheek and gave him her blessing. But on the way to his car, my brother stopped and rushed back to the house. He set down his briefcase, put his arms around our mother and began to cry. She embraced him even tighter and also wept. The cleaning lady's son had grown up.

As I watched this display of love and tenderness between mother and son, I realized the full extent of my mother's sacrifices. And today, I often think of my brother's warmth and generosity. He understood as a boy what it took years for me to learn. He knew how to express love, gratitude and affection toward his family. He also realized that certain opportunities come only once in a lifetime, and that if you don't grab them, they're gone forever. Mama passed away several years ago, and not a day goes by that I don't have her in my mind and heart.

How I wish I had gone to clean those offices.

Alejandro Díaz

Isabel's Final Chapter

My mother came to live with me before she died. Her name was Isabel, and she was with me during the final six months of her life, before she lost her fight with metastatic breast cancer and Alzheimer's disease. We never thought about having anyone but family care for her, which helped me focus on preparing for such a physically and emotionally challenging process instead of wasting energy figuring out what to do. Ironically, because of the Alzheimer's, she did not remember that she was dying, and in many ways she was more tranquil and cheerful than she had been since my father's death seven years before.

We wove our distinct lives together. Every day she complained that her *café* was too cold or too strong before heading off for the Alzheimer's day care center that we called "The Senior." She believed she was volunteering there, and it was one of the multiple redesigns of reality that I shaped to help us both cope with our daily losses. She was becoming more childlike than my eight-year-old twins; I was becoming my mother's mother. I was a caregiver, juggling my job, my kids, my *mamita* and my own sanity and self-care.

It was Memorial Day, 2003. Monday dawned with my mom's sharp cries of pain. "*¡Ay, ay, ay, caray! Me duele la cadera,*" she exclaimed. That very same hip had alerted us almost two years ago that her journey on Earth was beginning its final chapter. Being my mother's daughter, I went into task mode and began giving her more pain pills and checking in with the hospice nurse. The tender feelings I had unearthed over the months of caring for my mom made me both present to the moment and scared for what it foretold.

Before this episode, each pain medication adjustment had quickly relieved her aches so that we would continue with our delicate balance. I slowly comprehended that this time was distinctly different. Three days passed, and the pain did not subside, even though I doubled and then tripled her medication doses.

Mom relaxed on Thursday, staying in bed and reading the paper over and over again, oblivious to the efforts being made on her behalf. By nighttime, some liquid morphine had been delivered. I was instructed to give her a dose every hour until she was no longer in pain. After four doses, she became delusional. "Where is the letter from Colombia?" she repeatedly asked, looking at me with suspicion. This distrust was so different than the harmonious connections we had developed that it brought up great wells of anguish, which I futilely attempted to keep at bay.

Instead of going along with her train of thought, something I had become quite adept at, I fought it. I didn't want her to leave our sweet and crazy coexistence. Despite all the anxiety and work, I had come to appreciate giving her the comfort of being in my home.

After a few minutes, I found Mom in the bathroom squeezing the crinkly paper around a Kalonchoe plant, saying she wanted some candy, her hands pecking away at the sound her mind identified as belonging to a candy wrapper. I tried to wrest it from her strong grasp.

"It's not candy, Mom," I said, in a disapproving tone. "It's a plant."

She held on determinedly, but finally threw it in the trash and walked haltingly back to her bed. I rescued the *plantita* and hid it in my room.

In the morning, it was clear that she was rapidly losing her capacity to provide any self-care. I sobbed on the phone to my sister and brother, who quickly made arrangements to come join me.

By Saturday, Mom was not eating and had been reduced to wearing diapers and a morphine patch to keep her comfortable. I wasn't prepared for such a swift departure, such a momentous leave-taking. The intensity of her decline was profound to the friends who came to bring us food, give us hugs and visit her while she rested. There was no mistaking that my mom's body was letting go of the battle.

We called her *familia* in Colombia, letting them know the tide had turned and providing them the remarkable opportunity to share some last words with her. Of this I will always be proud, that her brother, sister, nieces, great-nephews and good friends were able to fill her soul with messages of love and *cariño* in her last days.

On Sunday, Mom slept for the most part, a few mumbles emitted at times. She was especially verbal when we disturbed her stupor to change her diapers. *"Brrruuuutaaaaasss"* would slip slowly from her mouth. Ah, yes, her final words were not very poetic, but they were definitely true to her feisty nature, a character that had served her well and had protected her in this country that she had adopted as her own over fifty years before.

In-between caring for her and managing the traffic flow, I was filled with the need to make Colombian *tamales*. It was an added chore in the midst of all the caretaking, but it seemed part of a natural sequence, to smell the chicken stewing in the cumin that she valued as a key flavor, the *masa* warm and moist, squeezing through my hands as it had done so many times through her hands. I have her hands, active *como dos pajaritos, volando por la vida.*

In the evening, her breathing became more labored, and my sister Susan and I doubted she'd make it through the night. Two *curanderas* taught us how to speak with my *mamita* and how to let her go. We burned copal and soothed her body with *yerbas y flores,* lit candles and brought flowers to surround her with beauty, just as she had always done in her home and garden. Peaceful music wafted in and around us as we held our vigil constantly now. The candles burned unhurriedly, echoing her slow breathing.

On Tuesday a priest gave her the last rites. He spoke in English and Spanish and reminded us that hearing was the last sense to leave, and that we should touch her with both our words and hands. Her space had become a sacred environment, the intersection of life and death for her and for all who came to sit and honor her passing.

On Wednesday morning, the *curandera* came to help reunite my siblings and I, as the stress of the moment had caused old tensions to arise among us. She told me as she left that it wouldn't be long, and that I would know when the time was near. I went upstairs at about 3:30 to sit with my mother and hold her hand. Antonio, my housemate, was there as well, holding her other hand. This is how we had been the last six months, the trio, experiencing our lives and struggles together *con mucho cariño.*

I wondered what else I could say to help my mom pass over. I promised I would continue to throw little *papelitos* at Antonio to tease him as she had done. I assured her I would put her favorite food on the altar for *día de los muertos*— *aquacate, mango, tamales, café.* I realized these are my favorite foods, too, part of my life, thanks to my mom.

Suddenly, she opened her eyes and looked at me. I looked back and saw her pupils were dilated. The color went completely out of her lips, and she closed her eyes. I knew without a doubt that it was time. I quickly asked Antonio to call the others to come, and they did, circling her bed. I held one hand, my brother Rosendo the other. Susan asked me to sing "Amazing Grace," and I said I would do my best, even as the tears flowed and my voice cracked.

"'Tis grace that brought me safe thus far, and grace will lead me home," I sang to my *mamita*, watching as her once strong pulse dissipated, the river of life finally letting go and departing.

I realized later that my mom was completely present in her passage, uncharacteristically patient in her final days. She let us love her and *acariciarla* like she never could while fully alive. She rested, as she hadn't during her life, with music and candles and *yerbas*. And my mom finally accepted the hand and heart I had extended to her for so many years to help her cross to the other side.

In return, I promised to value and learn from her complex relationships on Earth, her hilarity and her disappointments, her triumphs and her tragedies.

I let go of my fear of death that day in June and welcomed it as a natural process. That is a gift she gave to all of us present with her those last few days, one that I will carry with me forever.

Linda M. González

Learning to Appreciate Papi

In 1963, when we left Cuba and immigrated to the United States, my parents lost all their possessions. We moved to McAllen, Texas, where my parents had to start all over again. They both felt strongly about my mother staying home with us. This meant that my father had to work even harder to make ends meet. It also meant making many sacrifices as a family. Throughout my childhood, many of my memories are of my father working in the family fabric store. My father worked twelve- and fourteen-hour days, usually seven days a week. Occasionally, he would take a Sunday afternoon off.

Not once in all those years did I hear my mother complain about the long hours my father worked. My parents were in their late twenties, and I'm sure they missed not spending more time with each other as a couple. However, they were both committed to making it in this country, and they knew that unless they supported each other, they would not be able to accomplish their goals. My mother never spent money carelessly, buying only what was necessary. She cooked, cleaned and made all of our clothing.

My mother would remind us on a daily basis about how hard my father worked, about how much he loved us and about the sacrifices he was making so that we could establish ourselves in the United States. My mother taught us to be considerate toward my father, and as we watched the way that she always took care of him, we learned to take care of him, too.

When my brother and I misbehaved, she would tell us how disappointed my father would be when he walked into the house from work and found us punished, sitting in silence. I remember hearing my father's car coming up the driveway and my brother and I promising my mother that we would never fight again, pleading with her to let us get up before my father walked in.

For many years, we lived a few blocks from downtown McAllen, and on Saturdays we would walk to the fabric store. We would usually find my father standing behind the counter, bantering with a customer as they haggled on the price of a few yards of fabric.

I loved watching the way my father would make a slit at the end of a piece of fabric with his scissors and then rip the rest of the fabric with his hands. I can still picture him with his pencil behind his ear, a habit he still has, and his scissors sticking out behind his belt. And how proud I always felt that the man behind the counter was my Papi.

Saturday was the busiest day of the week, and my mother would always bring him lunch. The three of us would go into a small office that wasn't much bigger than a walk-in closet and sit with my dad while he ate.

Instead of resenting my father's work, we were taught to love what he did and to admire him for his commitment to success. We always understood that he was doing this for us. My brother and I love the family business because it is so much a part of who my father is. All the years of hard work that he put into the business paid off, and because of him our family has had a wonderful life.

I have so many memories of our doing things together as a family that when I became an adult and realized that those trips to the beach or picnics at Anzaldúa Park were few and far between, it was hard to believe.

In a family, children learn about relationships by watching how their parents behave and treat each other, as husband and wife. Part of being a parent is teaching your children to love your spouse. One of the most important things a mother can do for her children is to teach them to appreciate, to love and to respect their father.

María Luisa Salcines

Swim Like a Fish

El que nada no se ahoga.

Latino Proverb

Memories are like dreams, they are made of that same magical vapor. Misty and illusory, the details vanish in a fog. What's important in a memory is what you take from it, the way you remember the truth.

It was a cool autumn afternoon. The leaves on the palm trees were green and swayed in the breeze. There are no changes of season in Miami, yet it must have been autumn because I know for certain I was wearing sneakers and a sweatsuit, and that my *titi's* six-foot-deep, rectangular pool was too cold to use.

In the memory, I am seven years old. I'm all alone on the patio, looking into the pool at my reflection and the sky's. I have the sense I shouldn't be out here alone. I know I've been warned many times about playing too close to the edge even though my *tío* has been teaching me to swim. For Latinos, a *tío* is an uncle, but my *tío* has also been my babysitter, my *abuelo*, and sometimes even my dad. The men in our family have all functioned in each of the roles at one time or another.

I am looking at my reflection or a leaf, I can't remember which, when what my *titi* has prophesied all along finally comes to pass: I fall into the deep end of the pool. Normally, this wouldn't be such a big deal; just this past summer I had mastered swimming through the deepest parts. Of course, that was when my whole family was watching, when my older cousins were close by, and I was aided by inflatable orange arm floats and a two-piece princess swimsuit. Today I am wearing sneakers and sweatpants, items that become like dumbbells in the water, grabbing at my ankles and tiring me out with every feeble kick.

My uncle must have been watching from the sliding-glass doors in the living room, because within seconds he is standing on the edge of the pool as I thrash toward the surface. My long black hair is in my face. Like a black garbage bag, it suffocates and blinds me. I pant and cry out toward his brown leather penny loafers for help. My uncle does not jump in to rescue me, but the loafers keep pace beside me in the pool.

"Swim to the shallow side. You can do it! Keep swimming. Come on. You're almost to the other side. Just like I taught you. Keep going." His deep baritone voice is thick and soothing.

I spit and suck in water at the same time. "But . . . I can't . . . make it!" The words come out in spurts as I struggle to keep my head above water.

"Not like a froggy. Cup your hands. Face to one side, arm over shoulder. Face to the other side, again arm over shoulder. Your feet are fish fins; *swim like a fish!* Come on, Mama. Just like I taught you." He would accept nothing less than perfect strokes.

My panic gave way to exasperation as I grew more tired with each tiny kick. When I had made it to the other side, I got out of the pool and, catching my breath, looked up into my uncle's beaming face. My large dark eyes must have conveyed the fear and outrage of someone who is both angry at the outside world and embarrassed by her own stupidity. I began to cry, a cry that turned into a wail that did not subside until my *titi,* looking through the window in the kitchen and seeing me soaked and the green pool still rippling, ran outside, scooped me into her arms, wrapped me in a towel and carried me inside the house.

Some time after they pacified me, after the warm bath, the dinner and the hot Swiss Miss cocoa with the floating marshmallows that always melted too fast, I forgot all about it. I didn't even remember to thank my *tío.*

Years later, that memory surfaced. Maybe you've had a moment, a life-altering moment, whose meaning takes years to reveal itself to you. The events in our lives are not important because of the sequence in which they occur but rather because of the order in which we remember them. My uncle taught me a valuable lesson that day by the pool, the day I naively assumed he was letting me drown. He knew I would be able to save myself because he had already taught me how to swim. He knew that no matter what life had in store for me, no matter how many times I'd fall into the deep end of life's scariest seas, I could depend on myself to find my way back up to the light, to the surface, close to God and the sun.

It is only when we doubt our strengths, when we fear the sudden change in the current, that we take in water and begin to sink. We drown ourselves. And our family members, whose job it once was to protect us from harm's way, are our coaches, watching from the sidelines as we take control of our own lives.

Every decision we make, every kick of the foot and stroke of the arm, is a move toward our own destiny.

Melissa Annette Santiago

Hey, Mister!

If today brings even one choice your way, choose to be a bringer of the light.

Anonymous

On that morning in early spring, the track was cluttered with kids. They were dotted all along the path, and often I had to steer around them in order to pass. Some shuffled. They dragged their feet and raised a dry, red dust. Others, mostly girls, walked arm in arm, blocking the lanes and forcing me to skip off and on the trail.

They were in my way.

And it disturbed me.

But one boy in particular got under my skin. He walked alone, mumbling, and each time I passed him this kid called out to me. "Hey, Mister," he'd say, but I would just ignore him, picking up my pace and jogging by.

He did it without fail.

Repeatedly.

The boy stole my thoughts when all I wanted was to think about my son. We hadn't spoken in over a year, and

I needed now, this day, to figure a way to mend our relationship. But as I jogged, praying for God's advice, trying to feel his word, this dark, little imp kept interrupting me.

"Mister!" he'd say on cue whenever I passed him. "Hey, Mister!"

Once, as I glanced at him, I guessed that he was about ten years old, maybe eleven. The boy looked up at me with a tiny, wrinkled nose. It supported black, horn-rimmed glasses that were way too big for him. Like his sneakers, I thought. His shoes were also untied, and their lolling white tongues reminded me of thirsty dogs.

The next time I approached him, I noticed that he was knock-kneed. He was thin, stooped and, with a slightly oversized head attached to a long, slim neck, he looked . . . well, ill. It was then I first suspected that something was wrong with him.

With all of them.

Still, I didn't turn when again he called me.

I didn't want to see him.

I didn't want to speak with any of them.

But as I continued to run—even with blinders now—I couldn't deny that all these children were handicapped, disabled in one way or another, physically or mentally or both. Remembering where I ran, I realized that they were members of a special day care program run by Westwood Park, a Westside annex of the San Antonio Parks and Recreation Department.

Up ahead the boy kept turning. As I watched him search for me—the sun glaring off his thick, heavy lenses, and that wrinkled nose following me—he stumbled and nearly fell, having tripped over his own two feet. Now I couldn't help it. I wondered what he wanted. So I slowed my pace, coming to a tired and lumbering walk when I finally reached him.

"What?" I said, a little out of breath.

"Will you hold my hand?" he answered.

Instantly, my eyes welled. I nodded, yes, but I couldn't speak a word.

He then reached out. It was a sunny day. The sky was deep and blue and clear. In the trees all about us, the morning doves cooed. The boy grabbed my hand, and the two of us walked along in silence.

Rogelio R. Gómez

A Bridge to Freedom

I change myself; I change the world.

Gloria Anzaldúa

I must have crossed that bridge a hundred times, but it took the words of a stranger to show me what it really represented. Before our encounter, it was just a bridge, a way to get from one place to another. The stranger showed me that it was really a link between two worlds that were physically close, yet completely different. In one direction was a land of opportunity and freedom, while the other pointed to a land of hardship and pain. In all my crossings, I had never really thought of the old bridge that way, but this time there was this man standing on the Mexican side of a chain-link fence. He opened my eyes.

Dark, with Indian features, he had eyes like black pearls and hair like charcoal. His high cheekbones and elegant, strong nose told me that he had once been a proud man. But his hands were weathered, and time had not been gentle to him. In his arms, he gently held a peacefully sleeping baby swaddled in a multicolored *rebozo*. There was something about this man that moved me.

It wasn't as if I had never seen people begging on the border before. You know the ones I mean. I am ashamed to admit it, but sometimes I pass by and pretend that I don't see them. But I noticed this man in a different way. He stood on the other side of the fence as I began to make my way back to the bridge that would lead me to the states. My grandmother once told me that a healthy Mexican man would rather cut off his right arm with barbed wire than go out and beg in the streets. That's what got my attention. He was healthy and strong, yet he stood there begging, with his baby girl in one arm and a white paper in his hand.

"What's the matter?" I asked.

"We come from Puebla," he said. "We saved all of our money so we could come to the United States to look for work, but my wife fell gravely ill. We spent our savings on the doctor and a place to stay and eat. Please help us! I can't afford to buy her prescription." He waved the doctor's order in his hand. "I can't find any work here, and we don't know anyone. Please help! We come from Puebla. My wife is gravely ill."

His words were like bricks that weighed heavily on my chest. My heart sank, and his sorrow moved me to dig into my pockets and pull out what I had. He held out a large brown hand, callused from years of hard labor under an unforgiving sun, extending it through one of the openings of the chain-link fence. He didn't look at me, and I understood why.

"*Gracias, que Dios la bendiga,*" he said softly. I could feel that he spoke from his heart.

I wanted to ask for his name, but I knew not to. I didn't even look back. I wanted to leave him with his dignity. As I crossed that bridge back to the states, I knew that I would never know his fate. Tears filled my eyes, and I wondered why he had risked everything, including the lives of his family, to embark on such a perilous journey.

The currents of the Rio Grande moved swiftly beneath the bridge that day, ready to devour anyone who dared cut through its harsh waves. Yet in the distance, I could see people hunched in the bushes, waiting for the right moment to brave the strong waters. On the other side roamed the light green 4x4s, waiting to capture the members of the masses who might set foot on their shores. And I understood why the man behind the fence risked so much. He held the answer in his arms. For it wasn't too long ago that my grandmother, heavy with child, braved the same harsh river currents to get to the place where I grew up. But things were always so easy for me that I took that place for granted and never spent any time thinking about how difficult it had been for the others before me to get there.

My arrival home was bittersweet, as I had been touched and changed by what I had seen and experienced. I realize now that freedom is selective, and not everybody gets to taste it. Sometimes I look up and hope that there will come a time when the Earth will be like the clear, open sky, an immense space without man-made boundaries.

I found more than sombreros or trinkets that day on the bridge. I found a new understanding of what it means to be free and of what it means to wish for the well-being of all of God's children.

Jacqueline Méndez

Sadie Hawkins Day

I was squinting into the camcorder lens at a baseball game, our eight-year-old Vincent trotting past second base, when I noticed the limp. No one could have known, as Vincent began to favor one leg, that his strained gait was the first symptom of Fibrodysplasia Ossificans Progressiva (FOP), a rare genetic disorder that turns muscle into bone and leads, over time, to catastrophic immobility. No one could have known that FOP would go on to prevent our active son from combing his hair or tying his shoes. No one could have known, on that mild San Joaquin Valley afternoon as I pointed my camera at a spring green schoolyard, that Vincent would have no more seasons of sports.

We have lived with FOP for six years now, always hoping for a cure, for scientific miracles at the University of Pennsylvania, the focal point for FOP research. But until a cure appears, we pray for an average teenage life for Vincent, who has traded sports for trigonometry and a trumpet. And though a sense of loss stays with him, with all of us, this loss throws the small miracles of life, its happy coincidences, into sharp relief.

Last year, Vincent was invited to his first Sadie Hawkins dance by Clemencia, a pretty freshman girl in band, with shy brown eyes. One cold, clear February night before the dance, Clemencia's family came by to take Vincent on a Sadie Hawkins shopping trip. Clemencia's parents, I discovered, were from Mexico, so we spent a good while rattling off in Spanish, and by the time I had to explain FOP precautions, the teenagers had tuned us out, sparing Vincent the embarrassment of my recitations. A few hours later, he and Clemencia returned from a trip to Old Navy, happily holding up matching khaki camouflage gear.

The Saturday morning of Sadie Hawkins, the phone rang. It was Leonor, Clemencia's mother, with distress in her voice: "My daughter wants to apologize," she said. Clemencia had the flu.

Vincent quietly hung up the phone and retreated to the family-room computer. Our oldest son, Brian, was on his way to a friend's to have cornrows woven in his hair for the dance, and his younger brother Lucas was at a basketball game. While I was glad for our other sons, my throat tightened for Vincent.

But it was a sunny day, at least, a clear one in our normally white-skied valley, with the Sierra Nevada's dark rock suddenly visible, its snow shining like a grace. The day was so pretty that my husband, Walt, decided to cheer up our son with an outing.

"Come on, Vincent," he said. "We're going to the park to feed the ducks!"

"No, thanks," said Vincent, expressionless, at the computer screen.

"Come on!" called my husband, moving our eight-year-old daughter Celine and our four-year-old, Isabel, toward the garage with baggies of bread.

He extended the invitation again. Vincent refused again.

Walt tried again. No answer. Almost out the door, my husband asked once more.

"Okay," said Vincent abruptly, "but I'm staying in the car."

We found a spot for the van on the park perimeter, and my husband, the girls and I walked down a grassy rise to the oily olive lake patrolled by ducks and geese. Vincent stayed in the car. Our daughters had just started flinging bread chunks at the bustling birds when a swarm of seagulls began to loop and dive furiously for every tossed crust, setting off a family laughing fit. "Vincent has to see this!" said Walt after a while, and he jogged back to the parking area.

From where I stood by the rocks of the lake, I could see Walt rap on the car window and Vincent swing out his legs stiffly from the passenger side. A pretty young Latina with long dark hair and wearing sweats was running past. She stopped.

I could tell by his posture that Vincent knew the girl, and I saw my husband discreetly leave our son and his friend in conversation. After a while, the girl jogged off, and Vincent appeared at the lakeside. His face was transformed, radiant: "I'm going to Sadie Hawkins!" he announced.

The young jogger Vincent had just seen by chance was a friend from school. She had asked him if he would be at the dance, and when he explained that his date was sick, she invited him to join her large group, which was meeting at a brand-new arcade restaurant, John's Incredible Pizza, for a pre-party.

Vincent wore his khaki camouflage pants to Sadie Hawkins, and that night, instead of a first awkward couple's pose, our son brought home a professional photo of himself in the center of a crowd of friends.

I should add that—of course—Vincent never goes to the park, which happens to be on the other end of the city from his Catholic high school, far from our house. And the friend who jogged by lives in another town. The high school itself is a freeway drive away from our home, so, with the exception of Sadie Hawkins Dance day, Vincent has never coincidentally run into any classmates—many of whom live in different or distant San Joaquin Valley towns.

I said to my husband on that afternoon at the park that I know Vincent is surrounded by angels. Then Walt told me the name of the girl who jogged by at just the right moment: *Angelica!*

C. M. Zapata

The Ring

When I was growing up, my mother had a ring she never took off. It was the only ring I ever saw her wear during my childhood. It was made of a shiny silvery metal with an oblong penny-brown metallic piece upon which two hearts were attached in the center.

She wore it when she swept, when she mopped, when she made her large mound of golden flour tortillas, when she sewed on her treadle Singer sewing machine and when she washed clothes on the rubboard.

She didn't really have any other jewelry, and, in fact, I remember my father saying that he didn't even buy her a ring when they were married. He hadn't thought about it, and during the ceremony, they had borrowed her brother Charlie's ring.

The years passed. My father, who had come from Mexico in the 1920s to try to earn a living, worked long, long hours at the service station he operated. And my mother, who was also from Mexico, toiled at home, keeping house for her husband and eight youngsters. With his hard work and her thriftiness, they sent their first son off to college, then another child and then another. The older children helped with the expenses of the younger ones.

Just as the last two children were graduating from college, my father died suddenly of a heart attack, but my mother lived on for another twenty-three years. Their children had become lawyers, businessmen and teachers. In the last years of her life, my mother was finally able to enjoy the luxuries that had always been denied her. She was even able to buy some jewelry, which, I was surprised to learn, she really loved.

A few years before she died, she told me that she wanted her jewelry to go to her granddaughters. And when she died, it was done. A diamond ring to this one, a pearl ring to that one, an opal ring to another, and so it went.

Then I discovered it: her first ring. Now I could identify the metal. The ring was a thin, fragile thing by now, a small strip of stainless steel attached to two small hearts on either side of an oblong-shaped piece of copper. It had been worn so long that the copper had become unattached to the circle. Its value was naught.

I took the ring, polished it with a cloth and carried it to the bank to place in a safety-deposit box. To me, it was a gem that symbolized the sacrifices my mother had made for us and the values that she lived. How many years had she worn it? How many times had she denied herself so that we might succeed? Why did she save this ring when it seemed worthless? Was it a symbol to her, too?

The rest of my family doesn't quite understand this, but when I look at that ring, I see the priceless jewel of my mother's strength and the brilliance of the love that she showed us every day of her life.

Esther Bonilla Read

Lessons My Mother Taught Me

*L*et us love, not in word or speech, but in truth
and action.

1 John 3:18

It was Christmas time in Puerto Rico. A lady, a friend of
the lady and a little girl were among the many people with
a long list of gifts to buy for Three Kings Day.

They were shopping in an elegant, large mall. With life's
great irony, this luxurious building was located next to
one of the island's poorest government housing projects.

After a long, exhausting morning of gift buying, the
three of them decided to get a bite to eat. They went to a
small cafeteria on the first floor of the fancy mall. The very
small eating place was packed with people carrying bags
with assorted gifts. The lady, the friend of the lady and the
little girl were standing in line choosing between *empanadi-
llas, alcapurrias, rellenos de papas* and more, when they heard
a sweet and shy voice. It was coming from a skinny, dirty,
dark-skinned boy wearing a ragged blue shirt. He was
extending his small, empty hand toward the lady. He said:

"*Señora,* I am hungry. Could you spare some coins so I can buy some food?"

Without a moment of hesitation, the lady looked inside her huge black purse and grabbed as many coins as she could fit in both hands. Without counting, she placed the coins in the boy's outstretched hand. The lady always gave, so this action did not take the little girl by surprise. She was used to the lady's acts of kindness. As the coins were being passed from the lady's hand to the boy's hand, the little girl continued debating to herself between having a *bocadillo* or a pizza *empanadilla*. The friend of the lady did not find the lady's behavior as common as the little girl did. The friend of the lady called the lady foolish and naive.

"Do you really believe that the boy was hungry?" she said. "Do you really believe that right now he is spending that money on food? How can you be so trusting?"

By this time, with orange trays full of food in their hands, the lady, the friend of the lady and the little girl were trying to get through all the hungry Christmas shoppers toward the only empty table in the small cafeteria. Once they were seated, the lady turned to her friend:

"So what if he does not spend the money on food?" she said. "It's Christmastime. Let him get a brand-new toy or a comic book if that's what he wants."

The friend of the lady continued telling the lady how she still considered her foolish and naive.

Her reprimands were interrupted by the skinny, dirty, dark-skinned boy wearing a ragged blue shirt. In one hand, he was carrying an orange tray with a white paper plate on it. On the plate were a small chicken leg and a buttered biscuit. He was extending his other hand for them to see a dime, one nickel and two pennies. Then he said with his sweet, shy voice:

"*Señora,* I did not have enough money for a soda, see? Can you spare just a little more?"

With a wonderful, bright smile on her face, the lady got out of her seat and walked with the boy to the food counter. There she bought him a large soda, French fries and a piece of chocolate cake for dessert.

Years later, this episode is still fresh on the little girl's mind.

I am that little girl. I do not give skinny, dirty, dark-skinned boys money when they ask for some. I walk to the closest food place and buy them the whole meal, French fries and all. You see, I am afraid that I will not give these boys enough money for a soda and they might not have the courage to come back for more.

These boys owe those meals to a lady once called foolish and naive.

I am proud to call that lady "Mom."

Marta A. Oppenheimer

Hope, Thy Name Is Lina

Learn from yesterday, live for today, hope for tomorrow.

Anonymous

Two days before the now infamous events of September 11, 2001, our family gathered in our apartment in Manhattan to celebrate my daughter's first birthday. I was filled with all sorts of emotions as I remembered the past year and how quickly it had passed. From her early birth to the first time she laughed out loud, to her determined attempts at crawling and her loud musical renditions of *Maaamaaa*—the images sped by in my mind, and tears welled up in my eyes.

True to my neurotic form, I couldn't help but worry about the challenges still to come as she grew up a Latina girl in the United States. How could I protect her from the stares she already received as a newborn in upstate New York because of her dark hair and brown skin that refused to blend in with the white blanket of snow covering the valley? I stressed about how much English I was speaking around her and whether she would ever learn enough Spanish to communicate with her family members in Puerto Rico. How would I teach her to proclaim proudly "I am an American," when there will still be people who look at her and see a "foreigner"?

I put my worries aside, stopped myself from thinking about the ton of work that would be waiting for me on Monday morning and celebrated giving birth to the most beautiful little girl I had ever seen.

Two days later, on September 11, I found myself feeling a fear I had never known before and, for the first time, regretting my daughter's existence. How could I have so naively and selfishly brought a child into this world so full of hatred and violence? How would I explain to her the world my generation and those before us had created, a troubled world that she would inherit? I lost my sense of life's purpose: my own and my child's. I felt useless and helpless. How was I to teach my child about love when hatred seemed to be the order of the day? The hope for a better future that comes with the birth of a child was suddenly lost to me. Although I didn't personally lose a loved one on that fateful day, I grieved for all those who had, and I suffered moments of utter despair. I no longer believed innocence could exist in the world.

One day, as I walked home from work pretending that things had returned to normalcy, I passed by a local playground. Airplanes flew by, and I looked at them intently, thinking, *Is that airplane supposed to be flying that low?* But the children kept playing soccer, oblivious to the potential weapon of mass destruction flying overhead. They ran and giggled with each other, just as children have done for thousands of years. Overcome and overwhelmed by such a simple display of childhood innocence and joy, I breathed in deeply. How could I have not seen it before?

I ran home, picked up my little girl, looked into those

gorgeous, big, dark eyes, and there it was: the gift she'd been patiently storing for me. A vision of endless possibilities wrapped up in the wonder and wisdom of a one-year-old. And as she looked back at me, bewildered by my tears, I realized that hope was never lost. I know that all my daughter asks of me is that I have a little bit of faith, that I not let a troubled world rob me of the gift she gives me.

Hope, thy name is Lina.

Elizabeth García

Alma/My Soul

Alma—a little girl/young lady
whose name means "soul,"
touches my own soul with
her calm yet tenacious spirit.
Indian girl who must help
provide for her family, the
mission grounds her storefront.
She helps me for hours, though
we interrupt the work with a
few bouts of silent volleyball,
bumping a colorful beach ball
we find. She does not forget
her role and that her mother
will ask who bought what for
how much. As we finish she
says, "Now come see the dolls"
I buy.

Alma—silent child with soft
but piercing eyes, takes it all
in, saying so little but learning

so much. What do my actions
teach you, *mi'jita?* I hope it is
good. I hope it serves you
well. I hope I reflect the One
who brought me here, and who
made our lives touch in this
moment.

Alma—I watch your mother
teach you how to weave, as
she makes you repeat tedious
first missteps. I observe you
slowly, then more quickly,
cause colors to dance and
change on your tiny loom.
I study and think I understand.
I want to guide your hands
when you study the pattern
you are to follow anxiously.
Suddenly, I realize I have
thought too simplistically. I
give up trying to comprehend,
while you have mastered it.

Alma—who first refuses, then
after some thought, decides to
let me take her picture: a close-
up, so close I wonder if I am
wrong to cross this invisible
cultural line, even with her
permission. Alma—who later
sees another picture of her
Tarahumara face and dress
on a computer screen and
runs screaming from the room

three times before she finally
accepts an inkjet color print
of herself, passing from the
hand of the age of technology
to the hand of nomadic life
in an instant.

Alma—who lets me hug her one
day, and hold her close, who
accepts the blame for holding on
too long when it is really me
who can't let her go. Same
child who refuses to hug me or
even look at me on the day I am
to leave, but when I speak her
pain out loud, lets me hold her,
turning in to me with tears that
become my own.

Perhaps one day, Alma,
my own soul will be silent long
enough to learn from you, too.

Heather J. Kirk

On Teaching

*Real education should consist of drawing the
goodness and the best out of our own students.
What better books can there be than the book of
humanity?*

César Chávez

I am a primary schoolteacher. Growing up, teaching
was never high on the list of things to do with my life. I
had a world to conquer, I felt, and becoming a teacher
would not even allow me to conquer my own backyard.
Upon graduating from college, in order to pursue my passion for acting as much as I could, I worked as a substitute
teacher. I enjoyed the experience, but still something was
missing. Shortly after starting, however, I received an
assignment as a "long-term" sub wherein I took over the
last trimester (as this was a year-round school) of a kindergarten class. It was that trimester that a tiny light finally
went on inside of me. I realized that as a substitute, I
hadn't had the opportunity to cultivate relationships
with the kids, to observe their growth and foster their

development. To the kids, I was just another substitute, gone in a day or so; to me, they were just another day of work. As a long-term teacher, I was able to experience the true nature of teaching, and I began to fall in love with something that a few years earlier I would not have wanted to do.

The following year, I taught third grade full-time, and it was an incident from that year that affected how I viewed my job, my students, my community, my world and myself . . .

One evening I was visiting a friend in the area where my school is located. As I didn't live in that area, I never encountered any of my students outside of class. On this particular evening, my friend and I ventured to the local video store to pick up some movies. While inside, I glanced out at the parking lot and saw one of my students. I figured she was just accompanying her parent to the store and thought nothing more of it. Minutes later, as we left the store, I saw her again, a pretty, skinny, little thing, still standing just in front of the entrance. "Hey there, kiddo, what's going on? Renting some movies?" I asked. "No," she replied softly as she looked over to an old car parked a few meters away. I looked over and saw her mom standing outside the car. I waved. "So, what . . ." I didn't finish. I looked in her hands and realized that she was standing outside of that video store, at that time of night, selling crocheted toilet-paper covers, working to earn some extra money for her family. My heart sank. She grew embarrassed. I probed no further as I didn't want to humiliate her. I made a feeble attempt at pretending everything was fine. I uttered some informal good-bye, told her I'd see her in the morning and made my way to the car. On the short drive back to my friend's home, a thousand emotions came and went, a thousand thoughts followed suit. I was outraged that this little girl had to live in a world where fate, destiny, whatever, dictated such harsh life circumstances. I felt worthless.

The next morning, as I drove to school still ruminating about the events of the evening before, I remembered the lyrics to a song by Alejandra Guzmán dedicated to her daughter. *"El mundo es como es y no puedo cambiártelo, pero siempre te seguiré para darte una mano."* "The world is what it is, and I cannot change it for you, but I'll always be with you to give you a hand."

I couldn't change the life circumstances for this little girl and her family, but I was in a very special position that allowed me to make an impact. As long as she was my student, I had the opportunity to make a difference, to affect her life positively, to stir in her an endless thirst for learning and, maybe, just maybe, contribute, if even mildly, to her reaching her *más grandes anhelos.* Her biggest dreams. That year, and for as long as I could, I would *echarle una mano.* Give her a hand.

Today, this is how I view every one of my days with every one of my students. I believe firmly in what I do. I believe in the seen and unforeseen consequences that a good teacher can have on a student. Education, *mi gente,* is paramount!

I believe in the power of knowledge to effect change and create better lives. I believe in education, not just as a means to an end, but as an instrument of lifelong learning and relationship. I strive to leave an indelible mark on the life of every child I teach, and I never miss an opportunity to notice the beauty and the love in every step we take together.

Salvador González Padilla

4

LATINO IDENTITY/
LA IDENTIDAD
LATINA

*The very term Latino has meaning only in
reference to the U.S. experience. Outside of
the United States, we don't speak of Latinos;
we speak of Mexicans, Cubans, Puerto
Ricans and so forth. Latinos are made in
the USA.*

Marcelo M. Suárez-Orozco and Mariela M. Páez

NO RODEO®

NO RODEO © *Robert Berardi. Used by permission.*

From Tug-of-War to Dance

The customs and values that form the tapestry of our Hispanic roots should not get lost. It is our obligation to continue embroidering our heritage and to create a masterpiece.

Arelis Rocío Hernández

My life has gone from a tug-of-war to a dance.
And it's all been one big accident.
I didn't ask to be born Chicano or Latino or Hispano or any other Spanish-sounding word that ends in "o" that some census guy invented as a stamp to hammer on my head. I didn't draw up any plan that would have me speak Spanish first, English second, and then venture out into a world where I learned the "wrong" language first.
I am an American of Mexican descent, born and raised in Santa Fe, New Mexico.
Tug. Tug.
Safe within the protective walls of my family, I was never aware of any tugging. We flowed from Spanish to English and back again, unaware of which was which. If

we meant something in Spanish, we spoke Spanish. If we meant something in English, we spoke English. Reality depended on what we meant or felt, and language was just a means.

But when I began my Americanization in the public-school system, I rammed headfirst into all kinds of separation from my home life. At first, I knew no conflict as I spoke English as well as I spoke Spanish.

Until my father brought me a gift.

Tug. Tug.

He brought me a purple T-shirt that had a muscle-bound guy emblazoned across the front, wearing a white tank top and a blue bandana over his head. The *vato* had his fist raised to the sky and behind him were two criss-crossed flags: one, American, the other, Mexican. Underneath the tough-looking guy and the two flags were the words "Chicano Power."

I remember one kid, who I thought was my friend, really enjoyed that shirt. He mocked me and laughed every single time he thought about it. I was embarrassed to wear it. I wondered why he would laugh so hard at something that meant so much to me. At home, my dad told me that we were "Chicanos." I thought everybody would think I was cool because of my T-shirt. Instead, that kid gathered what seemed like a mob to laugh and tease me because of my shirt. He would say, "Hey, Chicano Power!" with his voice sounding like Cheech's in *Up in Smoke*. To hear kids teasing me about my Chicano Power T-shirt only made me want to rip it apart. That kid called me "Chicano Power" all the way through elementary school.

Of course, I eventually grew out of my T-shirt, but I don't think I really ever got over all the teasing and taunting. At home, we were Chicano. I loved it. And I hated it. I wanted to shed my brown skin and be like everybody else.

What was even worse was that I was the only kid in

the bilingual education class who could actually speak Spanish. In those days, bilingual education meant that kids would learn how to speak Spanish at school because, for whatever reason, they didn't learn to speak it at home. The ability to speak Spanish made me different. It was almost like I was a foreigner, someone from another planet. I wanted to forget that I had ever learned to speak Spanish.

I was losing my tug-of-war to Americanization and the English-speaking side of who I was.

Yet, my father loved for me to speak Spanish. No matter who was around or what was going on, he would implore me, *"Háblame en mexicano."* I always thought that it was a performance kind of thing where my dad would use me to show off and brag about how smart I was that I could speak Spanish. I never did it willingly. I felt like a monkey dancing around for a quarter, and my costume was a purple T-shirt. I was a dancing monkey every time my father pleaded with me, *"Háblame en mexicano."*

Only, I wasn't a dancing monkey. I was more like an umbilical cord. I was never performing; I was always reminding. I just didn't know it then.

One day, many years removed from those days of *mexicano,* my father and I were fishing at a pond. The weather turned bad. Rain hammered us, and wind knocked us around. We jumped into my truck to wait it out. Once in the cab, he asked me if I'd written anything lately.

"Yup," I said. "I'm always writing."

He didn't respond right away. Instead, he turned away from me and looked out his window. His eyes followed the raindrops as they fell. I wondered what he was thinking. I always thought that he didn't think much of me as a writer, like it wasn't something for him to be proud of. What added credence to my thinking was that while we were running to the truck, before he asked me about my writing, we were laughing and enjoying ourselves. But after he heard my response, he turned as dark as the clouds.

"The only thing I ever wrote . . ." he said, with his voice sullen and his head still turned to the window. His words barely rolled off his tongue. It seemed to hurt him to remember. He continued, slow and almost angry, ". . . was a letter to your grandmother when I was on the *USS Enterprise* heading to Vietnam. I wrote the whole thing in Spanish. I never wrote anything after that."

His head sunk.

No sooner had his words hit me than I knew that his mood wasn't about my writing. It was about his letter. To him, every time I spoke *"en mexicano,"* he heard himself writing that letter home. For me to speak Spanish was an umbilical cord that connected him to his own private Eden. I wasn't performing for him. I was reminding him of who he was before the marines and Vietnam took his innocence.

The day and sky cleared up. As suddenly as the lightning crashes into the ground, I no longer felt any tugs.

"¿Quieres pescar más?" I asked him. It had been years since I'd spoken to him in Spanish.

He must have noticed because he raised his head and looked at me with red eyes swimming in little pools of tears. It was like we had gone home. *"Sí, vamos."*

I don't remember catching any fish that day, but I did remember who I was before I became ashamed of my Chicano heritage.

And I learned how lucky I was to possess the tongue of my family's history and my father's heart.

Juan Blea

Not Mexican?

My wife, Veronica, and I have an ongoing argument. The subject? How I identify myself.

Before I met her, I never considered myself anything but a Mexican. Not a Mexican-American, or an American of Mexican descent, but simply, in a kind of ethnic short-hand, a Mexican.

I didn't mean that in the literal sense. I had never lived in Mexico, and I had only rarely visited it. In fact, most of what I knew of the place was limited to unsightly border towns that are no more representative of that country than are inner-city ghettos a fair reflection of my own.

And yet, growing up in a small farm town in Central California, that's how I saw myself: as a Mexican. Just as important, it is how others saw me and people like me. Adults pointed to the "Mexican" part of town or talked about how someone had once made history by being the high school's first "Mexican" quarterback or homecoming queen. Years later, when I was admitted to Harvard, my good fortune was scorned by less fortunate Anglo class-mates who informed me: "If you hadn't been Mexican, you wouldn't have gotten in."

Okay, so I'm Mexican, just like my friends in Boston—in more ethnic shorthand—consider themselves "Irish" and my friends in New York call themselves "Italian" or my friends back home in Fresno think of themselves as "Armenian." I'm Mexican, right?

Wrong, says Veronica. To her, I'm an American, plain and simple. Born and raised in the United States, how could I be anything else?

She's the Mexican. Born and raised in Guadalajara, Mexico, she came to the United States when she was nine years old with her mother and three sisters. Later, she returned to Mexico for two years of high school, and she stayed there for four years of college before returning to the United States. She speaks, reads and writes Spanish with an awesome proficiency that I could never hope to attain.

How can I be Mexican, she asks? If I went to Mexico and said that, people would laugh. They'd ask where exactly in Mexico I was from, and they'd expect me to answer in perfect, accent-free Spanish.

Veronica isn't the only one urging me to think of myself as an American. On the job, as a newspaper editorial writer and syndicated columnist, I write often about Mexican-Americans. When that happens, I get shelled with e-mails from furious readers. They have no use for hyphenated-Americans, seeing such things as a form of divided loyalty.

Veronica doesn't mind hyphens. As far as she is concerned, I can refer to myself as a "Mexican-American" to my heart's content. But if I decide to drop the hyphen and keep just one of those elements, then, by all means, I should drop the Mexican part.

I wasn't born in Mexico, she points out, and neither were my parents. Sure, my grandfather, Roman, came from Chihuahua, but he's the only one of my grandparents who came from south of the Rio Grande. The other three were all *Tejanos,* Texans of Mexican decent.

So I'm no Mexican, she says. That goes double for the other twelve to fifteen million Mexican-Americans living in the United States, even if many of them do live in what she disdainfully calls an "American Mexico"—those culturally rich neighborhoods and towns with taco trucks and rows upon rows of Spanish-language storefronts.

In fact, she admits, when she describes me to folks, she tells them I'm an American. Period.

Whoa there! What my wife doesn't understand is what it was like for me to grow up as a cultural nomad. I've spent my life feeling as if I was too Mexican to be 100 percent American and too American to be 100 percent Mexican. There's a lot of truth in the old joke about how a Mexican-American is treated as an American everywhere in the world except America, and as a Mexican everywhere except Mexico.

In Veronica's world, there was no need for identity crises. When she arrived here, there were Mexicans and there were Americans. But Mexican-Americans? She says that before she met me, she had no idea the species even existed.

She isn't alone. A few years ago, I was part of a delegation of Mexican-Americans that visited Mexico City. At a junior high school, we were surprised to learn that a classroom of eighth-graders didn't know there was such a thing as Mexicans who were born in the United States. For over 150 years, the Mexican government—still humiliated by the outcome of the U.S.-Mexican war in 1848—has seen no value in having its schools teach such things.

Nor am I alone in my identity crisis. For the most part, U.S.-born Mexicans aren't sure what they are. I would bet that most see themselves primarily as Americans. And yet many can also point to an uncle, aunt or parent who, as recently as twenty or thirty years ago, was made to feel like a second-class citizen. The culprit is usually the public schools, or government, or some other institution that saw them as "Mexican" and treated them as inferior because of it.

Sure, Mexican-Americans have distinct advantages over our distant relatives to the south. Overall, we have opportunities for more education, more freedom, higher living standards, fewer class barriers. But Mexicans do have one edge over us, their distant relatives to the north: They know exactly who they are.

Recently, Veronica threw me a curve ball. She explained that she did not think of me as a typical American. Her experience with that breed is that they are often arrogant, contemptuous of the rest of the world and prone to dismiss other cultures as inferior to their own.

That's not me, she said. I enjoy all sorts of people, and I always try to be open-minded to cultural differences. The reason, she suggested, must be that I feel a connection to what my grandparents and parents endured in America in an earlier time. That's great, she said. It's also one of the reasons she fell in love with me.

"*Mi amor*, you have the best of both worlds," she said with a smile. "You have all the privileges that come from being raised in the United States. You speak your mind, and you know you have the freedom to tell people exactly what you think. And yet, when you do that, you're always respectful and never look down on anyone.

"*Lindo*, you're very special," she said. "But you're still not Mexican."

Ruben Navarrette, Jr.

Hunger

The greatest thing you have is your self-image, a positive opinion of yourself. You must never let anyone take it from you.

Jaime Escalante

The gym floor gleamed. Tables were set up on each side of the room with books and projects assembled by the children and the staff. There were handmade maps of Puerto Rico and Cuba and glossy maps of Latin America. The children had proudly contributed examples of cultural items that were relevant to their backgrounds. There were colorful shawls, castanets, plates, pictures. And there were maracas: maracas made of wood, maracas honed out of gourds, maraca earrings, maracas made out of paper cups and seeds and even plastic maracas.

Nate is a musician, and I am a storyteller. Nate set up the instruments as I looked over my notes. I tell *cuentos folklóricos* with an emphasis on multicultural stories, especially stories of the Caribbean, where I was born. I am the Taína Storyteller, descendent of the Taíno Indians of

Puerto Rico. To the dismay of my parents, I chose to feature this aspect of my heritage and not just the Spanish
great-grandparents on both sides of my family. I wanted
to honor this long-ignored part of our greater heritage,
and the more I learned, the more joy I felt.

As we were setting up, several teachers and staff
stopped by to admire the conga drums and meet the
"artists." We shook hands, smiled and chatted with each
visitor. Not one was a person of color. A blonde, tall
woman of solid build and thick glasses introduced herself.
She told us how pleased she was to have us here. She
explained that she worked with these children every day.
The school was about 30 percent Latino or from Spanish-
speaking homes. Another 20 percent were black or Asian,
and the rest were "white non-Hispanic."

She told us how the children had been looking forward
to this day and how creative and artistic they were. She
wanted to expand on this, she said, because after all,
"we're not raising rocket scientists here."

Nate and I were stunned by her comment. He hit the
conga drum softly at first and slowly began a drumbeat, a
stiff smile on his handsome Dominican/African-American
face. I, who was usually fast on my feet and even quicker
with my mouth, stammered something akin to, "I am sure
that the children enjoy their artistic side, as I enjoy mine
in addition to my work as a teacher and scholar."

The children began to arrive. The first session was for
the kindergarten through third-grade classes. The gym
filled up with over a hundred kids, their teachers, teacher
aides, the "grandmothers" who helped out during class
time and parents. I took a deep breath and eyed the children. They were beautiful. I saw brown faces, tan faces,
black faces, white faces; most with smiles and lively chatter. A few shy children barely looked up. I tried to make
eye contact with them, to smile, to get the audience on my

side. I especially tried to search out the more obvious Latino faces.

We were introduced, and the stories began. Stories of brave *caciques*, lovelorn Taínas and the Taíno gods. Nate drummed a beat; I scraped some musical sounds on my *güiro*. I asked the children to raise their hands if they spoke English. They all laughed at what seemed like a ridiculous question to them. I then asked who spoke Spanish, and the excitement grew—some of the children were not content to raise their hands so they jumped to their feet to make sure they got my attention.

"Me, too," I said, "me, too."

Their excitement soared. I went on with stories of animals that speak Spanish, of a talking donkey, a story about my name and what it meant to me, and of boys named Juan Bobo. They listened, some with mouths open, as if they were being fed. They laughed, clapped and asked for more. We gathered for an interactive story, and in the front row, a red-haired girl named Yolanda and a boy named José competed with other students to be the first ones to hold my hand.

The afternoon session brought in another hundred children, who were older and seemed determined to be low-key. But I would not allow it. Soon, they were laughing and calling out the names of the countries their people were from. I was loud and barely needed the mike. I was vivacious and funny, and I even danced. They drank it up. Nate was musical, funky and electric; his bald head glistened with sweat as he smiled through it all. They loved it, and we loved them.

But it was later, wandering the halls looking for a bathroom, when my heart almost burst. I could not walk five feet without children stepping in my path, telling me proudly that they were "Spanish." The moment I said, "I knew you were because you're beautiful," they raised their arms to hug me. Some almost jumped into my arms.

As we were going down the hall to the cafeteria for a "Latino" luncheon prepared by the kids and their parents, more children came. They mobbed around our table as we ate. They brought us food to try, and they pointed out what they had made. A large fifth-grade girl with curly dark hair came over and asked me to taste her cookies. She firmly took my arm and led me to the table. Putting a cookie in my mouth, she watched carefully as I chewed and swallowed. I told her it was just delicious, as it truly was. She beamed and, with tears in her eyes, whispered "thank you." Struck by her emotion, I hugged this girl who was taller than me, and she clung to me. Nate brought out his drums, and the boys and girls stood in line to get their turn to play. The joy was intense.

We were surrounded by food of all kinds. Rice and beans, *pollo fricassee, guineas verdes, arroz con coco, tacos, burritos, frijoles negros*—all of which looked and smelled like heaven. Our hunger was quickly satisfied as we savored the foods of our ancestors, the foods of our living cultures.

But the children were satisfying another hunger that day: the hunger to see themselves in us and to know we are like them.

The hunger to be recognized as real people, with gifts and talents that the world needs.

The hunger to feel that they, too, could speak, dream, dance and eat in Spanish, without fear of being seen as different or less.

The hunger to be proud.

Nilsa Mariano

My Fundillo (All the Wrong Places)

Being Latina is a way of life, the way you feel and relate to others. It's a way of communicating, understanding and expressing yourself.

Claudia Yelín

There I was, sitting in a top-floor tenement walk-up in the Bronx, waiting for the '80s to be over. You remember the '80s? Bad clothes. Bad hair. For me, it was high school. Or more specifically, tenth grade, where my best friend, Joanie Boom-Boom, vogued through the girls' locker room in her new black lace bra like it was a trophy.

Believe it or not, I wasn't jealous. I know that for most people, the female rite of passage is getting your boobs, but for Latinas our body part of choice is the buttocks. This is the cheeky skeleton in the Latina closet, the five happy words to describe one's bottom: *culito, nalgas, fundillo, cheecho* and *delicioso!*

Now you might say everyone has a bottom, and of course they do. It's just not the perfect Latina bottom: not too wide in the hips, yet full and meaty across the beam.

Not as high as a bubble butt, but completely lifted off the back of the thighs. Picture two teardrop-shaped globes of firm, pliant, undimpled muscle, with built-in rack-and-pinion steering that allows each cheek to undulate separately from the other even when its proud owner stands completely still. There was no escaping this perfect posterior in my house. Every salsa album cover had one, and every merengue album had two. Every *novia* on every *novela* on Channel 47 had one. My sixty-year-old *abuela* had one. My thirteen-year-old cousin, Evie, had one. Every Latin woman in NYC had one. Except me.

I was a normal teenager otherwise. I just had this one problem. I didn't have a butt! And to the women in my family, this was a disaster that needed to be prevented, a catastrophe that needed to be averted, a disease that needed to be cured.

My *titi* Carmen said, "Pray for her." My *titi* Ophelia said, "Stop feeding her," and after I walked by, "Ay no, hide her till she's twenty-one." And then my mom said, "Listen to me, all of you. No daughter of mine is going to be a *gordita.*"

My mom, Lucy, was the Jackie O. of East 103rd Street. She never raised her voice, never cursed, and was never seen in public without full makeup, high heels and stockings. After twenty years of marriage and two babies, she still weighed exactly the same as the day she got married: ninety-eight pounds—seventy pounds of which was butt. And she was convinced that with the right makeup, diet and foundation garments, her little *gordiflona* would be transformed into *una gran mamichula.*

Now I wasn't really fat, they just thought I was because I didn't have a shape. Their shape. Pear shape. So I tried it my mom's way. I ate plain boiled chicken with no rice or beans. I let her buy me control-top panties. And still, no butt. I was sure there was something else wrong with me. Maybe I was adopted. Maybe I should go talk to someone who really knew about such things. And so I went to see my best friend, Joanie Boom-Boom.

Safe in the teenage sanctuary of Joanie's room, I spilled my guts about my lack of development. "You're just a child," she said. "You'll grow . . . someday." Then she started admiring herself in the mirror. I went into the bathroom, checked out my butt in the mirror and cried. No matter how far I twisted around, all I could see was . . . nothing. Joanie was right. I would be at least thirty before I looked like a woman, and by then I would be too old to enjoy it. I went back to her room to say good-bye and there she was, still enraptured by her reflection in the mirror, but now stuffing wad after wad of tissue paper into each cup of that black lace bra. Instead of being angry that she was cheating, I realized something about being a woman. If she could stuff her bra, why couldn't I stuff my bottom? Her secret would be safe with me.

I laughed, and Joanie turned around.

"How long have you been standing there?" she asked.

"Uh, I just got here," I lied. "Let's go get pizza."

For the rest of the weekend, I finally had something behind me I could be proud of. Sort of. It shifted around a lot, and I couldn't really sit down or it would flatten out, so I walked around the house as if I were holding a dime between my cheeks, just like my mom said a real *mujer* walked. But my family—who could spot unplucked eyebrows at thirty paces—didn't notice a thing, even when I shimmied it right in front of them. I couldn't believe they couldn't see the total and complete transformation of my body. But that was okay, because the next day at school, I was sure all my friends would.

Everything was fine until gym class, when I realized I would have to get undressed. I tried to hide in a corner, but of course Joanie saw me and came over. I turned around with my back toward the lockers and Joanie said,

"Hey, Michele, you got something weird hanging out of your . . ." And she pulled a ten-foot-long trail of Charmin out of the back of my underwear and into the cold fluorescent light of the locker room.

"Oh, my God!" she shrieked. "Michele stuffs her butt! Michele stuffs her butt!"

Everyone in the locker room froze. I knew my life was over, and there was only one thing left to do. I pushed Joanie over a bench, and as she fell, her black lace bra popped open and out flew enough pink Kleenex for every Ortiz funeral parlor in the Bronx and half of Brooklyn. As the entire locker room howled, Joanie leaped on me. She pulled my hair, and I tried to strangle her with what was left of my toilet-paper tail. Finally, a teacher pulled us apart. We were both suspended for three days.

My family didn't take it very well.

Titi Carmen said, "Take her to church." Titi Ophelia said, "Take her to jail." My mom just said, "How could you?"

I wasn't sure if she meant the stuffing or the fight.

And while everyone around me argued, I grew. Almost five inches in two years. The extra ten pounds around my middle somehow migrated just the right distance, and if I may say so, produced some of the finest *nalgas* in my entire *familia!*

Michele Carlo

NO RODEO®

NO RODEO © *Robert Berardi. Used by permission.*

NO RODEO, *Robert Berardi,* ©2005, *reprinted by permission of Robert Berardi.*

The Hardest Lesson

When I was five years old, my mother and father moved to the South Bronx, New York, leaving me in the care of my grandmother in Santurce, Puerto Rico. Although we were poor and food was scarce, I lived an idyllic life with my grandmother and my *tíos* and *tías* and cousins, surrounded by the loving faces of my extended family, emerald green oceans, trips to the countryside, to *El Yunque*, little kids' games and bedtime stories. I missed my mother and father, especially my mother, but I never wanted to leave the island. I was happy and loved, and I felt safe there.

When I turned eight, my mother wrote to my grandmother and asked her to send me to New York. She and my father were managing to scrape out a living, had a small apartment in a stable neighborhood and were making progress. It was time for me to join them, and so I went, sadly leaving behind the only world I knew.

When I got to the South Bronx, my mother enrolled me in the public elementary school, and although I didn't speak a word of English, I found myself stuffed into overcrowded classes of English-speaking children and teachers. Luckily, there were some other Puerto Rican kids, although they were very different from me, most of them having been born in the United States and speaking much more English than Spanish. But they were able to communicate with me, and the little conversations that we shared at recess really kept me going. I was scared and I felt alone, like nobody else in the world had ever gone through what I was going through. My parents weren't any help since they didn't speak much English. In fact, they were pressuring me to learn the language so that I could help them handle daily transactions that had to be carried out in a language they didn't speak. It was a tough time, and I remember it very well.

A month after I started school, things started to get better. I was beginning to understand some English, I had made a few friends, and I was feeling a little more at home in my new surroundings. But that was about to change. One day, as we were getting our daily math lesson, I felt the kid behind me nudging me on the back. When I turned slightly to see what he wanted, he stuck out his hand and showed me a small piece of paper that was sloppily folded into a little square. I understood that he wanted me to take the paper from him, so I did, and I put it on my desk. I didn't realize it at the time, but the teacher had observed the passing of the "note," and she was quickly standing over me at my desk.

I remember feeling scared and small as my tall, blonde teacher reached down and grabbed the folded paper out of my hand. Mrs. Jones's face turned red and her squinted eyes seemed to get smaller and smaller as she glared at me. Although I couldn't really understand the fast string of staccato words that came out of her mouth, I did hear her call me a "Dirty Puerto Rican." I didn't understand the word "dirty," but whatever it was, it felt like an accusation. And I had no idea what I had done to earn my teacher's wrath.

The next thing I knew, Mrs. Jones yanked me up in front of the class and announced that I was being sent home. Soon my mother appeared, and I watched as she came in through the hall door and started making her way toward me. I was so relieved to see her that I ran as fast as I could and buried myself in her waist, holding on to her desperately. But my sense of security was quickly shattered as she pushed me from her, unfastening my grip on her waist and staring down at me with fiery eyes. My mother's face was redder and angrier than the teacher's; she was furious and didn't ask me any questions. I could see her eyes filling with tears although she was trying hard to blink them back.

"*¿Por qué lo hiciste?*" she screamed at me, demanding to know why I had done what I had "done." I knew it had something to do with the paper that the teacher had snatched off my desk, but I didn't know how to begin to answer her. And then, without another word, she slapped me in the face, hard.

I felt so betrayed by her and so humiliated in front of my classmates. I ran out of the room and hid under the water fountain down the hall. My mother came out and found me, wiped my tears, hugged me and took me home.

When we got there, she asked me why I had been so foolish as to pass around a note with filthy words on it. This was the first clue I had about what had happened and why I had gotten into trouble! It didn't help me feel any better about things. I hadn't even opened the note, and even if I had, I wouldn't have understood any of the cuss words that the boy behind me had written on the paper. I didn't even know bad words in Spanish, let alone in English!

When I explained to my mother exactly what had happened, she was filled with sadness and remorse; she explained that a lot of people in New York didn't like Puerto Ricans, and that I would have to be careful about that. She said that in order to avoid these "problems," I would have to behave better than the Anglo kids. I would have to look cleaner, neater and more decent than them, always speak properly and only when spoken to, and never bring suspicion on myself or my family. How I missed my life on the island right then.

Looking back on this incident as a grown woman, I understand what my mother was trying to do for me. Although she definitely made the wrong choice that day, I've come to understand that "choices" don't come easily when people are living under stress. I was also able to understand that my mother did what she did, ironically, to try to protect me. She wanted Mrs. Jones and the class to know that I came from a "good" Puerto Rican family, and that I would be disciplined harshly by her if I crossed any lines. My mother meant well; she just didn't have the resources to make a better choice.

Racism is evil. It isn't something that anyone should have to put up with. It is one of the ultimate injustices of life. But still, I am grateful that my mother set me straight at a very early age so that I could better deal with the life that she and my father had chosen for me. I learned so much from that one experience and from others that followed, and I have become much better equipped than my parents to struggle for myself and my family. As a Latina, as an American and a Nuyorican, I always remember that my greatest resource is believing in myself, believing in us, in our inherent dignity, and in our right to live and thrive in this country.

It's a life worth struggling for.

Caroline C. Sánchez

The Power of Our Family History

My roots have provided me with a peculiar sen-
sitivity and wide lenses through which I can
contemplate the entire world and its different
hues. I'm very proud of this.

Claudia Yelín

Notebook in hand, my nine-year-old son Michael
plopped down on the sofa in our living room where I had
been paging through a writer's magazine and said, "What
did Grandpa Leal's father do for a living?"

I was startled by his question. He had never shown the
slightest interest in his ancestors. When I asked him why
he wanted to know, he explained that his fourth-grade
teacher had given the class an assignment to research
their family histories. I felt an excitement stir within me.
There was almost nothing I loved more than talking about
my family's roots since I had recently researched and written genealogies about both sides of my family. But I also
knew that my son had a typical nine-year-old's attention
span, and that he would drift off in boredom if I started a

lengthy discourse about his ancestors.

My son is of Irish, Hungarian and Mexican descent—a "melting pot" American. I knew little about his father's Irish-Hungarian side, but enough about his Mexican side to keep him writing for days. This, I realized, was the perfect time to tell Michael the story about his Mexican roots.

He asked again. "What did Grandpa Leal's father do for a living?"

I put my magazine on the coffee table and leaned back into the cushion of the sofa. "That would be my grandfather, your great-grandfather, Agapito. He was a field laborer, and later, he became a groundskeeper at a high school. He loved to work outdoors. His flower garden at home was gorgeous. Whenever I smell jasmine, I think of his garden."

Michael looked up at me, his brown eyes wide and round. "What do you mean by a field laborer?"

"He picked cotton, vegetables, fruit—you know, whatever was in season."

"Like out in the fields?"

"Yes, like out in the fields!" I smiled, amused at his incredulity. "In fact, your grandma's father also was a field worker for a while." I suddenly realized that the lives of his great-grandparents were as alien to Michael as if they had been born on another planet.

"Where were these fields?"

"Your grandfather's dad worked in the valley, near the Texas-Mexico border. There are a lot of citrus orchards down there, also commercial vegetable fields, with acres of beets, carrots and tomatoes. Every kind of vegetable you can imagine."

"What about Grandma's dad?" He stopped writing and looked up expectantly.

"He worked for a little while as a picker, but then he went into business as a labor contractor. He took field workers with him all over Texas and Mississippi to pick cotton."

Michael bunched up his eyebrows. "By hand?"

I nodded.

"Anyway, back to your grandfather's father, my *abuelo*— that's the Spanish word for grandfather—moved to Texas in 1912 because of the Mexican Revolution. He was seventeen at the time. He got a job helping to clear the land in the town where he lived. After his field work, he got a job at a packing shed, washing, gathering and then packing thousands of pounds of fruits and vegetables into crates for shipping. After he retired from that job, he worked for many years as a high-school groundskeeper.

"His wife, my *abuela*, was a strong woman. She was the same age as Grandpa and was born in a little ranch in south Texas, though her parents were from Mexico. Grandma and Grandpa Leal were married in the early 1920s. They lived in Weslaco, north of the Missouri Pacific railroad tracks, in a pink, three-room house on the Mexican side of town."

"On the Mexican side of town?" Michael interrupted.

"Yes, in those days, Mexicans lived on one side of the railroad tracks, and the Anglos lived on the other side."

"That's weird."

"Yeah," I said.

"If I lived then, where would I have lived?" He put his notebook on his lap, his eyes intense.

"You mean being part Mexican?" I crossed my arms.

"Yeah."

"I'm not sure, but since your dad is Anglo, probably on the Anglo side of town."

He nodded, then picked up his notebook.

"Anyway, neither of your great-grandparents could read or write, but they were responsible and wise. They were married for more than fifty years. My grandmother died seven years after their fiftieth anniversary, and then Grandpa died just a few months later. Before he died, *abuelo* often roamed around the house calling for her."

"That's creepy."

I smiled. "He missed her. They were married a long time."

He frowned.

"Anyway, even though my grandparents were not educated, they were honest, God-fearing people who expected their children to better themselves and to be good American citizens."

Michael looked down at what he had written. "I didn't know I had relatives who were field workers and one who was a janitor."

"Does it bother you?"

"No . . . I mean, I just never thought about it, about what it must have been like to have to work in the fields."

"People still do that kind of work today, and many of them are Mexicans who travel all over the country. It's hard work. During the time your great-grandparents were alive, they had few choices but to work in the fields. But they didn't complain about it. They knew that one day their children, grandchildren and great-grandchildren would have a better way of life."

Michael pursed his lips. "Wow, this is really something. My great-grandparents worked in the fields." He slapped his notebook shut. "I'm done. I'll type it up later." He jumped off the sofa, walked over and plopped down on the recliner, then turned on the television with the remote control.

I felt strangely deflated. Had anything I said meant anything to him? As I reached over to pick up my magazine, Michael turned to me.

"Mom, the janitor at our school is Mexican. I've never talked to him before. I think I'll say hi to him tomorrow."

That day, because of a fourth-grade project, Michael learned about his immigrant forefathers, and I learned about the power of our family history. The story of our ancestors can have a positive effect on how we view others—the men and women working in fields, in restaurants, in hotels, in the multitude of menial labor jobs our society gives to new, uneducated immigrants—no longer faceless individuals, but people who want to achieve the American dream. People like our own ancestors. People like us.

Cynthia Leal Massey

Raising Our Family at the Cultural Crossroads

When my husband and I were thinking of names for our baby son, we knew we wanted a Spanish name that English speakers could pronounce easily. It needed to be short, preferably two syllables. We came up with Diego, which gave our son the same initials as his dad, D. S. The S is for Spielman.

Thinking about names was my family's first conscious effort to blend our multiple cultures. I was born and raised in Puerto Rico; I have lived in the United States for fourteen years, and in Philadelphia for the past seven. I am a product of twelve years of Catholic schooling, but I haven't practiced this faith in a long time. My Jewish husband, a Philly native, comes from a nonreligious family that observes the major holidays. These seemingly different cultures did not stop us from finding love and common ground in our shared values, professional interests and social concerns. These differences are now helping us figure out how to raise our son in an environment that blends our languages, cultural traditions, family rituals and perspectives on life.

We've decided to take what we like from each other's cultures—and from other cultures—and mix it up in flexible, nonprescriptive ways. What some scholars call "cultural syncretism," we like to call our homemade rice-and-beans-matzo-ball soup. For example, when it came time to put together our baby's welcoming celebration, I bought the book *How to Be a Jewish Parent* by Anita Diamant and looked up "baptism" on Google. Grounded in my Catholic-derived belief that babies need to be blessed when they are born, we agreed to create our own ceremony. Using my sources, we put together a celebration that combined reading a poem by a Lebanese author, some verses traditionally read at the Jewish "bris," and a special blessing written by our son's Puerto Rican grandparents. Our community of family and friends blessed water as it went around the room in a bowl before being poured over our son's head.

Another ingredient in our homemade cultural blend is the collection of family stories that we plan to share with our son. We hope that these stories will give him a sense of history and belonging. There's the story of his Puerto Rican great-aunt, Mercedita, who helped raise my mother. She was the oldest of ten children living on a coffee farm in Puerto Rico. After a hurricane destroyed the farm, she moved with her family to San Juan and learned to sew beautiful dresses for carnival queens and brides. He will also hear stories about his Jewish great-grandfather, Leon, who had a gift for working with wood and a palette of colors. Most important, we will share stories about Carol, his paternal grandmother, who passed away three months before he was born. She loved to tell the story of the birth of her sons. She would have given anything to tell Diego the story herself. We will retell the story in her memory.

The mix of stories, rituals and beliefs that we share with our son will shape his perspectives on life, people and the world that surrounds him. We hope that our homemade "soup" will nurture the seeds of curiosity, tolerance, fairness and hope. I am sure he will meet other children growing up in similarly mixed families, as the blend of cultures and traditions increasingly becomes the norm in many American homes.

During our son's first holiday season, we lit Hanukkah candles with my Catholic family in Puerto Rico, and my husband and I agreed, after some negotiation, that the Three Kings could come to our house in Philadelphia. We also talked about and remembered the people and life stories that made it possible for us to celebrate our blended holidays together. These are the people and stories that we hope to honor as we mold, shape, blend and bless the rich cultures of our families in our everyday lives.

Liza M. Rodriguez

Child of the Americas

I am a child of the Americas,
a light-skinned mestiza of the Caribbean,
a child of many diaspora, born into this continent at a
    crossroads.

I am a U.S. Puerto Rican Jew,
a product of the ghettos of New York I have never
    known,
an immigrant and the daughter and granddaughter of
    immigrants.
I speak English with passion: It's the tool of my
    consciousness,
a flashing knife blade of crystal, my tool, my craft.

I am caribeña, island grown, Spanish is in my flesh,
ripples from my tongue, lodges in my hips:
the language of garlic and mangoes,
the singing in my poetry, the flying gestures of my
    hands.

I am of Latinoamérica, rooted in the history of my
   continent:
I speak from that body.

I am not african. Africa is in me, but I cannot return.
I am not taína. Taíno is in me, but there is no way back.
I am not european. Europe lives in me, but I have no
   home there.

I am new. History made me. My first language was
   spanglish.
I was born at the crossroads,
and I am whole.

Aurora Levins Morales

5

CHALLENGES/
LOS DESAFÍOS

*Look for your passion and follow it, come
what may, but do it from a Latino
perspective, where you are guided by the
effect of what you do on your family and
your community. Being Latino is emotional,
is spiritual, and to me it means moral
structure: what is good, what is right, what
is justice. All this will become more
important as we go through some tough
times ahead. We need to build on that.*

David Hayes-Bautista

Eggs, 1930

It's the fall of 1930 in a small apartment in Spanish Harlem, the home of Lola and Manolín Morales, my abuelos. This is one of a series of homes through which every cousin and uncle and aunt fresh from the island will pass on their way into life in the United States, a kind of family consulate where they learn to ride subways, wear coats, and find apartments and jobs of their own. My grandparents were married a little over a year before, and they boarded a steamship for New York the same day in September of 1929, which means they came north just in time for the great stock-market crash. They walked off the gangplank and into the Depression.

In the years ahead, my grandfather will walk ninety blocks to work in order to save the nickel of the bus fare. He will feed his family on institutional cans of ham and giant jars of jam "liberated" from the elementary-school cafeteria, where he is a stock clerk, and his supervisor pretends not to notice what's missing. My abuela, who loves color and style, will own a single brown dress she jokingly calls "wash and wear" because you wash it and wait for it to dry so you can wear it again.

In 1941, when the U.S. enters World War II, Manolín will be recruited by the International Brotherhood of Electrical Workers, whose apprenticeship program is actively seeking out workers of color, looking to strengthen the union in a time when patriotism is being used as an excuse to undermine workers' organizing efforts. He will become a Navy Yard electrician, wiring battleships in Brooklyn. He'll go on to become a skilled and well-employed worker, a craftsman proud of each detail of what he knows, who delights in sending his grandchildren transistor radios that arrive in Puerto Rico smelling like new cars, boxes of Jordan almonds packed up with bottles of giant orange vitamins, and a special high-tech nylon rope as thin as a pencil, but strong enough to hold a swing for a ten-year-old child. And in 1969, he will retire with my grandmother to the Flamingo Terrace housing development in Bayamón to tend his plants and try to keep my grandmother locked inside the wrought-iron gates of their house.

But this is October of 1930, and my newborn mother is suckling at the breast of my starving abuela. Manolín has been unable to find work, like millions of others. Abuela Lola is faint with hunger. She hasn't eaten anything in several days, but her body continues to empty itself of nutrients to feed her child. I imagine the minerals draining from her bones and teeth, how they start to crumble. Imagine strands of protein breaking in her muscles, like elastic threads stretched too far. I have seen malnutrition. I know the sucked-in look of it. Hour by hour, she is going there.

I don't know who knocks on the door—one of the compadres or comadres, that small group of Puerto Rican immigrants who know each other, who act as family in this foreign place where the autumn air is growing chill and everyone is desperate. One of the men has been promoted. No longer a janitor, he will now supervise maintenance at the office building where he works. The others have gotten together to decide who they should groom for his old job. The consensus is that Manolín should get it because he and Lola have a new baby. So the former janitor takes Abuelo down to the building at night and teaches him how to use the big industrial vacuum cleaner. In the morning when he recommends Abuelo for the job, they will both be able to say he has experience.

The manager approves him, hires him and advances him a week's pay, and when Manolín leaves work in the early morning hours, he buys eggs and butter and hurries home to Lola and my infant mother. He cooks her scrambled eggs, a specialty of his that will be famous to his descendants, his way of expressing love and also exercising his perfectionism and authority in the kitchen. You beat the eggs just so, dice the onions in the most efficient Morales way, put the chopped tomatoes in at just the right heat, stir at the exactly correct speed for the perfect texture.

But in all his cooking career, there are no eggs as perfect as the ones he cooks for his wife that morning, blessed with the compassion of the comparientes, seasoned with hunger and hope, and spooned carefully into the mouth of a woman too weak to hold a utensil. Fifty years later, my abuela will still be able to describe what it was like to eat those eggs, buttery and soft and delicious beyond words, the warmth of them entering her stomach, the surge of strength returning to her limbs. For those eggs were more than eggs—one mouthful after another, they were golden bites of life itself.

Aurora Levins Morales

The Clinic

Mami was not a small woman. But that day, sitting up in her hospital bed, she looked tiny. It had been only six months since the diagnosis. I looked at her sitting there, all smiles, busy making plans. The only signs of her struggle with the disease were the deepened creases around her eyes, her bald head, now carefully wrapped in a colorful scarf, and the acrid smell of antibiotics that permeated the room. She had tried to camouflage it with perfume, but the odor of the medicine oozed from her pores, sank into the bedclothes and hung in the air like an evil spirit.

I was doing her nails. In place of the usual clear polish, she asked me to apply the third coat of a scandalously red nail polish, *Apasionada*. I looked up at her questioningly.

"I just love the name, so full of love and life," she said. She leaned forward and took my hand, giving it a long squeeze. She looked into my eyes and held me. There were so many ways that she could do that—hold me when all I wanted was to move on. And in the past, she had let me. There had been so many things I didn't want said. Now, the intensity in her eyes made me uncomfortable.

I tried to pull my hand away, get back to the business of grooming, but she wouldn't let go.

"*Nena*, when death is near," she said, "you've got to hang on hard, *real* hard, any way you can. You've got to savor each day, roll it around in your mouth before swallowing it. And each day, each minute will nourish and sustain. You've got to learn to hang on to the good and even the not-so-good. It's the hanging on that counts, the relishing the moment." Then she looked down at our hands and added almost inaudibly, "and I'm trying to hang on, to *every* single moment, in *every* way I can." When she looked up again, her face was rigid with effort. But the tears sitting in her eyes made their way down, carving agonizingly slow paths down her cheeks.

She was fifty-eight years old. She never saw fifty-nine.

*   *   *

The nurse touches my shoulder. I jump, upsetting the vase full of flowers. I look at her and notice that she, too, wears white. My eyes wander down to her breasts. I understand the compassion in her voice. It shelters her own fear. My body rises, pushes into the heavy air, legs leaden, and goes through the door. I've lost the room. *Breathe in.*

"I'm sorry to have to press so hard, but we must get a good picture."

The nurse adjusts the lever. I hold on as the vise closes down on one breast. *Hold your breath.* I look away from the machine. My flesh clings to the glass plate even though my torso wants to back away. The cold at the bottom of my stomach has become a solid block of ice. *One more time, hold it . . . breathe.* The technician releases the levers, slides my breast off the shelf and disappears. I pull the robe around my shoulders, hoping to find warmth to counteract what is going on inside. *Breathe out.*

Then come the fingers, the poking and prodding and squeezing. The doctor wants to be thorough. I look at her mouth moving. I hear only the sounds of the technician in the developing room behind her. *Any questions?* Back in the waiting room, I hold on and wait some more. *Breathe in.*

Seemingly hours later, the doctor calls me into a glass-enclosed alcove. She looks once again at my old X-rays and then the new. She puts them down in the center of her desk and begins to speak. Quietly, she gives me the results, squeezing my shaking hand. My shoulders release. The block in my stomach begins to melt. *Breathe out.*

The women in the room look at me through the glass. I smile as the words wash over me. The eyes of the women outside go over me like searchlights. They are happy for my relief. One woman in the corner stares at me, darkness playing on her face. *What's that all about . . . ?* The thought plays in a distant part of my mind. I revisit my own fear of this afternoon, and I understand. She doesn't know yet, and it takes so much strength to just sit and wait. She cannot afford kindness, not yet. In truth, it is only now that I can be generous.

It takes me a few moments to get up and collect my things at the desk. When I am alone in the paneled dressing room again, I let my weight fall against the wall. *Breathe in.* I close my eyes and go within. The ice continues to melt. The pressure has slackened. The fireworks come more slowly now. Their colors are beginning to fade. I take in a gulp of air and try to find my normal breathing again. I have a reprieve. *Breathe out.*

I stand naked before the mirror and examine the sight of my breasts. They are misshapen, tender and pendulous, certainly not as firm or smoothly round as they used to be. But they are whole, intact. And I am thankful for that.

I look at myself in the mirror as I begin to dress. My

fingers follow the length and trace the depth of the old scar. I search for temperature changes and feel the textures. I look at the shades of pink and purple. I stay with it, know it. There will be no repeat of this on my chest, not yet, maybe never.

But I know this place will become familiar. The doctor had said, "Clean bill of health. See you next spring."

I dress quickly.

Before leaving the room, I catch sight of my face reflected in the mirror. I stop for a moment before digging in my purse. I fish out my lipstick tube, *Apasionada*. My mother flashes through my mind. Mom, who didn't have another spring, and still she hung on. I stare at the tube of red for a long time and let myself listen for my mother's voice and remember her struggle. I let her memory wash over me and feel it charge me with resolve.

I know that I will come here every year, and I will wait. I will fear the bad news and hope for the good each time. I will hang on. And I will be thankful for every additional year. I will take that thankfulness with me into the world and let it propel me through my life. *And if one year the news is not so good, I will hang on anyway because it is all that I can do, because it is what she left me.*

In the mirror, I seek out the lines of her face in mine. I fill in the contours of my broad lips. I look closely and find my mother's superimposed on mine deep in the mirror. "We won," her lips say. Slowly, they pull into a smile.

As I walk out, the woman behind the desk waves. "You have a good day, now."

"I will," I say. The ice in the pit of my stomach is gone now. I feel my face moving to accommodate my smile as I step into the elevator. I am still smiling as I walk out into the lush green of the busy street.

Dahlma Llanos Figueroa

In My Classroom

It is possible to become discouraged about the injustice we see everywhere. But God did not promise us that the world would be humane and just. He gives us the gift of life and allows us to choose the way we will use our limited time on Earth. It is an awesome opportunity.

César Chávez

Sobbing silently to myself, I gripped my older sister's hand as tightly as I could as she rushed me down the long corridor of Theodore Roosevelt Elementary School in Indio, California. It was the late 1950s, and at five years of age I was about to enter the frightening dimension of a new world: first grade. Since my birth date was in November, and because my older siblings had taught me my numbers and the English alphabet—so I could read a few simple words—I was able to skip kindergarten.

Depositing me inside the first-grade room, my sister, Elodia, quickly disappeared, scurrying on to her sixth-grade classroom. Scared and missing the warmth of my sister's hand, I nevertheless obeyed the teacher's instructions to sit at my assigned desk. The cold, wooden seat offered little comfort as I now imagined Mama's brown, soft face and longed for her familiar arms and soothing voice. *"No tengas miedo, Angelita."* I could almost hear her whisper. Soundless tears dried on my sticky cheeks as I waited for the next turn of events. The look on many of the other kids' faces mirrored my own distress.

The teacher's voice addressed her roomful of dazed children—all shades of white, brown and black. It didn't take long before I realized that the sounds emanating from her mouth were from that "other" world. It was not the Spanish that filled the home where I grew up with nine siblings. A few of Mrs. Miller's words sounded a little familiar—like the English my older brothers and sisters often spoke at home. But panic set in as the storm of English hitting my ears became a rain of darts, and I felt like such an unwelcome foreigner. With sweaty palms and racing heart, I sat there frozen . . . and needing to go to the bathroom.

Mrs. Miller's smile and blond doughnut hair appeared friendly, but her vague speech was vinegar to my ears. I could not just bolt out the door, like my feet were trying to make me do, so I scanned the room for a calming spot to gaze upon. I noticed a colorful bulletin board displaying a farm scene: large red barn, cutouts of farm animals and a dungareed farmer on a green tractor who seemed to gaze down on me. Since I was from a family of migrant workers who picked seasonal crops, the farm scene offered an odd sense of familiarity, reaching out across the cultural barrier I was experiencing. Somehow, I managed to read the caption on the bulletin wall: *Life on the Farm.* I felt grateful for my summer instruction, when Elodia had insisted on teaching me my ABCs. The vivid colors of the construction-paper cutouts on the bulletin board calmed me. I grew accustomed to the four walls of the room where I was to spend countless hours away from home, but it would come to feel more like a sentence than a privilege.

In that long productive school year and ones that followed, I gradually became an excellent student. I'm not sure how long it took or even how it happened, but I acquired English in a forced way—we were punished with a slap to the hand whenever we spoke Spanish in the classroom or school grounds. I have a vivid memory of two Mexican boys in my classroom returning from the principal's office, sobbing loudly as they slid back into their seats. Corporal punishment was a regular practice at that time, and paddling was administered for continuously breaking the "no-Spanish" rule. Forbidden to speak my home language, I understood the message: Spanish was not acceptable, and neither was I if I chose to speak it.

A newfound feeling of shame toward Spanish and my Mexican culture made me eager to blend in with my Anglo peers. In an effort to be accepted by the dominant society, I complied with school rules. Then, determined to speak English only, I eventually forgot how to speak Spanish altogether as the school years progressed. By the time I graduated from high school, I could no longer hold a clear conversation with either of my Spanish-speaking parents. My older brothers and sisters became translators for my three younger sisters (who were also losing their ability to speak Spanish) and me. I acquired a mixed sense of pride and shame for being able to speak English without the accent that many of my Mexican-American friends so shamefully and helplessly possessed. Back then, an accent was erroneously linked to a sign of low intelligence. It was an age when "English-only I.Q. tests" were regularly administered to students for placement and tracking. Those who failed to pass the tests were permanently labeled "retarded" in their cumulative file. When the word got around of their test failure, these children were cruelly teased by their peers. I was terrified of ever being labeled mentally retarded. I felt great pride in speaking like an "American-born citizen" and sounding "smart" to my teachers, but ashamed for turning my back on my own people—and on a part of myself I would later find I could never deny.

It was not until many years later, as a college student at San Jose State University, that I came to the realization that being bilingual and bicultural could be valuable assets. I applied for a minor in Mexican-American Graduate Studies, a newly established college program of study, in an effort to acquire knowledge and understanding of my ethnic roots. I took Spanish courses to relearn my mother tongue, and delved into the study of Hispanic history and culture, trying to make up for lost time.

I became an elementary bilingual teacher, teaching in the lower grades for fourteen years. During my career, I lost count of how often I recognized the confused look on the faces of my non-English-speaking students as they entered my classroom for the first time. Their dazed faces reminded me of my own traumatic first day of school. Unlike my fearful initial school days, my students always had the comfort of being able to hear and speak both Spanish and English in their classroom. And they were never shamed into denying or abandoning their home language or rich heritage, something that made their transition into the English-speaking world quite different.

Alas, the shame I had acquired over too many earlier years would not be easily erased. It took a long time for me to obtain a new sense of pride toward my ancestry and ethnicity, a pride that gradually replaced the hollow that had accompanied me far too long.

Today, when I stand in my classroom, I am relieved and

happy that my students have a learning environment in which they will never have to lose the sense of ethnic pride and wholeness that they bring with them on that first day of school.

Anjela Villarreal Ratliff

A Mother's Love

A mother's love is instinctual, unconditional and forever.

Anonymous

Think back to the early '90s, before Ellen "came out" and *Will & Grace* was not yet all over prime-time television. Before Matthew Shepard received national attention, and being gay got the public support it has today. Imagine a nineteen-year-old Mexican son coming out to his mother and seeing the heartbreak in her eyes. Picture her heart breaking into pieces so small they could fit through the eye of a sewing needle.

Living in Texas, growing up Catholic with a strong Mexican ancestry and influence, it was difficult coming to terms with my own homosexuality. I can remember many nights when I prayed the entire rosary and begged God to change me. As the years pushed on, I gradually accepted who I was and learned to love myself despite my machismo-rich heritage. However, that was only the first step.

All Latinos know how important family is, and I am not any different. Accepting my sexuality was a big move for me on my journey to self-discovery. Yet, the burning question was, would my family accept me as well? The thought of losing them and being disowned frightened me more than death.

In our culture, we are taught that family is everything. I could gladly meet any of life's challenges as long as I had my family by my side to face them head-on. Nonetheless, the time had come, and I needed to be honest with them.

Easing into the task, I came out to my younger brother first. Surprisingly, his reaction was good and more or less indifferent. He was of the mind-set that I was his brother, and my sexual orientation was not important. Feeling particularly confident about the experience, I decided to come out to my mother.

It was October 11, 1994, National Coming Out Day. She cried, yelled, screamed and ultimately blamed herself. It was a nightmare. By the end of the night, our eyes were red and puffy from all the crying, and our noses dripped with *mocos*. We were exhausted and retired to our respective rooms without saying good night. I never expected her to react the way she had, and I worried that our relationship was forever damaged.

That night I lay in bed and thought about a TV talk show that I had seen earlier that day. The focus of the show was National Coming Out Day, and the guests were a variety of non-Latinos coming out to their families. Their experiences on the show were much better than mine that night, and I could not comprehend why my mother had reacted so awfully. For the next few days, the house was covered with a blanket of awkwardness.

The next day I came out to my sister, and a month later I came out to my dad. I was able to delay telling my father as my parents divorced when I was in middle school. I could not bear another episode like the one I experienced with Mom. Nevertheless, their reaction to my news was much like my younger brother's, and I was very much surprised by my father's kind words. He said, "You're my son, and I'll always love you no matter what."

I wish I could write that my mother soon thereafter came to her senses and we promptly mended our relationship. The truth of the matter is, the road to her acceptance and understanding was a long one. In the months that followed, we had many emotional discussions, and she had several questions. She was determined to figure out what went wrong. Mom would encourage me to continue to pray, and I know that HIV and AIDS were huge concerns for her. A lot of people, especially at that time, believed that being gay was equivalent to an AIDS death sentence.

Today, eight years later and thanks to a lot of determination and persistence, my mother and I have a very healthy and open relationship. In a lot of ways, she is my best friend. Recently, we've watched movies with gay themes as she tries to gain a better understanding of my life. Her favorite is *The Broken Hearts Club*.

As far as my seemingly open-minded brother, sister and father and our relationship today, they have adopted the philosophy, "Don't ask, don't tell." We are all still close, and I now have a sister-in-law, a three-year-old niece and one-year-old nephew. But they turn a blind eye and deaf ear to those things they choose not to know. Unfortunately, that means there are parts of me missing from their lives. My mother and I had a rough start as 1994 came to an end, but today she is the only one in my family who knows me completely.

My Mexican-proud mom had survived an impoverished childhood on the north side of town, coupled with years of adolescence tormented by Texas-style bigotry and hatred for our race. And just when she probably thought she was in the clear, her first-born son professes he is gay. But falling back on our faith and cultural importance of family, that no longer matters to her. Come what may, we promise to be there for one another and to stand together.

People's reactions vary when I come out to them today, but as long as I have my mother supporting me, I am happy. What more could a son ask from his mother than her continued support and love? Nothing can compare to a mother's love, and being a mama's boy is a good thing. My mom has been the rock in my life, *y no puedo imaginar mi vida sin ella.*

¡Gracias a Dios por ti mamá, gracias por quererme sin límites!

Johnny N. Ortez, Jr.

I'll Always Remember You

I watched her as she lay there, propped up in the bed by sanitized hospital pillows and covered by numerous white sheets and blankets. Her body was swathed in the unattractive, thin material of the hospital gown. The hospital bed, with all its railings, made her look like a small bird in a large cage.

I had expected her to be sitting up, laughing and talking to the nurses in her broken English and requesting her beloved rice and beans and *café con leche*. I wanted to hear her say, "*Hola*, Norma." I wanted to talk to her about my day. Instead, I saw a tiny elderly woman with a quizzical, frightened expression in her eyes. She looked at my face, trying to place me. The more she struggled to remember me, the more her eyes would mist.

It was only yesterday that I had been in this very same room, but a different woman had occupied that bed. She was the woman I knew, who knew me—not this frail, scared and confused woman on the verge of tears.

At first I thought it was as simple as just telling her who I was. I thought that she would laugh and say she remembered me. Unfortunately, it wasn't that simple. It only added guilt to her confusion, and it just made her eyes (and mine) mist even more.

I couldn't bear her discomfort or the pain of that unconquerable struggle, so I changed the subject. We talked about minor, insignificant things like the weather, gradually shifting the conversation to all the cards and flowers in the room. She agreed that they were pretty, but sadly admitted that she didn't know who they were from. I read to her from the cards, but she didn't recognize the names of any of her children so, emotionally worn, we talked about the Jell-O on her tray.

The afternoon passed as we made small talk, trying to ignore the pink elephant in the room. I had planned on just a short visit, but the child in me found it hard to leave without some type of acknowledgment from her. So I lingered until visiting hours were over. As I was leaving, she said, "Norma came to see me yesterday."

I kissed her good-bye and said, "I know, Mom. And she'll be back again tomorrow."

Norma Oquendo

Reeling In a Boy's Dream

In 1962, my husband and his family were living in a cramped apartment in Miami Beach. My husband's family had arrived from Cuba only a year before, and like most Cubans who left the country during this time, they were struggling to make a new life for themselves.

My husband was ten years old, and his brother was eleven. Every week, when my mother-in-law would go to the grocery store, they would wait for her in the fishing and tackle shop next door. The boys would walk around the store admiring the fishing supplies, and eventually would end up in front of the fishing poles. There was nothing they wanted more than to own their own fishing pole and reel.

My mother-in-law would find her sons in the same place every week, staring at the fishing poles, and it broke her heart. She knew how much the boys missed living in Cuba. They had grown up spending weekends and summers on their grandfather's ranch, where they enjoyed horseback riding, hunting and fishing.

My father-in-law had two jobs, but every chance he got,

he took his sons fishing. The pier was only six blocks away from their small apartment, and on weekends it was filled with fishermen. You could tell who the Miami residents were and who the Cuban refugees were by looking at their fishing gear. The Cubans fished with a spool of fishing wire, a hook and a small weight tied to the end of the line.

For the Cubans, fishing was fun. It was also one of the few activities they could share with their children for free. And if they were lucky, it could also provide dinner for their families.

My father-in-law also used fishing as an opportunity to practice his English. While they fished, he would talk to the people he met on the fishing pier. Many of them were retired Jewish businessmen who had moved to Miami Beach.

One Sunday morning, they walked the six blocks to the pier, and after finding an empty spot to fish, they swung the string over their heads and threw the lines out as far as they could. They fished most of the morning, but except for a few bites, no one caught anything. Then my brother-in-law felt a tug on the line.

He began to reel the wire in, and as he did he could feel the fish at the other end trying to pull free. It was enormous. Slowly, he continued to reel him in. By this time, people on the pier had put down their fishing gear and stood around my brother-in-law, waiting to get a glimpse of the monster fish he had at the end of the line.

Just when he thought he couldn't hang on any longer, out of the water popped a fishing pole and reel covered with seaweed and mud. Everyone groaned in disappointment except my husband and his brother, who couldn't believe their eyes.

The fishing pole looked like it had been in the water for months. The reel was rusted and in bad shape, but that night on top of the dining-room table, my father-in-law took it apart, and began to clean and grease every single inch.

The next weekend when the brothers went fishing, they walked to the pier carrying a fishing pole. It wasn't like the ones they had seen at the store, but for two young Cuban refugees it was just as good.

Finding and fixing that fishing pole gave the boys hope that their new lives would get better, and it provided a very important lesson for my husband: Life gives us what we need, even though blessings don't always come in the shiniest packages.

María Luisa Salcines

The Power to Shine

Anyone who saw me standing at the podium during the awards ceremony that June day would have called me a success. At thirty-five, I was the founder and sole owner of a multimillion-dollar business. I traveled the country speaking to businesspeople. I had three beautiful sons and was prosperous enough not to need to work another day in my life. But I had spent so much of my early life feeling lost and powerless that I wasn't able to savor my own good fortune.

As a girl, growing up poor in the South Bronx, I wasn't sure what success looked like, but I was pretty sure it didn't look like me. There was no chubby, freckled, bespectacled Puerto Rican girl in any movie I'd ever seen or book I'd ever read—nor had I ever heard of a Latina CEO or scholar. And there weren't too many successes on view outside my window either. The women I saw were worn-out domestics and shop clerks, carrying groceries to their walk-ups, trying to scrape together enough energy to make it through another day. Without realizing what I was doing, I began putting together a model for myself from bits and pieces of those around me—that one's straight back, and this one's spirit—a kind of rag doll I kept by my side.

As I grew up and moved out into the world, I worked hard to overcome the impoverishment of my childhood years. But early versions of myself were stacked inside me like Russian dolls: the four-year-old who was beaten up the first day of school because she was mistaken for white; the frightened teenager at a South Bronx high school where police stood in riot gear; the college freshman at Wellesley whose roommate requested to be moved because she didn't want to room with a kid from the ghetto. I couldn't get rid of them entirely, nor did I want to. They were part of me, reminders of where I was from, although I made sure to keep them hidden. Then completely by chance, at seventeen, I found a niche for myself in New York after dropping out of Wellesley. I landed a job as a customer-service clerk at a company that made umbrellas and tote bags. Business fascinated me—all the gyrations of people and product, the ups and downs, the whole cycle of making something out of nothing. Eventually, I decided I wanted to move into sales, but the company turned down my request. Not to be deterred, I called in sick one day so that I could call on the Museum of Natural History, a potential customer. I left there with a huge order and a new customer. After I brought the order to the office, I met with the company president and asked, "Are you guys gonna let me sell now or what?"

They did. A few years later, when I was twenty-one, I was promoted to account executive and put in charge of my own category of business. Two years after that, I went to work for a rival firm in California to expand their umbrella business. I was making a lot of money for someone my age, and with a goal in mind, I consciously lived well below my means. After working for that company for a few years, I had enough money to step out on my own.

Suddenly, I was an entrepreneur without a salary. Flying by the seat of my pants, I was losing money, but I didn't let my early mistakes discourage me. I continued to move forward, doing what I felt I had to do, even when I wasn't sure whether I was right.

By this time, I was married with two young children, and my world was split down the middle. I kept the professional strictly separate from the personal, and never spoke about my background in business circles. It was lonely being a woman CEO, but I was used to that. I was vaguely aware that I was hiding, but I didn't feel ready to take the risk of revealing myself.

My company, Umbrellas Plus, continued to grow and expand, landing several major retail accounts. Eventually, I relocated to New Jersey to be closer to the industry action. One day as I was flipping through a magazine, I came across an announcement for the Women of Enterprise Awards sponsored by Avon and the SBA. The award was given to women business owners who had overcome significant odds to build a successful enterprise. It sounded right up my alley. As I filled out the essay questions, it occurred to me that this kind of award might bring me smack up against my carefully constructed identity, but I completed the application anyhow. Who said I was going to win? A month later I opened a notice from Avon, read the first word—Congratulations!—and whooped out loud. This Puerto Rican, a one-time public-housing resident, was going to be honored in front of fifteen hundred luminaries during a reception at the Waldorf-Astoria! I'd been awarded a stay in New York, with theater, dinner, media appearances, a cash gift and a makeover. I was on cloud nine.

The day of the awards luncheon, I felt like Cinderella as I walked into the legendary Waldorf-Astoria, surrounded by well-wishers. But once I was seated in the hotel's grand ballroom, looking around at the crystal chandeliers, the linen tablecloths and the impeccably dressed crowd, I grew increasingly anxious. When it was my turn to speak, my ears roared and my legs shook as I made my way to the podium. Looking out over the glittering crowd, the old voices I had battled all my life came thundering back at me: *Who do you think you are? What's a ghetto girl like you doing here?* By this point in my life, I "had it all"—the well-tailored suits, the fine jewelry, the business, the family, the house. What was still missing? I stared out beyond the crowd to an illuminated patch of floor at the back of the ballroom. . . .

And then an amazing thing happened. A vision of an old woman with a bucket and rag flashed before me: a widow who spoke no English, whose only option had been to leave her children and homeland to work as a domestic in the United States. That woman was my great-grand-mother, Juanita. You see, my great-grandmother had left Puerto Rico and found a job at a large, fancy hotel in New York—this hotel, the Waldorf-Astoria. She had worked on her knees, in this very building where her great-grand-daughter was now standing in a place of honor. As I looked out over the audience, I felt such a connection to Mama Juanita, her spirit of fortitude and resolve, and all the other women who came before me, women who worked hard without knowing how it would affect future generations. If they could push through their fears and achieve so much, then so could I. I would let my real life shine, not only for my great-grandmother, but also so that other women could see it for themselves. With my sons, parents and business associates looking on, I spoke. For the first time publicly, I shared, with pride, my true story, not a sanitized version. As I gave that speech, I came to terms with where I came from and where I was going. In embracing my own history, I was connecting to a story larger than myself.

To this day, whenever I feel discouraged, I stand at the kitchen sink and wash dishes. When I make that circular motion with a brush or cloth, I feel the power of so many women before me, whether they washed dishes at a river or cleaned the floors of a hotel. I think about my children and their children, and their children's children. I think of my great-grandmother Juanita and how she scrubbed floors on her knees, so that one day, I might shine.

Deborah Rosado Shaw

Transforming Tragedy

The point is not to pay back kindness, but to pass it on.

Julia Álvarez

A while back, I went through the best and worst year of my life. My husband got his first full-time job, I became pregnant with twins, and we bought our first home. We felt truly blessed. Unfortunately, our good fortune did not last long. I went into labor when I was only twenty-three weeks pregnant and had to undergo an emergency caesarean section. I gave birth to two sons: Alejandro and Nicolás. Both children were extremely premature and were kept alive by machines.

With each minute that passed, I felt more helpless. Fortunately, I had a great deal of support. At the hospital, I was surrounded by friends and family. My mother was constantly by my side. Being a good Mexican mother, she brought my husband food so that he could keep up his strength and not have to leave my room in order to get something to eat.

My friends were incredibly supportive. Since I had a caesarean section, I was unable to return to graduate school to finish the semester. While I was consumed with the survival of my children, *mi comadre* Marta said, "I'll take care of everything at school." At that moment, I couldn't have cared less about school. Marta filed the necessary paperwork to grant me incompletes in the classes I couldn't finish. Her support enabled me to return to school later and pick up where I had left off. Thanks to her, I was able to pass all of my courses, not jeopardize my funding and eventually graduate.

Other people tried to lift my spirits by sharing their miracle stories. Tía Rosa told me about the little girl at church who was born weighing less than two pounds and was now a healthy eight-year-old able to run all over the place. These stories gave me hope as my husband and I desperately waited for any signs of improvement from my near lifeless children, whose tiny hands we held every day. As each minute passed, I saw my miracle slowly slipping away.

Shortly after I was released from the hospital, the doctor called, saying, "You need to come to the hospital immediately. Nicolás is deteriorating quickly."

We drove to the hospital as quickly as we could. As I rocked Nicolás in my arms, I felt my mother's presence. She stood in the doorway, staring at my son, and her eyes quickly filled with tears. "*¿Qué haces aquí Mamá?* I asked.

"*Sentí que me necesitaban,*" she replied. Nicolás died in my arms within an hour, having lived only four short days. Nine days later, we received another call urging us to get to the hospital quickly. As we drove frantically to the hospital, I saw a shooting star in the sky—a sign perhaps of a spirit returning back home. Alejandro died on the operating table shortly thereafter.

My biggest fear was that my sons would not recognize

me in heaven since neither one of them ever opened their eyes to see what I looked like.

Despite the terrible loss we endured, I realize now that we were also greatly blessed. The kindness from friends, loved ones and strangers sustained me. During the short time that our children were in the hospital, they received constant blood transfusions. The hospital asked us to find people to donate blood in our sons' names. We informed our supervisors of our situation, and they sent out campus-wide memos. A few days later, my husband and I went to the blood-donor center to donate blood. When I gave the nurse my name, she said, "Are you the babies' mother? The Alvarez babies?"

"Yes, I am," I replied. "How did you know?"

"So many people have called wanting to donate blood for your babies that we had to stop taking appointments." My eyes filled with tears at the kindness of so many people, many of whom I did not even know.

Many other people personally reached out to us. Professors, colleagues, students and family members all shared stories with us about other children who had died. It made me realize that losing a child is more common than I thought; the problem is that no one talks about it openly. I felt as though I had joined a secret society where it was safe to speak the unspeakable. No one in that group shuddered at the mention of a dead child. It was very comforting to be able to talk to these people.

I also had strange experiences. One day, I was at the station waiting to take the train home. I saw a humble-looking woman holding a baby in her arms on the other side of the station. Everyone around her froze as she floated directly toward me and lifted up her baby as an offering. She said, "Here, you can have my baby. You can take better care of him than I can." I stared at her in disbelief, unable to understand why she would give up her baby, but grateful that she had chosen me. I lifted my arms to accept the baby when suddenly everyone in the station started moving again; I realized that the woman I thought was giving me her baby was still standing on the other side of the station. I buried my face in my hands and cried. I had imagined all of it.

I have replayed the day I went into labor over and over again, trying to understand why it happened to me, but unable to find an answer. Nevertheless, this experience has changed the way I live my life. I have learned that the human spirit is very resilient; time has reduced, but not eliminated, my pain. I also realize the importance of nurturing relationships. My husband and I no longer work as hard in order to spend more time together: Life is too short to spend it working all of the time.

We have also tried to live a purpose-driven life. Since we do not have children of our own, we try to help others. We offer scholarships to Latino students; we have established college funds for our nieces and nephews; we provide assistance to relatives who are struggling; we comfort people who have lost loved ones. These small gestures have brought us many blessings. Even though my children are not with me physically, they are with me spiritually.

Their constant presence in my mind and heart inspire me to live life helping others.

Maya Álvarez-Galván

The Christmas Train

In 1963, I was a ten-year-old girl living with my parents and four-year-old brother in Madrid, Spain. We were poor Cuban refugees who had left our country just a few months before.

Our stay in Spain would be brief as we waited for our U.S. residency to be approved. My maternal grandfather and uncle had sacrificed their little savings—they were recently arrived refugees to New York—to send us a meager monthly stipend for our humble lodgings. Our only meals came from a soup kitchen where we lined up in the late morning along with dozens of other Cubans.

That particular winter was bitterly cold in Madrid. Our hospice room was freezing during the day, so we would spend our time walking Madrid's magnificent boulevards. We marveled at the architecture and the large plazas and the snow! We missed our homeland, but the promise of a fresh beginning beckoned, and *la madre patria* was a magnificent start for a new life.

The Christmas season arrived. Overnight, Madrid lit up. Every corner was awash in sparkling holiday lights, *los madrileños* were busy bustling about buying gifts and looking forward to *la noche buena,* and *el día de los reyes.*

Every storefront was a winter wonderland full of dolls, trolleys and every imaginable toy. The storefront at the *Corte Inglés* department store had a fabulous Christmas village full of enchanting chalets, snow-covered peaks and a shiny red train that circled the town, hooting its horn at every turn.

My younger brother, Santiago, was born during the first year of the Cuban Revolution, and he had never seen such a wondrous toy. Toys were considered a luxury then and were very hard to obtain.

My brother fell in love with that train. Every day he would push his nose against the glass in the window and ask: "Do you think *los reyes magos* will bring me that train? Do you? Do you?" My parents' pain was apparent as they looked at their son's hopeful face. They knew that no matter how hard their son wished for that train, his wish would not be granted.

Looking at my parents, I just wished Santiago would stop asking. But I also didn't want to destroy the innocence of a hopeful four-year-old. So the next time Santiago ran up to the storefront window and asked the question, I pulled him aside.

"Santiago, you know that we left our country and we are in a strange land," I said. "The three wise men are pretty smart, but since we are only here in Madrid for a little while, they probably don't have our address. I don't think we'll be getting any toys this year."

I also told him that once we were settled in the United States, the three wise men would find us once again. To my utter surprise, he accepted my explanation without question, and our excursions up and down the main boulevard continued without any major interruptions.

A year later, we were settled in Union City, New Jersey, the town we had moved to upon entry into the United

States. Both my parents—a teacher and an engineer—
were working at factory jobs. Santiago and I were adapt-
ing to a new school and quickly learning English.

That Christmas was modest, but my parents bought a
silver-colored Christmas tree, and we put tiny, sparkling
lights on it. They also bought the traditional pork and
turrones for the *Noche Buena* meal.

On Christmas day, I woke up early, and to my surprise
and delight found several presents underneath the tree
with my name on them. But even better than that was
watching my brother's face as he opened a square box
with a large red bow and his name on it.

Inside was a shiny, brand-new train! The locomotive
and caboose resembled the one that had so enthralled
my brother a year before. Santiago's face lit up like the
Christmas tree. He looked at my parents and me, and his
eyes shined with happiness and surprise.

"Babby, you were right!" my brother told me eagerly.
"The three wise men found our address, and they gave it
to Santa Claus!"

Barbara Gutiérrez

NO RODEO®

NO RODEO © *Robert Berardi. Used by permission.*

NO RODEO, *Robert Berardi,* ©2005, *reprinted by permission of Robert Berardi.*

Love in Shadows

It's past noon on a hot Sunday in July. I am with my sister, who rarely gets out, only for doctor appointments or for short visits with her daughters. We are going to a nearby museum. She is in the beginning stages of Alzheimer's disease, and while she does recognize me, at times she calls me by another name. Still, she looks at me with love and affection. According to her daughters, she functions best in familiar surroundings; in public she gets antsy, nervous, and can be difficult to handle. But I like a challenge. I'm determined to make this a fun day for my eldest sibling, who bought my Easter bonnets and winter coats when I was a kid. She was the sister who taught me about "good furniture" and good table manners, the 1940s "career girl" whom I always wanted to emulate.

She wears a cotton shift and, although it's hot, a heavy sweater. On her feet, once adorned by ankle-strap sandals, are white shoes like those worn by nurses. High white socks cling to her skinny ankles. She is slowly losing weight, so that when I see her after a time, the weight loss is more apparent. Yet, if allowed to, my sis will eat all day, a common occurrence among Alzheimer's patients; they forget when they last ate. I find it scary that with all she eats, she continues to lose weight.

Her complexion, once flawless, is pale and pasty from lack of sun. I'm surprised to see she wears blush—too much blush. (In her days, they called it rouge.) The effort to make her look healthy fails; she just looks made-up. The round red spots remind me of circus clowns. But the dark eyes and long eyelashes I still envy retain their freshness. Wound around her head is a bright scarf like that worn by Lana Turner in movies. She smells nice.

Just getting her in and out of the car begins to test my patience. Because my vehicle is a bit high (a 4-Runner), she needs help getting into it. She confuses the door lock and the handle, and when she's able to locate the lever that adjusts the seat, she pulls it. Her head is now close to the windshield. Worse, the seat belt is too tight! She is irritable, and I'm in a sweat—and we haven't even left! I take a deep breath, turn the ignition key and off we go.

As we hit the freeway, she appears tense, almost frightened. Traffic on the I-5 is treacherous, even for a seasoned California driver. Cars doing at least seventy-five miles per hour fly by on my left; a truck comes to a screeching halt in the middle lane; a bus cuts in front of me. I'm beginning to panic. What if I have an accident and we get hurt? Will my sister know her name? Home address? It dawns on me that she carries no identification. I won't panic. I slow down, stay in the slower lane. As cars zoom by, I pull back, relax. I turn on the radio and pat my sister's shoulder to reassure her. She says nothing, only stares out the window.

What does she see? I wonder. Can she tell we're on the freeway? Does she feel the sun's warmth? Not long ago, I took her on an outing. After the usual hassles with the seat belt, we drove to nearby San Fernando Mission. I wanted to help her recall days past, when she and her friends—and boyfriends—strolled (and kissed?) through the pretty and romantic mission gardens where a stony-faced *Junípero Serra* looks on. We had a lovely time. At lunchtime, I ordered a large pizza with everything: pepperoni, Canadian bacon and loads of cheese. She liked it, and I was pleased. I hope today turns out like that day.

At long last, we arrive at the Gene Autry Heritage Museum. It's near the Los Angeles Zoo, which, if things go right today, we might someday visit. Perhaps the sight of pretty birds or a polar bear will interest my sister. My sister used to be interested in everything. She is an intellectual and bookworm who no longer reads, but who once subscribed to the Book-of-the-Month Club. I read most of the books before she sent them back; they were my introduction to English literature. At age ten or so, I read *The Razor's Edge* and Gothic novels by Daphne du Maurier. Once hooked on real books, I never read comic books again.

The museum's current exhibition, "Images of Mexican-Americans in Film," focuses on movie stars from the 1940s, my sister's era. I want to jog her memory. We view the display of clothes based on movies of social bandits like the Cisco Kid and Zorro (as in *The Mark of Zorro*). Dark cape flying, black mask on his handsome face, Zorro fought the evil ranch owner and won the pretty *señorita*, a blonde in a *mantilla*. I'm anxious to see everything, but my sister walks so slowly! An image of her gliding into church in a polka-dot dress and straw hat (with cabbage roses) comes to mind. *Who would have thought?* I ask myself. *Who can predict whom this disease will strike?*

The exhibit is extensive. She lingers before a photo of Gilbert Roland, the handsome (Mexican) rascal with a thin moustache. The cape worn by Tyrone Power (as Zorro) glitters through a wall of glass. She enjoys the Old West display: the gun collection, chuck wagon and leather chaps.

Suddenly, she takes a wrong turn and is lost from view. I call her name in a frightened voice, but she does not answer. Once I find her, I vow to stay close.

She appears to take an interest in women's calico dresses and movie paraphernalia, laughing at a replica of a 1940s farmhouse replete with washboard.

"I scrubbed on one of those," she tells me, her eyes merry. When she smiles, her face lights up.

"Hungry?" I ask. She nods, pulls at the buttons on her sweater, then follows me to the museum café. We split a chicken sandwich and dig into chili-cheese spuds. The sister from whom I learned table manners is chewing with her mouth open. In one hand she holds the sandwich; with the other, she digs into the mound of chili. Gently, so as not to startle her, I remove her hand from the chili and go for dessert.

"I'm cold." She tugs at her sweater. "I don't like it here," she says, looking around, uneasy with the cafeteria crowd. "I don't like it here." She shakes her head up and down, a now familiar gesture, but I'm startled by the screech in her voice.

"Where are we?" she asks me.

"At the Gene Autry Museum," I say.

"I don't like it here."

Today's museum program features Arturo and José Luis, two good-looking brothers who sing (and record) the '50s tunes popularized by Los Panchos during the "Golden Years" of Mexican music. What wonderful luck! Quick-as-a-wink I find two seats in the third row. We settle down to await *los músicos*; this is their last show.

"I have to pee." Quick! I rush my sister to the elevators, to the bathroom across the wide patio. I push her into the stall for the handicapped, then pace the floor, anxious to get back. We're missing the concert! She's out. I run water, splash soap on her hands, then pull her to the hand dryer.

Out the door we go, back to our seats, which—thank goodness—have not been taken.

The music begins. Strains of "Piel Canela" fill the room. I'm intoxicated by the guitars and songs of love; *los músicos* caress every word. Next to me, my sister, suddenly alert, sits straight up. In a wispy voice, she begins to sing! She knows all the words. She remembers! She is not that far gone. I squeeze her arm, but she ignores me, lost in another world, *en otro mundo,* of '40s print dresses, wide-brimmed hats and ankle-strap shoes.

"Creí," a song of love and longing, is followed by "Historia de un Amor," a tune that brings tears to the woman on my left. As the song ends, my sister leans over to whisper: "Joe used to play that one." Joe, her husband of more than forty years, recently died, and I see that she remembers.

Once the concert ends—and after I buy a CD and cassette—we check out one last exhibit.

"I want to go home," my sister cries, pulling at my arm. But I want to prolong the day.

We might not have this chance again! Will she remember today? The Cisco Kid? Zorro?

As we exit the museum, she pulls her sweater tight, although it's at least ninety degrees in the shade. Once more we go through the motions: the door, lock, seat belt—then we hit the freeway.

I pop in the new cassette of Arturo and José Luis, and my sister and I sing all the way home.

Mary Helen Ponce

Gift of Jehovah

El hombre propone y Dios dispone.

Latino Proverb

I miscarried for the second time on the evening of my forty-fourth birthday. Not exactly encouraging for a middle-aged mother of one—but unbeknownst to me, God was working.

Seven years earlier, after eleven years of marriage, my husband and I became the parents of a healthy, beautiful girl. Sarah was a blessing in our lives. However, within a few years, we longed for another child. I was very open to the prospect of adoption, but my husband, having worked in the field of social services for many years, was not so keen on the idea. I had my first miscarriage two years after Sarah was born, then put the idea of another child on hold. Of course, the longing for another child to love as a part of our family just grew stronger over the years.

We decided to go ahead and adopt. I had worked as a teacher for many years and knew in my heart that loving "the child of another" as my own would come naturally for me, especially a child from my own Latino culture. Well-meaning friends and doctors thought differently. I heard words of wisdom from many arenas: "You're not too old to get pregnant," "Try to have your own child one more time," and "How could you love someone else's child?" I took stock of my age and doubted whether a woman in her forties would be able to carry a child. Fortunately, I verbalized these thoughts to my seven-year-old.

"Remember Sarah? She was a really old lady when God gave her a baby," my own wise-beyond-her-years Sarah said to me. "If God can bless her, God can bless you. AND YOU'RE NOT TOO OLD!!" she scolded.

She was referring to the story of her namesake in the book of Genesis. Sarah was barren and did not have a child until the ripe old age of ninety! I decided to try to become pregnant one more time. I miscarried again. A tragedy? No. Merely a message that made it clear I needed to accept my own humanity and let God be God.

We reignited the adoption process, but this time with fervor. Over the next several months, our portfolio was shown to several birth mothers, but no child was forthcoming. I grew concerned over the issue of my age. Would any young woman in her right mind choose me as the person to raise her child?

A few months later, we received an urgent phone call from the director of the adoption agency. There was an incredible shortage of birth mothers with babies available for adoption. Would we mind locating a birth mother on our own? We were dumbfounded, flabbergasted and shocked. But we still desperately wanted a child.

We met with a local attorney a few weeks later to pursue finding a birth mother on our own. In fact, he had met with a possible birth mother right before speaking with us. We even saw her as she headed out and we headed in. She looked adorable. But . . . she wasn't Latina. We left encouraged by the possibility that we could have a baby in a few short months, only it would not be Latino. That would be fine, but it was not our first choice and not what we were hoping for.

We received another call the very next day from the director of the adoption agency. A young single woman from El Salvador had come out of nowhere, given birth to a healthy baby boy and had just signed adoption papers. Were we interested in letting her see our portfolio?

We told only a few family members and friends about the possibility of a sudden addition to our family. There were twenty other families on the waiting list. Most were probably much younger than we were. We didn't expect much to come from the recent news. However, five days later we received a call stating that I was the only Latina mother available, and the birth mother wanted a Latino family to raise her child. We were ecstatic.

We named our son Jonathan after the biblical hero and friend of King David, but had no clue as to the name's meaning. During the adoption ceremony, the director of the agency stated that the name Jonathan means "Gift of Jehovah." Tears welled up in my eyes at the realization of the great gift that God had indeed given me. The gift was not on my timetable, but it was given at the perfect time nonetheless.

At the age of forty-five, half the age Sarah was when she gave birth to Isaac, God had remembered me.

Melody Delgado Lorbeer

6

OUR LANGUAGES/
NUESTRAS LENGUAS

*By the year 2050, I do not know what
language we will be speaking in the
United States, but it will be called English
and will sound a lot like Spanish.*

                                                    Mark A. Trevino

Long "i," Silent "e"

I knew she would eventually trap me. I would be caught, snared in my own educated ignorance. I knew that she would leave me wondering about her unschooled intelligence—which always seemed to make as much sense as the things I had worked so hard to learn.

We had been through this before, many times. And now it was a complex assignment to try to make sense of the things that seemed so unexplainable, ineffable and mysterious to those of us who have grappled with teaching and its often-reluctant dance partner, learning. These were elusive issues that, as an educator, I had to face. I also knew that when dealing with a challenging student, there was the possibility of my being pinned to the mat by my frustration at my own inability to share abstract ideas.

My sense of duty obliged me to try, and in the short drive from my mother's home to her favorite restaurant, I did try.

"It's not pronounced like that, Mom," I said carefully as I continued with my cautious explanation. "It's *prime* rib, not *prim* rib." In pronouncing the correct usage of the word, I jerked my head forward a little, thinking that somehow it might help get my point across.

"*¿Qué?*" she said, confused. Confusion annoyed her. And when she was annoyed—about anything—she lashed back at whomever or whatever caused the perplexity.

"*¿Cómo que* it's not '*prim*' rib? I always been corrected by you, *Señor* Big Shot. But I remember when you told me that English is like being a *mexicano*. You say that the English language is *mestizo* like us, mixed up with other things that came from someplace else. So how it comes I need to know anyway? I been asking for *prim* rib for all these years and nobody says nothing to me about that. I see them smile, and maybe they laugh a little when I make my order, but I always get my *prim* rib. Just like I like it, too! I do good with my own language my own way."

To bring her back to the avenue of my explanation, I offered gently: "You see, Mom—and I've taught you this before when I tried to teach you to read—in a word like 'prime' the 'i' is long and the 'e' is silent."

Of course, she protested as most students do when learning is imposed upon them. "*¡Ay, Dios mío,* the professor wants to '*splain* to his *tonta mamá* how smart people should talk!"

I started off by reviewing the two types of letters I had once tried to teach her: consonants and vowels. She remembered none of it and didn't mind telling me so. I proceeded anyway, with overdramatic images of Anne Sullivan flashing through my mind.

"When you have a word that has the letter 'i' in it and the letter 'e,' and those two letters are separated by a letter like 'm,' the 'i' is called 'long'; think of it as being LOUD. You could say the 'i' is loud; you can hear it, can't you?" With emphatic lecturing, I showed her how the long "i" could be heard: "Pry, pry, pry. Do you hear the loud 'i' in pry?"

"*¡Qué estúpido, hijito!*" she said, commenting in a tone similar to that of the self-absorbed young people who filled my classrooms with their own unsolicited and apathetic points of view about the world, education and long "i's." "*Pry* is a word?" she then asked, testing the grip of my lesson with each honest question.

"When you put *pry* together with 'm' and 'e,' we say the 'e' is silent. It's just a *regla,* a rule, but it's helpful to know. It'll eventually improve your language."

Silently we drove on busy streets. Having raised a number of children single-handedly, my mother could figure things out for herself; she always had. Her answers came to her on her own terms, and if they fit the question, that was sufficient. So when she had reflected on the unsolicited lesson I offered, when she started to see the language at work in her head, she put forth a genuine hypothesis.

"I think I know the reasons why they do that," she offered, her face scrunching to show that her brain was seriously at work. She nodded her head, as if she were carrying on a conversation with herself. I sensed that my mother's linguistic theory would be impressive, and I listened closely.

"You see," she began, "the letter 'e' is *redondo,* round. It's short, too. The letter 'e' is *chaparrita y panzona.* And you know when you see people who are *chaparrita* and *panzona,* they are quiet because they feel embarrass about being short and fat, 'specially womens because mens make them feel that way. Look at your tía Panchita. She is so quiet and she barely talks loud enough to hear her; she is like a silent 'e.' But you look at her husband, your uncle Silvestre. He is like a loud 'i.' The 'i' can be loud because it is *alto y delgadito.* The little dot is like the head, and if you have a head you have a mouth, so it even has a way to be loud. But the *pobre* 'e,' she don't have no head or no way to speak up.

And people who are tall and skinny think they are so big shots, and they talk loud and laugh loud like they want everybody to look up to see them, *muy presumidos*. That's why the 'i' is loud. It stands *muy macho* and with too much *confianza*. It probably makes the others feel like they have to be silent. *Y aunque confianza te da asco*, there it is anyway, the loud 'i' for everybody to hear him. It's too bad some have to be the quiet ones and there are others that are loud and think they know everything."

As we now sat at the table waiting for someone to take our order, I decided not to tell her about silent "i's" and long "e's." Nor would I expound on the other vocalic citizens in the community of expressive and inexpressive English letters. My mother's own methods—rules or no rules—were obviously enough to get her through a mixture of language and ideas.

At dinner we both ordered *prim* rib.

Rick Rivera

Home Sweet Caldo de Pollo

My home language starts to simmer
In a hot pot
Under high butane flames
The smell of *caldo de pollo* wakes me up
Calls me
Makes me go to the kitchen
Amá tosses chopped vegetables into
Boiling broth
Tomate, cebolla, calabacitas, chayote, zanahoria
Dance around the chicken
A new day forms in my mouth
Last night's taste is forgotten

We decorate the table with ingredients
Turn on the fifties model radio to Ramón Ayala
Playing on *La Que Buena*
Take out the two-liter Coca-Cola plastic bottle
My mother sits across from me
Talks the language she learned in México
While she waited for her mom to flip
Tortillas

Two feet away from our conversation
Yellow corn tortillas heat on a metal *comal*
Dad made at his job in the factory
Las tortillas de maíz wait for their turn
To be rolled up into long flutes
Puffing steam, smooth tunes
Nothing like the garden-red chile
Who spills the knowledge learned
From the Earth's own mouth

With every spoon full of *caldo*
I can taste the fire of her words
Dancing on my tongue

Outside, a summer evening
Lets the sun go to rest
Birds rustle in their nest
Make the leaves on the tree shake
Put a smile on my face
Tires on a car screech
Interrupts the peace
We don't care
Let them say all they want
We. Don't. Care.
Keep the conversation going
With a coffee
With a smile
With my six-year-old niece Gabby
Who comes over from across the street
For some *caldo*

A cool breeze picks up
Opening the screen door next to our refrigerator
Flies sneak in
 Like always, to examine our lives

The plate left empty
A broken wishbone
The shell of the *aguacate*
Turned brown
The small yellow *limones*
Exhausted
Speckles of salt
On the green table counter
That I try to gather and pick up
With my index finger

Now that the *caldo de pollo* is in us
We are allowed to further speak
Our language
The language of love
The language of home

Alvaro Garduño

Chuleta

My husband, Mike, is Italian, and I'm Puerto Rican. Mike is always trying to understand Spanish, and whenever my mother and I speak Spanish, he tries to pick up words. One day, he heard us say that a woman we noticed was *chula*. He asked what it meant, and we told him that it meant "pretty."

When we went to my mother's house for her birthday party the next week, he walked in the door, gave her a big birthday kiss and said, *"Feliz cumpleaños, mi chuleta."* He danced her around the kitchen, calling my mother his *chuleta*, all the while thinking he was flattering his mother-in-law and impressing her with his Spanish.

My mother, who is soft-spoken and shy, raised an eyebrow and looked over her shoulder at me, but she didn't say anything. The problem is, *chuleta* doesn't mean "pretty" in Spanish; it means "chop," as in "pork chop." In some places it has a double connotation; it's something a boyfriend would say to his girlfriend, but certainly not a son-in-law to his *suegra*! But Mike's intentions were so sweet: He was trying to let my mother know how much he loved her and that she was still beautiful in her old age.

I'm not sure what my mother thought he was doing. I just smiled and enjoyed the irony.

Pretty soon my brothers and sisters gathered in the kitchen to watch the dancing as Mike continued to call my mother his "little pork chop." We didn't tell him what he was doing because we didn't want to embarrass him. But every time he left the room, we would laugh so hard that tears would start rolling down our cheeks.

Michele Capriotti

Cleaning Crackers

A group of women have been unfolding their lawn chairs every afternoon for about fifteen years to powwow on my grandma's stoop. Dominoes in their carrying cases on the ground, *agua de limón* in my grandmother's hand, iced tea in the grips of her native English-speaking friends who flaunt sundresses and hats to match. This daily congregation of women does what most people do when they get together: They talk about other people. Husbands, neighbors, brothers, sisters, mothers, fathers, aunts, uncles, sons, daughters, pizza boys, grocery checkers, pool cleaners or pretty much anyone who has anything going on in their lives could become the topic of conversation.

My grandmother was raised in Latin America and moved to the United States on her fifteenth birthday. Sometimes she confuses people with her use of English. It's most hilarious when she translates a Spanish saying into English verbatim. Apparently, she thinks colloquialisms can be universally translated.

One afternoon, I walk outside and, acting like a brat, tell my grandmother that I am going to run away from home if she doesn't let me go to the dance at the community center. She erupts with anger because I am challenging her authority in front of her friends (something you don't do in my family . . . not if you want to live, anyway). My grandmother looks at me with rage in her eyes and yells:

"I will enter you to clean crackers!"

It sounds like a line from *The Exorcist,* and my grand-mother's friends look frightened. Eyes dart around the circle of lawn chairs, trying to see if anybody else under-stands what exactly is going down. They probably think it's some peculiar way that Latinos punish their children. My grandmother is still foaming at the mouth, and I'm standing frozen on the porch. I'm scared to go inside, scared to go outside, and scared to get too close to my grandmother, who is trying to regain her composure. Now, you'd think that her friends would know she has a knack for screwing up the translation of Spanish sayings, but my grandmother is a wild card. She has been known to say some pretty crazy things that she *meant* to say; that's why her friends never know when she's speaking literally or when she's mixing up a Spanish saying. I'm paralyzed, my grandmother is trying to suck the saliva back into her mouth, and her friends are caught in the middle of a Latino standoff.

My grandmother has told me many times that she was going to "enter me to clean crackers," and I know all too well what it means. However, her friends obviously don't. She finally calms down, and I lean over, as I always do, and tell them what my grandmother meant was, "I'm going to slap you," or *te voy a entrar a galletas limpias.* Simul-taneously, the women give a loud "ohhhhhhhhh" and go back to playing dominoes without a care in the world for my safety. As long as my grandmother isn't going to liter-ally enter me to clean crackers, they don't care whether she hits me or not. As a matter of fact, I was such a *travieso* as a child, I'm sure at that point they all wanted to enter me to clean crackers, too.

Well, I bid you farewell, or as my grandmother always says, "It already was" (*ya estuvo*) or translated figuratively, "That's all she wrote."

Colin Mortensen-Sánchez

NO RODEO®

NO RODEO © *Robert Berardi. Used by permission.*

NO RODEO, *Robert Berardi,* ©2005, *reprinted by permission of Robert Berardi.*

The Hurricanes

I knew some English when, at the age of eighteen, I came from Cuba to the United States. My father had a friend from Barbados who taught my sister and me the basics of the English language while we were still living in Cuba, but we still needed a lot of conversational practice.

My first job was working in the tomato fields in Homestead, Florida, and there were a lot of Hispanics, so not much English was spoken. After several months, I started working at the University of Miami School of Medicine as an office clerk, and there I had to speak English very frequently.

During my first week, one of the supervisors went out to lunch and left me in charge of the phones in the reception office. A lady called asking for the "schedule of the hurricanes," and I immediately told her to call the Weather Bureau, since this was the Admissions Office for Medical Education and she was obviously mistaken. The lady, very upset with me, hung up the phone, saying (among other choice words), "You think you are funny, eh? Damn Cuban!"

When Mrs. Romano came back, I explained what had

happened and offered my apologies for any wrongdoing, but I could not understand why the lady got so upset with me—and insulted my Cuban heritage!—when I was truly trying to help her. As I told the story, Mrs. Romano was choking with laughter. I was even more puzzled then.

After a while, she explained to me that the University of Miami had a football team called "Hurricanes" and that "the schedule of the Hurricanes" the lady was inquiring about was the schedule of the season games of the team. Then I started laughing along with Mrs. Romano. I told her I was glad to know that the University of Florida also has a team called the Alligators, so I wouldn't direct callers to the Everglades National Park!

Xiomara J. Pages

A Lesson More Important than Math

That's the point. It goes like this: Teaching is touching life.

Jaime Escalante

It was a hot, muggy day in mid-September in a bilingual classroom at Wilson Elementary. In spite of the heat, the room bustled with active, energetic second-graders. Over the duration of an hour, I observed a math lesson that gave me wisdom well beyond anything I could derive from mathematics. I was conducting research for my doctoral dissertation on the two-way bilingual education model. Mrs. Gamache, a dedicated, white bilingual teacher, was applying a kinesthetic experience-based method in teaching as she began a new math unit on sets and subsets. Our class comprised six students from Spanish-only families, six students from bilingual families and eleven students from English-only families.

Mateo, the class monitor for the week, turns over our blue Señor Pato language symbol at the front of the classroom. Now a red Mr. Duck reminds everyone that instruction has changed from Spanish for social studies to English for math.

On the whiteboard, Mrs. Gamache writes three potential subsets of the complete set of second-grade students in our class: kids wearing tennis shoes; kids who speak Chinese; kids who have brown eyes. She then asks the students to think of other possible subsets of the whole class set. The children call out their ideas as she writes them in red: "kids wearing black," "kids with green eyes," "kids who speak French," "kids who are Mexican-American," "kids wearing striped shirts."

"That's enough ideas for now," Mrs. Gamache says. She writes the names of the three subsets she had initially introduced on three large sheets of chart paper. Then she invites the class to choose two of the subsets from their brainstormed ideas written on the board. As María calls out "Mexican-Americans," and Martin chooses "striped shirts," Mrs. Gamache creates two more charts, neatly printing their titles in big red letters at the top of each sheet. Then we tack up the five subset charts, strategically spacing them around the classroom.

It is time in the lesson to check students' comprehension of the concepts. Mrs. Gamache walks over to the tennis-shoe chart and instructs the students.

"Raise your hand if you belong to the subset of kids in our class who are wearing tennis shoes." A number of hands fly up.

"Why are you a member of this set, John?" asks Mrs. Gamache.

"I got black tennis shoes on," John replies, lifting his recess-muddied foot above his desk.

"Yes, I see clearly that you are a member of the tennis-shoes subset." She repeats her comprehension checks, moving around the classroom from one chart to the next, asking for children's rationales for being members of each particular subset.

When she comes to the Mexican-American chart, she asks Marcela, "Why are you a member of this subset?"

Marcela responds, "Because my family has Indian blood."

"Mine does, too," Delia chimes in.

"My mom and dad were born in Mexico," Daniela proudly volunteers.

Mrs. Gamache affirms their rationales for belonging to the Mexican-American subset, and she praises their "wonderful attention while learning the math concepts today!"

The lesson progresses. Mrs. Gamache directs the second-graders: "Now, go around the room and sign your name on the charts, but *only if you are a member* of the subset, *only if you belong* to that particular subset title on the chart. Do not sign your name if you are not a member of the subset. We'll check the names on the charts at the end of the lesson to see if we all get right answers as members of our subsets. Then I will know if you all have learned our math concepts for the day: set, subset, member of a subset, empty set. Okay, I'm starting the timer. Take your pencil with you. Go!"

Twenty-three eager, noisy second-graders scramble in all directions to sign their names on the charts as members of subsets. The Chinese speaker chart remains blank. Toward the end of the chart-signing phase of the lesson, Mrs. Gamache and I exchange communicative smiles as we watch Clark join the long line of students waiting to write their names on the Mexican-American chart. He has light blond hair and bright blue eyes. He often and unabashedly expresses his self-confidence in becoming a Spanish speaker.

When the timer goes off, Mrs. Gamache directs the students to sit down at their desks and count the number of members in each subset. They enthusiastically count with her in chorus, anxious to see the results of their math lesson: fifteen students wearing tennis shoes; seven wearing striped shirts; zero who speak Chinese (ah ha, an empty set!); fifteen with brown eyes; seventeen Mexican-Americans.

Students who indicate they belong to the Mexican-American subset include seven students whose surnames and skin and hair coloring clearly indicate Mexican ancestry, seven students of blended ancestry who could easily "pass" for Anglos, and three Anglos whose heritage is clearly not Latino, none of whose parents are Spanish speakers. Mrs. Gamache, noting that the Mexican-American chart is the only list of names representing errors, offers an extension of the lesson.

"You know what? Students whose family members or ancestors have not come from Mexico are not really members of this subset. It's great that you all are learning to read and write and speak Spanish, but of course that doesn't make you a member of the subset of Mexican-American students in our class set of students, does it?"

Susan ventures a rationale for having written her name on the chart, saying, "I think I have a cousin who came from Mexico somewhere in the country. I have cousins all over the place!"

Clark timidly adds in an unusual-for-Clark quiet voice, "I really do think my mom's aunt might be Mexican." He looks up at Mrs. Gamache, eyebrows raised, arms outstreched and palms upturned, begging for a confirmation that he qualifies in some way to be in the Mexican-American subset. A second knowing smile is exchanged between Mrs. Gamache and me. Clark's mother teaches fourth grade in the school, so we know her family beyond mere acquaintance. The third student in error remains silent, resigned to simply accept the correction as an unfortunate fact.

Through the lesson skillfully delivered by Mrs. Gamache,

the students had clearly mastered the math concepts of sets, subsets and members. There were only three certain "errors" written on the subset charts. Why did such brilliant students portray inaccurate information on this singular chart designated as the Mexican-American subset?

This is the answer, the lesson I learned on that hot, muggy September day: The Anglo children *wanted to belong* to the Mexican-American subset. They *wanted to identify* with their Latino peers in the bilingual classroom, where the Spanish language and the Latino culture were valued and validated by an inspiring teacher every day. In short, the Anglo children desired to be in the cultural and linguistic group that held *status* in their classroom and in their school.

Children learn the lessons we teach them, but when we create the right conditions, they learn something much more important: how to love, respect and belong to each other.

Dr. Ellen G. Batt

Wrong Channel

Hablando se entienden las cosas.

Latino Saying

Barbarita waited impatiently for her ride as beads of sweat dripped from her eyebrows into her third cup of cold, syrupy espresso. She was headed for the bathroom when she heard the knocking sounds of Mima's old Impala.

"About time you got here!" yelled Barbarita from the Florida room.

"It wouldn't start this morning."

Barbarita got into the car, tilted the rearview mirror and applied enough rouge to her face for a healthier look. She wanted to make a good impression on the doctor who would approve her medical records for her green card. On the way to Jackson Memorial, Mima talked about her grandchildren.

In the waiting room at Jackson Memorial, Barbarita knocked down all the Bibles and *Reader's Digest*s on the table when the nurse finally called her name.

"Sorry, ma'am, but you can't come in," the nurse said to Mima.

"I am her interpreter," replied the polyglot.

Mima and Barbarita entered the doctor's office together. *"No bueno,"* said the doctor grimly as he walked in with Barbarita's X-rays. He told Mima, "Ask her if she had TB."

Mima turned to Barbarita. "He says, if you have a television?"

"Tell him yes, but in Havana. Not in Miami. But my daughter has a television here."

Mima told the doctor, "She says she had TV in Cuba, not in Miami, but her daughter has TV here."

"In that case we need to test her daughter for TB, too."

Mima translated, "He says he needs to test your daughter's television to make sure it works, otherwise you cannot get your green card."

"Why the television?" asked a puzzled Barbarita.

"How many times did I tell you that you needed to buy one? Don't you know, Barbarita? This is *América.*"

Roberto G. Fernández

NO RODEO®

NO RODEO © *Robert Berardi. Used by permission.*

NO RODEO, *Robert Berardi,* ©2005, *reprinted by permission of Robert Berardi.*

7

REAL HEROES/
HÉROES VERDADEROS

*Y*oung people are hungry for real heroes,
people who overcame challenges and
changed their lives and then, the world. . . .
One of the most important gifts we can give
our children is to read stories about those
who went before them. Our children need
to know about the sacrifices César Chávez
and others made for them and their
responsibility to give back to future
generations. Who will they learn this
from—if not from us?

Edward James Olmos

La Brava

Her name was María de Jesús Galván, and she was my paternal grandmother. She was a rather tall woman, especially by Mexican standards, but she appeared even taller with her erect posture and no-nonsense demeanor. Her stature was accentuated by her dark complexion, deep black eyes and the long black hair that she always wore in an Indian braid style. There was a natural sense of dignity about her, as if she were a holy woman. She was also blessed with an extraordinary memory, a photographic memory that I utilized many years later in my genealogical research.

I once asked her if there was an incident in her life that stood out for her as a defining moment—a "make-or-break" kind of moment. She responded that there had been many highlights, as well as tragedies, in her life. But my question must have been one that she had already contemplated because she wasted no time in describing what she told me was the most poignant incident in her life.

The year was 1914, and it was a time of great civil unrest. Mexico was ripped apart by revolution. The war left many towns and villages in Northern Mexico even more isolated than before and at the mercy of the rival armies. Still, even in rural Méndez, the news of the war traveled quickly. Although Méndez was of no strategic significance, it was situated in the midst of the revolution. Far from the reach of the government, the armies of Pancho Villa controlled the vast uninhabited and desolate areas of this northern Mexican state.

Little María had heard the hushed tales that little girls of ten were not supposed to hear—stories of rape and of murder at the hands of heavily armed marauders. Her own father had died two years prior, and she feared for the men of the village. These same poor and humble men had been so generous to María and her widowed mother after her father's death. Without their help, God only knows how they would have ended up. Her fears were fueled by word that all the men in a nearby village had been executed—shot down in cold blood—in the town square. Rumors were spread that the rebels were behind the atrocities so as to terrorize the populace. Others argued vehemently that only the government could be so cruel.

Still, life went on as well as could be expected. It was August, and there were fields to tend to, livestock to feed and meals to cook. It was little María's daily chore to fetch the water. Now, this was no small job. Her family was poor and did not have the benefit of a personal well. Rather, she had to lug the earthenware vessels to the town square several blocks away. There she would fill the containers and struggle with them all the way home. Fortunately, on most mornings some kind man would usually help carry her heavy load home.

This particular day María hauled two empty vessels to the square. It was early, perhaps no later than eight o'clock, but the sun was strong, and it was already hot. She had filled one vessel and was struggling with the second when she first noticed the commotion. Men were shouting and directing the women to run home immediately. Apparently, a field worker had reported that a large column of armed men was a few miles away and headed toward town. As the men rounded up the horses, wagons and donkeys to hide for safekeeping, María contemplated her situation. With all the men running off to protect their families and all the women hiding, there was no one to help her. And she wasn't going to leave her water vessels unattended. She was infuriated at her misfortune. Alone with no one to help or defend her, she decided right then and there that she was not going to take it anymore. There was no choice but to stand her ground and fight. The second vessel full, she looked up to see the cloud of dust in the distance. Her hope that perhaps the men had been wrong vanished. She decided to pull up the last bucket of water before facing her enemy. She contemplated how she would die, and after deciding that she would be brave, she said her prayers as best she could.

Before she had finished her mental rosary, the rebels arrived. The thundering hooves of a hundred warhorses announced their arrival. There were so many! It appeared to her that these riders weren't men at all, but giants! And the deafening roar of the horses' gait was almost overwhelming. Still, she stood her ground; no one would steal her water.

She must have been quite a sight to the young commander as he gestured his troops to halt. The dark little girl with long black braids and cold black eyes was standing between him and the water well. She refused to budge even as his stallion moved within a couple of feet in front of her. For a few moments there was absolute silence. *El Comandante* and the little girl locked eyes for some time before he finally asked, "Is there no one else here to greet the army of Pancho Villa?" She refused to answer, and the silence continued.

El Comandante finally nodded and smiled before he

dismounted. His spurs jingled as he stepped her way. He wore a full *sombrero* and *bandoleros*. Two guns and a sword hung at his side. He was dusty from the ride, but he was also clean-shaven, with clean black hair and the most awesome full mustache she had ever seen.

Now standing right in front of her, *El Comandante* looked down at the child. Defiantly, María had never broken eye contact. She could see deep into the officer's brown eyes as he towered above her. After a few torturously long moments, in which no words were spoken, María at last closed her eyes, expecting death to strike immediately. *El Comandante* waited for the little girl to open her eyes again. Then, with just the hint of a smile, he removed his *sombrero* in a gesture of respect and went down on one knee and spoke.

"Little girl," he said, "my men are tired and thirsty. Would you be so kind as to share your water with us?"

"Perhaps I could do that," said *La Brava*. "But if I do, will you help me refill the jars and take them home?"

"Why, of course, my *princesa*. It would only be fair to do so."

And with that he affectionately cupped and caressed her head and directed his men to approach the well. María offered *El Comandante* her bucket of cool water from which he took a long quenching drink before pouring the rest over his head. She stayed there and helped the rebel soldiers draw water until their thirst had been sated. Then she helped water and care for the horses as the men rested.

Soon it was time for the army to move on. As the troops remounted, *El Comandante* ordered two soldiers to fill the water vessels and accompany María home. As the young commander mounted his horse and prepared to lead his men to war, María, now confident in the righteousness of the revolution, shouted out to him, *"Viva la revolución!"* To which he replied in a loud and triumphant voice, *"Y viva México!"*

María never saw him again, except in her dreams, but she never forgot him. She would later tell me: "That day *El Comandante* taught me that it is better to die standing on one's feet than to live on one's knees." She carried the fire of the revolution in her heart all the days of her life. Then she leaned over to me. "I have only one regret," she said.

What was *La Brava's* only regret, you ask?

"I should have gotten his name," she winked. "He was gorgeous!"

Robert Suarez

Abuelita, Abuelita . . .

If each of my words were a drop of water, you would see through them and glimpse what I feel: gratitude . . .

Octavio Paz

Stirring the *arroz con habichuelas,*
She's cooking on the stove.
The fragrant smell of the
Different spices blending,
The smoke rising from the *olla*
The golden beauty of age
Radiating from her face,
Her wrinkled hands reaching
For the *sazón* so she can feed
The family she still takes care of.
Straight from the *isla del encanto*
She came,
Ready to make a better life for her family
In the "land of the free."
Never taking into account

That she was in a strange
Land where she didn't even
Know the language.
Working in a box factory
For practically nothing
When she couldn't
Even say "box" in English.

Abuelita, Abuelita,
Bringing her sons over from
The only home she knew,
Working hard to pay the bills
Too hard to play with her kids
Because she came home
Tired at night.
Never taking a day off,
Never late,
Not being able to help them
With their homework because
All she knew was where to sign
For the rent check.
Trying to get ahead in life
To make a life for her children,
Struggling every day
To make ends meet
And still keeping the rhythm
In her soul and in her heels to
Clear any salsa dance floor.
Never once did she pat herself
On the back for a job well done.

But it was *Abuelita, Abuelita,*
In her golden years,
Hanging in her neighborhood
In the South Bronx on 172nd and Walton Avenue,

Jugando sus números en la bodega
De la esquina o bochinchando
Con sus amiguitas,
Getting pleasure out of
The simpler things in life
Like visiting her sons
Or being brought a piece
Of *pastel de guayaba,*
Never once thinking
"Damn, I'm bad!"

Abuelita, Abuelita . . .
Taking two buses to
My house every week,
Never once complaining about the ride
So she can cook to make sure
Her granddaughter eats well.
The swiftness of her hands as
She puts the food together reflecting
Her years and years of experience.

Abuelita, Abuelita,
I wish you could stay with me forever,
Showing me you love me through the
Flower of the food and the little
Consejitos you give me when you
See that life is hitting me
A little too hard.
Mi segunda madre,
Giving a new meaning to the
Word grandmother, but I'd
Rather call you *Abuelita*
than grandma.

Trajiste la pasión de la
Isla del encanto contigo,
Y me has enseñado más fuerza
Que nadie en esta vida.
Te quiero muchísimo, abuelita.
Bendición.

Lauren Perez

NO RODEO®

NO RODEO © *Robert Berardi. Used by permission.*

Don't Do It, Willy!

My *abuelita* was a huge baseball fan. Huge. A fanatic about the game, the players, the show. In her hometown of Santurce, Puerto Rico, "Mama Bi," as her grandchildren called her, had been a pretty good shortstop on her girls' high-school baseball team. She was also a big fan of her fellow *boricua*, Roberto Clemente, the great star of the Pittsburgh Pirates, and she followed his career very closely. I remember her talking not only about what a great baseball player he was, but also what a good man he was, how he always tried to help poor people back on the island and in other Latin American countries. When Clemente died tragically in a plane crash in 1972, he was on a mercy mission to Central America, taking medical, food and clothing supplies to earthquake-stricken Nicaragua. Mama Bi was brokenhearted when she heard the news; she felt like she had lost a close friend.

My *abuela* admired great achievers like Roberto Clemente, but in her mind, the greatest and most noble people in the world were not necessarily superstars—they were people who show great compassion and share what they have with those who are most needy. Mama Bi grew up in a humble family that worked very hard just to pay the rent and put food on the table for her and her four siblings. I remember Mama Bi telling me that her mother, my great-grandmother, always shared the little food that they had with the neighborhood children who came to the door hungry. When my grandmother complained that her mother was giving away food the family desperately needed, my great-grandmother would say, "We always have something to eat, even though it isn't much. But if we don't give these children something, they will not eat today." This lesson stayed with Mama Bi all of her life. It didn't matter to her if you were rich or poor; she saw the humanity in all of us, and was always ready to reach out to anyone who needed it.

Growing up, I shared a bedroom with Mama Bi, and she and I would stay up late (on the sly—my mother would have killed us if she'd known) listening to Vin Scully announce the Los Angeles Dodgers home games on the radio. We would huddle together on her bed, our ears close to the radio, watching each other's reaction to Scully's dramatic interpretation of the game. When our favorite Dodger, center fielder Willy Davis, would come up to bat, we would get so excited, always hoping he would hit a home run. On a lucky night, we would hear Vin Scully say—after hearing Davis's bat slam into the ball—"it's a long fly ball to center field; it goes back . . . a-way back . . . to the wall . . . IT'S GONE!!!!" We would jump up and down on her bed, arms reaching up in the air, hugging each other in a silent scream of joy.

The summer I turned twelve years old, we had the opportunity to go to a lot of Dodgers games because a friend of the family who was also a big fan had a car. We would leave early in the morning and arrive in time to see the ground crews comb the grass, line the baselines, and install the bases and home plate. We got there early enough to watch pregame batting practice and to catch a glimpse of our favorite players close-up. Since we always arrived several hours before the game started (believe me, the only people there at that hour were the stadium workers), we were able to get really good seats. We often found ourselves sitting right on the third base or left-field line, not too far from the field. This made it pretty easy to get autographs and shake hands with some of the players.

I had followed in Mama Bi's footsteps and was an avid Bobby Sox softball player in our local league; I played shortstop. I would bring my baseball mitt to the Dodgers games, and each time we went that summer I'd get an autograph on the mitt from one of the players on the starting lineup. The last autograph I needed to get was Willy Davis's, but we couldn't seem to catch up with him. He often came onto the field well after the other players, and he wasn't as likely to mix with fans as some of his teammates.

One summer evening, we attended a late afternoon game at Dodger Stadium; this would be our last game for that season since the friend with the car was moving away. I was determined to get Willy Davis's autograph, no matter how long I had to hang around before or after the game. When he didn't appear with the other players in the usual autograph "spot" after the game, I panicked and said to Mama Bi, "What will we do now? I'll never get his autograph!"

My grandmother had a solid idea. "I think I know where he parks his car," she said. "Let's go find it and wait for him there."

We finally found the right parking lot and headed toward a crowd of fans who were already there waiting, like me, to get an autograph. The game had been really close, and we had lost by one run, so there was a bit of rowdiness among the fans. When Willy Davis finally appeared, we all rushed toward him. He was pretty good-natured about it, even though he was obviously tired, and he had finally made his way to me when an angry fan, standing in a group of noisy young men, yelled at him from the back of the crowd.

"You're a bum, Willy! You're a stinking bum!"

Davis paused and looked up, but then he shrugged and seemed to brush the comment off. He took my mitt from me and was about to sign it when the rude fan persisted.

"Did you hear what I said, BUM?" he shouted.

I saw Davis's eyes narrow, and he slowly handed me back my mitt and started walking toward the young man. My grandmother, sensing that violence was about to erupt, jumped in between Davis and the fan, pleading with Davis in her thickly accented English.

"Don' do eet Guilly! Don' do eet!"

Her plea stopped Davis, but only for a second. He looked her in the eye and seemed to think about what she was saying, but then he kept moving toward his heckler. At this point, Mama Bi summoned up all her strength and, with her arms straight out in front of her, pushed Davis away from the young man. Willy Davis looked stunned! He gazed at this little Puerto Rican grandma who had just given him a fierce push toward his car. He looked at her, at first confused, but then, with what appeared to be affection, he began to smile. Mama Bi moved closer to him, looked him gently in the eye and pleaded, this time in almost a whisper.

"Don' do eet, *Guilly*," she repeated, and she gestured to him with her head that he should continue moving in the direction of his car.

Willy Davis paused, and I wasn't sure what was going to happen, but then I saw his eyes shine with understanding as he said to her, still smiling, "All right, Grandma. All right." He moved back, got into his car and drove off.

After he left, I looked at my grandmother in amazement. "I can't believe you just pushed Willy Davis into his car!" I said. "Oh, my God! I can't believe you did that!"

She looked at me like she didn't understand and said to me, simply, *"Tuve que ayudarle."* She just had to help him, and that was that.

The following summer we went back to Dodger Stadium, and we brought a big sign with us (we smuggled it in, actually, because they won't let you in with signs) that said in huge red letters: DON'T DO IT, WILLY! Every time Davis ran onto the field that night, we would hold up the sign and try to get his attention. It took a few times before he saw us, but during the last inning he waved at us from center field. After the game, I was thrilled to see Davis come running in off the field. Instead of going down into the dugout with the other players, Davis walked right up to us.

"I think I owe you an autograph," he said to me.

I nodded in disbelief, silently handing him my mitt. He signed it and handed it back to me. Then he turned to Mama Bi, took her hands into his and said, "You know, Grandma, you were looking out for me that night. Thank you." She looked at him, with the matter-of-factness of someone who sees nothing special in what she does, and said, *"No hay de qué, Guilly, no hay de qué . . . ¿Si no nos cuidamos uno al otro, Guilly, quién lo hará? Por algo Dios nos puso en esta tierra . . ."*

Davis looked at me for the translation, and I paraphrased what Mama Bi had said to him.

"My grandmother says we have to stick together and take care of each other because that's what God intended us to do," I said.

And as my childhood hero turned and walked away, Mama Bi looked over at me with raised eyebrows, nodding her head and pursing her lips like she always did when she wanted to accentuate her point, and said, "He's a good boy, this Guilly . . . *que Dios lo bendiga . . .*"

Susan Sánchez-Casal

Living the Dream

As we grow up, we often fantasize about the future and what it holds for us. Some of us want to become professional athletes; others want to be astronauts, policemen or firemen. But often our dreams don't quite come true. So what's the next best thing?

The next generation.

We grew up in Fajardo, Puerto Rico, playing baseball and basketball from dawn to dusk. Baseball was my thing, but I also played quite a bit of basketball. Early on, I knew I didn't have the tools to become a great basketball player, but that didn't deter me from going out there and spending endless afternoons playing hoops with my friend Alberto Arroyo and the rest of the neighborhood kids. Alberto was a much better player, fundamentally sound, and a pretty decent shooter. The only drawback was that he often stopped the game to teach us the fundamentals and most of us didn't care; all we wanted was to play.

This knack for teaching the key points of the game would eventually be instrumental in his children's future.

As we grew older, Alberto—who has a couple of years on me—got married first. He married my cousin Glorián

Bermúdez, and a year later, on July 30, 1979, she gave birth to twins. The twins were baptized, Carlos Alberto and Alberto Carlos—after the two of us, of course. Immediately after their birth, Alberto and I began to make plans for the twins. I suggested baseball, but Alberto's passion for basketball was overwhelming, so basketball was the sport of choice. Before they could walk, Carlitos and Albertito would learn how to balance themselves on a basketball. They were both fascinated by the leather sphere. By the time they turned two—that is, two months old—the twins became a permanent fixture at our pick-up games. They would sit there and watch us play, argue, then play some more and argue some more. Unfortunately, by the time they turned a year old, it was time for me to leave my little town in pursuit of bigger and better things.

At the time, I was having dreams of my own of one day going to Hollywood and becoming a television writer. Alberto thought that was a good idea because by the time the twins reached college age, I would be a famous writer and they could come live with me while attending UCLA and leading the Bruins to the final four. We went on and on daydreaming about how the twins were going to carry the team through March Madness.

Once I finished college, I headed for Los Angeles to pursue a writing career. I would go back to Puerto Rico every couple of years and check on the twins' progress, which was right on schedule, but it wasn't until the twins were ten years old that I saw them play organized basketball for the first time. They were both very good, but there was something very special about Carlitos; his ball handling was exceptional, his move to the hoop unstoppable, and his jump shot was poetry in motion—*swisssh*. He had a confidence on the court that made him a very special basketball player for a boy his age. After the game, I turned to Alberto.

"I'm sure UCLA wouldn't mind having him," I said.

We took a second to think about it, then simultaneously, we shook our heads, laughing.

Years later, I saw them play again. The twins were now seventeen and playing for Santurce in Puerto Rico's superior league. With Albertito at his side, Carlitos led the team to five championships in six years. The dream of going to UCLA didn't materialize, but Carlitos went on to play college ball at Florida International where he made a name for himself. In his senior year, there was a possibility that Carlitos would be drafted by an NBA team. After he went to camp in Arizona, scouts were so impressed with his performance that he got invited to camp in Chicago, but a week before camp, he fractured an ankle and couldn't play, ending his chances of getting drafted.

The resilient young man got over his injury and went after his dream. He worked hard and was invited to preseason camp by the Toronto Raptors. A month later he made the team, and Carlos A. Arroyo Bermúdez became the fifth Puerto Rican ever to play in the National Basketball Association. There he was, a boy who carried my name, measuring his skills against the best in the game from Michael Jordan to Kobe Bryant.

On December 1, 2001, Alberto, Glorián, Albertito and I met in Miami. It had been a long, long time since I had seen them all. My hair was now graying and receding, and I had lost a step or two, but the dream was more alive now than ever. Fulfilling my own dream of becoming a television writer/producer and creating my own sitcom was peanuts compared to what Carlitos was about to do.

As we entered the American Airlines Arena, home of the Miami Heat, we looked at each other in awe of what we were about to witness. We didn't say much. No words could describe what we were all feeling. My skin was bristling with goose bumps. As we walked through the tunnel and out to the other side, a basketball court appeared, the parquet floor shining under the lights. It reminded me of one of those early evening pick-up games twenty years ago when we played under a lamppost and could barely see the basket. If we had had this much light, I would've never missed a shot, I thought. So much light, so much life, so much excitement—and then the announcer stepped up to the microphone and announced the Toronto Raptors. The team ran out of the tunnel and there he was, number 21, Carlos Arroyo, jogging behind All Star power forward, Vince Carter. Alberto, Glorián, Albertito and I all exchanged silent glances.

Carlitos was living the dream.

Carlos R. Bermúdez

[EDITORS' NOTE: *Today Carlos Arroyo is the point guard for the world champion Detroit Pistons and a member of the Puerto Rican national team.*]

A Hero's Story

Al bien hacer jamás le falta premio.

Latino Proverb

This is the story of an uncle I never knew.

I grew up looking at the beautiful painting of him on my living-room wall, wondering who he really was and what he was like. He was a young, handsome Latino man with dark hair and a clean-cut look. My family tells me that his walk had a sure stride and that his face was always blessed with a gentle smile. Just by looking at his picture, you might think he was an ordinary man, but nothing could be further from the truth.

Primitivo Garcia, or "Tivo" as friends and family used to call him, was extraordinary.

Like many other immigrants in search of the American dream, my family had left their hometown in Mexico and settled in Kansas City, Missouri, ready to embrace a new life of opportunity. Tivo's dreams were to become a U.S. citizen, buy his mother a home, develop his artistic abilities and to one day have a family of his own.

But on November 15, 1967, Tivo and his brother Alfredo were outside of the building where they attended adult-education classes when a gang of six young thugs assaulted his five-and-a-half months pregnant English teacher. An ordinary man might have walked away, but Tivo, enraged by the ugly sight and unconcerned for his own safety, rushed to her defense. His brother Alfredo was two steps behind him, and he watched his older brother go from calm to crazed as he jumped into the middle of the violent scene and began to fight off the attackers, using his boxing skills to an advantage. "Go call the police!" he yelled to Alfredo in Spanish as he drew the attention of the boys toward him and away from his teacher.

When the gang attacked her, Mrs. Kindermann had been standing in the cold wind, waiting for her ride after giving her last English class of the evening at the inner-city Westport High School. She was caught off-guard by her attackers and yelled at them in anger as they spat obscenities, tore her purse away and knocked her to the ground. She embraced her heavy belly as she prayed for God to save her baby, only months away from entering the world. "Be careful," was all she could mutter to her brave students as she managed to pull herself up from the cold and dirty ground, grab her purse and run to safety. As she ran, she heard one of the boys yell, "Shoot him! Shoot him!"

Suddenly, Alfredo, still at Tivo's side, heard three shots. A cold sweat bolted through his body, and his worst fears were confirmed as his brother crumpled to the ground, and a pool of blood began to form on the sidewalk. The last of the three shots had pierced Tivo's stomach, and he remained doubled over on the ground as the thugs disappeared.

Guilt and pain filled Alfredo as he held his wounded brother.

"Don't tell Mama," Tivo begged. "She is old, her heart is weak, and the pain would be more than she could bear." Tivo kept thinking of others, even when his own life was in jeopardy. Alfredo listened to Tivo's words and felt his own heart breaking at the sight of his dying brother.

At the KC General Hospital, Tivo fought a courageous battle for his life. He lost large amounts of blood and was subjected to multiple surgeries. The community lit candles, united in prayer, gave blood transfusions and raised money to help pay for his medical expenses. There were lines of people waiting to give blood. But in spite of the best efforts of general hospital's medical team, Tivo died thirteen days later from complications stemming from his wounds.

The community gathered to support the family, pay their respects and mourn his loss. It was a very difficult time for my family, and my grandmother struggled bravely to face her loss. But Tivo was right about her weakness. With his death, grief seemed to consume her. First, it took over her heart, and then it overpowered her mind. Later, we just called it Alzheimer's, but we all knew it was the never-ending grief over the loss of her beloved son.

While researching this story, I discovered that Primitivo was the first local Latino hero in my hometown of Kansas City, Missouri. At the time of his death, the governor of Missouri, Warren Hearnes, declared him an honorary citizen of the state and declared December first as Primitivo Garcia Day in Kansas City, Missouri. He also dedicated a memorial site in his name at a prominent community park. The Carnegie Hero Fund Commission awarded Tivo a Carnegie Medal in recognition of an outstanding act of heroism; the Missouri House of Representatives granted him "posthumous American citizenship"; The Catholic Youth of the Diocese of Kansas City-St. Joseph dedicated their 1968 yearbook to him.

During the winter of 1967, my uncle became a hero. Unfortunately, his legacy lay dormant and forgotten by the public for twenty-five years until a local reporter did a two-part televised story in memory of Tivo. On April 27, 1993, the reporter and Tivo's family and friends convinced the school board to name a new elementary school the Primitivo Garcia World Language School. This was a proud day for the Garcia family.

At the school, his legacy lives on daily through the students. They tell visitors about the legend of Primitivo Garcia, and the children have recorded a song and video about their school's namesake. His spirit lives on in the school walls, in the community and in the people he touches even today. Every year, the school celebrates his life and heroic death on that cold night in 1967. The Garcia family unites at the school along with the community to remember Tivo and to see traces of his soul in the eyes of every child who sings his song. My uncle is gone, but the power of his heroic act lives on.

To me, as that little girl staring at the living-room picture, Tivo looked like a dreamy movie star with beautiful eyes and a warm smile. He was the uncle I always longed to meet.

He is the uncle who now inspires me and others to search for the hero within us.

Mónica García Sáenz

Amador

My grandparents, Vicente and Juana, emigrated from Guanajuato, Mexico, to the United States in the early 1900s. My grandfather worked on the railroad. When the couple became a family with three sons and three daughters, they worked as migrant farm workers throughout the southwest. They picked cotton in Texas, tomatoes in the Central Valley of California, grapes in the Napa Valley, apples in Washington and harvested sugar beets in Idaho. In the winter, the men pruned trees. In the spring, they planted the crops they would harvest in the summer and fall. They eventually settled in the Central Valley of California.

My mother's brother, Amador, was the youngest of the six children. He was the first to graduate from high school. He had dreams of going to college and becoming an engineer. He pursued his dreams in a quiet but persistent way. In 1942, the year he graduated from high school, he was called to military duty. He was eighteen years old.

Amador smells the rich scent of ripe tomatoes on the vine. The aroma fills the hot, dry air as he makes his way down the row of small, bushy plants, each row a perfect line into the distance. The plants hide their fruit behind dusty leaves. His hand reaches in and searches. The fresh morning dew is long gone in the summer heat. He feels a tomato and gently tugs. The plant reluctantly lets go.

With tomato in hand, he looks up and sees his mother in the distance. She is making her way from their home during the tomato harvest, a cluster of tents next to the levee. A little cloud of dust rises with each step. It must be lunch time. She shifts the weight of the bucket she is carrying from her left to her right hand. He goes to help her. The duty of the favorite son. The one with promise. The one who will go to college.

He makes his way to the wide, dirt road. They meet. She hands him the bucket. The food is covered with a faded washcloth. The weight is shifted from her to him. Her responsibility complete. He can feel the moisture of her perspiration on the washcloth she has wrapped around the handle of the bucket. He looks down and sees the worn gray and pink fabric that was once red and blue. "Gracias, m'ijo," she says as they make their way to the shade of a lone tree in the distance. At this moment he feels content, almost serene.

He wakes to the damp air. For a moment he wants to cry, but only a few tears escape in the morning darkness. The rough blanket and hard ground feel harsh. He is in the Philippines. World War II. His reality gradually comes into focus. Just another couple of weeks, and he completes his tour of duty. The longing and the loneliness in his chest sometimes feel unbearable. As the time draws nearer, the dull pain becomes sharper. The memory of the smell of tomatoes warmed by the sun and his mother's tortillas dissipates as he crawls out of his tent into the humid morning air.

Amador completed his four-year tour of duty. He returned to a freshly painted bedroom and a new bed. The return home after the long separation seemed surreal not only for him, but also for the entire family. His boyish innocence had been replaced by a man's demeanor. His previous energy replaced by periods of silence and solitude. He explained that he had become infected with malaria in the Philippines and had spent the previous months in a military hospital. He hadn't sent word because he didn't want the family to worry.

Amador's life plan remained intact; he enrolled in college and registered for classes. His course schedule was set for the next semester. The week before he was to start classes, he went shopping for new shoes, the shoe box next to his bed a symbol of a dream about to become a reality. But tragically, Amador passed away just a few days before he was to start college. Two months after his homecoming, he died of complications related to malaria. The shoe box next to his bed transformed into a symbol of a dream never to be fulfilled.

I didn't know my *tío* Amador. Fortunately, I have come to know him in the stories my mother has shared with the family. She remembers him as a kind and gentle young man with big dreams. His military photo brings him to life—a teenager with a shy smile and sparkling eyes. We visit his grave and ponder the vacuum created by his absence. The stories he might have shared. The professional accomplishments he might have achieved.

On Veteran's Day, a little flag distinguishes his gravesite. We leave the cemetery knowing that Amador is part of a long and distinguished legacy of Mexican-American participation in the defense and protection of the rights and privileges of all U.S. citizens.

Maria Luisa Alaniz

Cop by Destiny

I loved my job. I loved every minute of it for thirty-six years—because I was never supposed to have it. In a few weeks, I will be retiring from a law-enforcement career that spanned five decades. Since 1966, I've been a deputy constable, police officer, patrol sergeant, district attorney investigator and finally a labor standard investigator for the California Labor Commissioner. I have worn five badges.

My last job has taken me back to the same agricultural fields that I worked in as a six-year-old boy in 1947. Back then, I carried water to my parents and brothers as they worked. My father gave me that job. But he didn't give me hope that I could have the job I really wanted. I was about eight years old when I told my father I wanted to be a policeman. I had seen a storybook at school called *Dick and Jane* where a police officer in a blue uniform helps get a cat down from a tree. I thought to myself, *That's what I want to do—help people.* My father smiled, shook his head and told me it could never be. It was the end of the 1940s, and he never imagined there could be Mexican policemen. Besides, he thought I was too small.

"Estás muy pee-wee," he said.

My father, who was born in Chihuahua, Mexico, thought only about providing for his family. He had no idea about what his children could do in life nor did he have the desire to look that far into the future. Maybe if he had, he could have warned me about what lay ahead. I experienced my first obstacles in grammar school. I could not learn as fast as other kids. I had learned to be resourceful, alert and quick-witted, but those skills didn't benefit me in the academic world. It didn't help that I didn't speak very good English—or even very good Spanish for that matter. I used to mix both the Spanish and English words whenever I felt comfortable. I'm also left-handed. The teachers in the second and third grade would grab my left hand, spank it with a ruler and try to force me to write with my right hand. I never finished my lesson, and I would always get a black star, never a gold one or even a silver one like other kids got.

And, of course, growing up in the 1940s and 1950s, I had to deal with racism. In the seventh grade, I volunteered to be in a school play about the South. I asked the teacher in charge if I could be one of the gentlemen, a part that appealed to me because I could wear a top hat and white gloves and carry a cane. The teacher told me that I was too dark to play a gentleman and suggested that I be one of the slaves. Soon, my face was all painted up, and I was standing next to three other dark-skinned slaves. I was only about twelve years old then, but I caught on quickly. I asked the teacher for permission to go to the restroom, and out the door I walked. I never went back.

No matter what obstacles I faced, I never let go of my dream of helping people. Today, I find myself doing a job that combines all the others I've had, a job where I can put my life experiences into practice. I'm working in the same agricultural fields as when I was a boy, but in a very different way. I'm enforcing labor laws. I make sure that the workers—most of them Mexican immigrants—are protected from abuse and low wages, and I make sure that they are protected by worker's compensation insurance. It's my job to see that workers are not taken advantage of. As I walk the fields and approach these hard-working people, all dirty and sweaty, I sometimes think I see my father's image and feel his spirit around me.

When I approach the workers, I try to put them at ease. They're scared, and some think I am with the INS. I greet them with a smile and tell them, in Spanish, that I'm there to help them. That's when my father helps me. I tell them that, a long time ago, my father (*"mi apá"*) came from Chihuahua and worked these same fields. The only difference, I tell them, is that he had nobody looking out for him. Around me, I see sad faces that, all of a sudden, have a little bit of trust in them. I spot the face of an older man, *un viejito,* standing with the younger ones, and he cracks a smile. I put my arm around his shoulder. I tell him things are going to get better, and I hand him my business card, which has a small emblem of a badge. His face lights up. A few seconds later, a dozen or so other workers come closer to me. They're smiling and laughing and thanking me for the visit. Soon, they all have business cards.

Then I talk to their supervisor, the field labor contractor. I make sure he knows what the law says and what his responsibilities are. I also make sure he knows that there is a dark-skinned angel looking out for these field workers. As I walk to my pickup, I look back and see the old man waving good-bye to me.

Right about then, I am that eight-year-old boy who wanted to wear a uniform and help get a cat down from a tree. I can feel my father's spirit again. But this time, instead of telling me I'm too small for the job, I hear him telling me: "Son, I'm very proud of you. And I respect you for following your dream."

Ruben Navarrette, Sr.

My Puerto Rican Grandmother

Here's to Grandma's unanswered prayers.
Here's to the saints and the Virgin that
comforted her through millions of salty tears,
cried through long, dark and tempestuous nights.
Here's to Puerto Rico, the family she left behind,
all her belongings in a suitcase, on a ship, Brooklyn bound.
Here's to her elusive dreams, her seamstress hands,
strong will and nerves which stood on end.
Here's to a religion that never did recognize the
toils of its women, to the children she fed,
clothed and sacrificed herself for working day and night,
lost in the humidity and futility of Panamá.
Here's to the Great Depression and the war,
to can rations and soup bones.
Here's to a woman who held on so that myself and
others would enter this world.
All things said and done, her prayers were answered
and life she might have never imagined manifested.

Patricia L. Herlevi Balquin

Patricio Flores

We can choose to use our lives for others to bring about a better and more just world for our children.

César Chávez

In the heart of Texas lives the sole Mexican-American Catholic archbishop in the world. At seventy-five, this gentle man stands only about 5'2" tall, yet his stature in the community is beyond measure. As Archbishop of San Antonio, he pastors some 660,000 Catholics. He has dined with presidents and politicians, with the poor and with the pope. He is equally comfortable communicating in English or Spanish, and he fosters a community of collaboration that transcends religious boundaries and ethnic traditions. This letter, written to his late mother (who died in 1957 and is, no doubt, *en el cielo*), honors the man who Latinos can be proud to call one of their own.

Dear Mrs. Flores,
      You and your husband would be proud of the man your

son, Patrick, has become. He was the first Mexican-American to become a bishop, and he is currently the longest-serving archbishop in the country. In this, the twilight of his career, many people are stepping back to appreciate the scope of your son's accomplishments, some of which are discussed in the paragraphs that follow. I write this letter to honor you by honoring him, and to glorify God for making these things possible.

You were with your son at his ordination in 1956, and you were at his side during his first pilgrimage to the Basilica of Our Lady of Guadalupe in Mexico City in 1957. Your death later that same year had a profound impact on your son. Through the pain of losing you, he grew as a man and as a priest. In the 1960s, your son experienced another great blow: the death of his father, Patricio. Your son turned his heavy heart into a renewed faith in the promise of the Resurrection of Jesus.

This strength guided him as he served a number of parish communities. Though he still encountered prejudice—such as an admonition from one of his pastors to refrain from speaking Spanish to his parishioners—he not only overcame it, he also transformed it. He was among the first priests to coordinate "Mariachi Masses," bringing the music of la gente into the sacred halls of a church.

In 1970, your son was ordained as a bishop. Not long afterward, he stood with César Chávez in boycotting grapes and founded the Office of Catholic Services for Immigrants. He also cofounded the Mexican American Cultural Center (MACC), the nation's premiere training ground for those involved in ministry to Hispanics. He made a huge impact on the face of higher education when he jump-started the National Hispanic Scholarship Fund. Your son had his first brush with death when he was held hostage with several others while attending a bishop's conference in Ecuador. He eventually became Archbishop of San Antonio in 1979.

During the 1980s, your son spearheaded much growth and development in his diocese. Guided by the principles he set forth in his first pastoral letter, "A New Pentecost: A Vision for the Archdiocese of San Antonio," he strived to meet the goals he had set forth: a call to ministry; parish development; preference for special needs; a reorganization of diocesan structures; and increased service to rural areas. In the midst of all this, he traveled to Cuba for a pastoral visit and hosted Pope John Paul II during the pontiff's own pastoral visit to the state of Texas. The '80s also included a second brush with death as he underwent surgery for Ménière's syndrome.

Your son has continued his ministry through the 1990s and into the twenty-first century. To be certain, there have been dark, lonely times for him along the way. He has made his fair share of mistakes and has even stared down the face of death, not once, but twice in these last fourteen years. (He was held hostage a second time, and he underwent septuplet heart bypass surgery.) But you must know all of this, as you have no doubt been his guardian angel throughout!

Mrs. Flores, all these things are wonderful, but they are not what make your hijo truly remarkable. Anyone who spends a few minutes talking with him comes away with the sense that this man is special. He is a believer that "hablando las cosas se entienden." Take, for example, his response to the church's "crackdown" on liberal Catholicism that has gone beyond the scope of Catholic teaching. Your son does not condone behavior that goes against Church teaching, but he does not condemn the person either. "We have to pray for guidance," he says. "We were sent to deal with sinners—which we all are. We have to ask, 'What would Jesus do?'" He believes that it is more important that we listen to one another and pray for each other than to close the door on others.

This "open-door policy" is something he practices on a daily basis. People in need come to his office looking for help. What does your son do? If they are hungry, he offers them a voucher for free groceries at a local grocery store. He gives them information about shelters in the area and agencies that assist the poor on a long-term basis. In some cases, he shares a meal with them himself. And do you remember the second incident in which he was held hostage? The man involved was apparently distraught by immigration and financial difficulties. After his ordeal, your son did not shut his door. Instead, he saw to it that the man's family received financial and legal assistance.

I believe we owe you a word of thanks for raising your children to respect other people and other cultures, reminding them that every connection we develop with another person is an additional opportunity to see the face of God. This is quite evident in your son. Ask him what he thinks about people of different religions, and his response is simple yet eloquent: "There are those the Lord wants in heaven through us (Catholics), and there are those he wants in heaven through others. Either way, it is in God's hands so we should not worry." As to people of different cultures, he talks about his appreciation for what they have to offer (traditions, music, food, etc.). Regarding illegal immigrants, he quips that the members of the Holy Family (Jesus, Mary and Joseph) were undocumented people simply in search of safety and shelter. With a sparkle in his eye, he adds, "I'm just a cotton-picking bishop, too, you know," referring to his years as a farm laborer.

The sick and the imprisoned have a special place in your son's heart. In fact, they are the ones who will benefit the most from his retirement as he hopes to minister to them more in the future. "Es un ministerio que se puede hacer y que no hay excusa por no hacer," he says emphatically. He cites the beatitudes as his source of inspiration for this outreach. He says, "You can summarize it (the beatitudes) by saying that Jesus came to love us, and he wants us to love one another." He has translated this teaching to his episcopal motto: "I will work not for myself, but for others." It is something he does con todo corazón.

Though he never had any children of his own, your son is very much "un abuelito" for many young people in this diocese. His patience with children is unswerving, his concern for them unmitigated. Shelters, services, schools—your son supports these and many more systems that serve our youth. He is a firm believer in the value of an education, and he never wastes an opportunity to convey this to children and parents alike. You know what it was like for him to drop out of high school when he was a teenager, and how hard it was for him to eventually earn his degree. Every chance he gets, he urges young people to learn from his experience.

The parents he talks to receive a loud and clear message from him as well: "Parents, love your children. Tell them you love them. Mamás and papás, you must tell them of your love for them, even if it seems like they are not listening." Your son sees that the greatest gift a father can give his family is to love his wife and children; the same can be said for the greatest gift a mother can give her family. Gracias, Sra. Flores, for sharing that gift with your family!

Your son is indeed a remarkable man. But he is also just as human as the rest of us, and thus he has his share of failings. He is the first to admit this. Even now he insists, "I hope my successor will be someone different from me, someone who can make up for the areas in which I fell short."

We celebrate a man who, through the years, has struggled to overcome his shortcomings, who has remained faithful to his priestly vocation, who has defended the marginalized and oppressed, who has appreciated all cultures and religions, who has preached the gospel of Jesus with humility and humor, who has inspired others by his faith, and who has engaged people with compassion and service. We celebrate your son, Mrs. Flores, in whom we have had the privilege of seeing the face of God: We celebrate Patrick F. Flores, Archbishop of San Antonio.

Mónica González

"I Am a Curandera"

It was a miserable morning: cold, drizzling and gray with no promise of sun to warm the frigid mountain air. The sun was hidden behind ominous, dark rain clouds. My teeth chattered, and I trembled under my lightweight rain poncho. A huge droplet of rain hit my forehead, rolled directly between my eyes, then dribbled down to the tip of my nose. I wished I were somewhere else—anywhere else.

We were gathered in this mountain village in the highlands of Peru to hear midwives speak about their work. We were a mixed group of healthcare providers on a holiday under the guise of continuing education, and the course was a study of alternative healing in South America. We arrived from different parts of the world, bringing with us varying degrees of belief in medicine, alternative and traditional. But everything we had seen in the past week had changed us. Even the skeptics in the group were beginning to examine the possibilities of other views in the realm of healing.

Two men spoke to us first and explained their work as midwives. I was surprised to learn that men in this culture can be midwives; I had mistakenly stereotyped it as "women's work" since that's what it is in the United States. Both men had been trained by their fathers, who had been trained by their fathers before them. I learned that although a *curandero* or *curandera* is often called to the profession by a dream—the *curandero*'s or someone else's—most *curanderos* pass the vocation down from one generation to the next, so it often runs in families.

Each man told of similar techniques he employs when delivering babies. Their deliveries involve indigenous practices such as rubbing a woman's stomach with a urine-soaked stone for protracted labor and checking fetal position by reading the mother's pulse in her feet. By tradition, they both cut the umbilical cord with a shard of pottery broken in the home at the time of delivery.

Agripina was the last of the three midwives to address us. In contrast to the men, who wore brightly colored woven ponchos of hot pink, flaming orange and brilliant red, she was dressed simply in a long, gray wool skirt and dark green sweater. Her dark hair hung in a single, thick braid under her gray fedora and fell almost to her waist. She had been sitting quietly, with her head bowed, while the men spoke. When they were finished, she rose and began to speak in a quiet, soft voice that had an almost mystical effect on the small crowd.

"I am a *curandera*," she said, and our guide translated for us. "I have always been a *curandera*. Many years ago, when I was only eight years old, a mother sheep told me. It is not something I chose. It is something that chose me."

The crinkle of rain gear ceased. Those who had been moving about or rubbing their arms briskly in an attempt to get warm stopped moving. Her words were enough to pique my curiosity, but it was her voice—a low, melodious hush—that held me spellbound. It had a timelessness and tranquility that seemed not of this world. It was as though an angel was mesmerizing me with her words.

Glancing around the small crowd, I saw that her voice had captured us all. The entire group leaned forward in rapt attention. Agripina had something special, something precious to say, and no one wanted to miss her message. But a sheep telling her that she was a midwife? The doubting Thomas had questions. What could she possibly mean by that?

She went on to explain that when she was eight years old, her family had left her home alone for several days. She didn't explain where they went or why, only that she was left behind to tend the small flock of sheep. In this communal culture, children are small, responsible people who work hard from the time they begin to toddle. Everyone must participate in the flourishing of the community. So it was not at all unusual that Agripina was left alone to tend the herd.

Her job was to lead them to the stream each day, once in the morning and again in the evening. In between they would graze. It was not yet time for the lambing season. It would be easy. Besides, her family was not going far away. "They had only gone 'around the corner' and would return in a few days," she told us. Of course, we had learned this week that "around the corner" is an expression that may mean literally just that, around the corner; or it could also mean a journey of many days. Time and distance mean different things to different people.

"But," she continued, "even though it was not the lambing season, a mother sheep began to birth her baby. She cried and she cried for so long, and I became very frightened. My heart started to beat very fast. I looked, but I could see only one foot extending from the mother. What could I do?"

As she told her story, Agripina's eyes opened wide. Her speech became more intense, though she never changed her slow, melodious pace. She had us hooked. We waited impatiently for our guide to translate her tale.

"What could I do? I was only a child. I was only eight years old. But then the mother sheep spoke to my mind.

"She said, 'Help me,' and I knew what I had to do. I took hold of that tiny foot, and I pulled and I pulled with all my strength. And the mother cried to me, 'Pull harder!' And I pulled and I pulled and I pulled until I thought my arms would break. But the baby lamb still did not come out. My heart was pounding like a loud drum in my ears.

"Then, little by little, a calm and peaceful feeling surrounded me. I could no longer hear my heart beating in my ears. And I knew what I had to do. In my mind, I said to the mother sheep, 'Don't be afraid. I am here. I will help you.' My mind spoke to her mind, and she became still. She no longer fought me. She no longer fought her own body.

"Now two tiny, wet, slippery legs protruded from the mother. I took one leg in each of my hands, and I pulled until finally a tiny, perfect lamb was born, and I knew then that I was a *curandera*."

Agripina went on to explain that when her parents returned home and heard what had happened, they too understood that she was a *curandera*. She began then, at age eight, to train with the village midwife. Over the years she has continued to learn from the old healers of her village and the other villages nearby. But, unlike the two other midwives who practice exactly as their fathers did, she has also learned "modern" midwifery and medicine from the nurses and doctors from other countries who come to teach in her village.

"I am a modern *curandera*," she told us, with a proud smile.

When the presentation was over, I made my way toward this lovely woman and, with the help of the guide,

I asked how could I help her practice midwifery in her village. "Is there anything that you need that I can send to you from the United States?" I asked.

Shyly, she smiled, then reached into her bag and pulled out a roll of brightly colored hand-woven cloth. She unrolled it and revealed a set of basic medical instruments—hemostats and scissors. She explained, "I boil these in water for every delivery. Then the baby and the mother will not get sick. But these are borrowed from a North American nurse. I must return them. I would very much like to have my own set of tools. If I had my own tools, I would not have to cut the cord with a piece of pottery," she said honestly.

Such a simple request. I purchased the instruments when I returned home, and our guide took them back to the village six months later when the next tour visited. Agripina will never again cut the cord with a pottery shard.

I am filled with respect and admiration for this woman. Agripina will be a teacher for the next generation of midwives. This self-proclaimed modern *curandera* will teach indigenous birthing practices that date back thousands of years, while incorporating what is useful to her from other birthing traditions. In her isolated village, Agripina spans the centuries and bridges cultures.

With one foot planted firmly in the past and the other just as steadfastly planted in the present, this *curandera* will continue to work for the health and well-being of her village.

Nancy Harless

Face to Face with My Childhood Hero

*It is not enough to know how to ride; you must
also know how to fall.*

Mexican Proverb

I can remember only one thing about the year 1967. I
was five then. That was the year my hero shined the
brightest in his Major League career.

The Baby Bull we called him, with his strutting walk, his
long, towering home runs, his flashy plays at first base, his
charisma. I will never forget my father patiently translat-
ing Jack Buck's colorful comments into Spanish every time
Orlando Cepeda stepped to the plate. I held on to my dad
firmly as the ball was hit into the air. My dad's rough "play
by play" was full of emotion as the ball kept going back,
"Atrás, atrás, atrássss y la bola se llevó la cerca!!!" I can remember only the ones that went out, twenty-five of them that
year. Each and every one of them forever engraved in the
sacred annals of baseball history.

Orlando excelled for sixteen years in the majors. There
were others—Clemente, Aparicio, Marichal—but Cepeda

was the star in my eyes. Every night, I went to bed dreaming of one day stepping into his shoes to carry on his tradition of excellence. On December 12, 1975, that tradition turned into a cruel nightmare. My hero, the man that I and hundreds of thousands of other kids idolized, was sentenced to a term in federal prison for a drug-law violation.

For years I mourned my hero as if he had died. It was beyond my understanding to put this occurrence into perspective. "God couldn't make mistakes, so how could Orlando?" The question lingered in my mind for many years to come, until one day in 1986, fate brought me face to face with my childhood hero. Eleven years had passed, and time had answered many questions. I wasn't bitter anymore, but I was still disappointed.

At a friend's party on a Friday night, I met Orlando Cepeda, Jr., or as we knew him from television commercials, Orlandito. We began talking and hit it off right away. The twenty-year-old Cepeda was a funny character, never at a loss for words. We spent the night reminiscing about his father's career. It was a dream come true to hear all these stories from a source who had experienced them firsthand. At the end of the party, we exchanged phone numbers, and he invited me to lunch at his house the next day. That night I didn't sleep one bit—I was about to come face to face with my idol.

Saturday morning, I made my way to a very humble yet charming apartment in Burbank, California. I always pictured myself meeting Orlando at a run-down Little League field in my Puerto Rican hometown, Fajardo. In my fantasy, I would have just finished a doubleheader in which I went six for eight with two homers, five RBIs and a couple of stolen bases. I had played it through in my mind so many times: Orlando coming up to me, saying, "You've got what it takes, kid. I'll see you in the big leagues." This had to be the longest running daydream in my entire life.

As I approached the doorstep, I could smell the aroma of red beans seasoned with homemade *sofrito* and fried onions. This wonderful smell reminded me again of my childhood days when every home smelled that way around suppertime.

With great excitement, I finally rang the doorbell. The door opened, and there he was. He stood tall, looking pretty much like I remembered, perhaps a few pounds overweight. "Come in. Orlandito will be right down. You're Carlos, right? Put it there, partner," he said with a deep voice and warm smile.

"Yes sir, Carlos Bermúdez," I replied, and shook the hand of a legend. Time stood still, and the electricity of those yesteryear dreams flashed back through my mind at light speed.

I entered the house and looked around, admiring all the baseball memorabilia on the walls and shelves: Rookie of the Year Award, 1958; National League MVP, 1967; Comeback Player of the Year, 1966; Designated Hitter of the Year, 1973. It was a wonderful trip down memory lane. He walked behind me and answered all my questions. I was overwhelmed by the strangest of feelings; here I was talking to a man I'd never met before, but one I felt I knew so much about. Even the men in the pictures felt like old friends: Mays, McCovey, Maris, Mantle, Perez, Brock, Musial, most of them Hall of Famers. My eyes suddenly focused on one of the photos depicting Willie Mays and Orlando Cepeda standing side-by-side, holding their bats in a batting stance.

"Greatest player I ever saw," he said. The comment struck me because, for me, Orlando was *the greatest,* and his father, Perucho, was probably the best Latin player in the history of the game. Unfortunately, he never had the chance to measure his talent against the big boys in the Majors because the American leagues still excluded dark-skinned players.

Orlandito came down the stairs, and we headed for the kitchen to dig into the succulent *arroz, habichuelas y bistec encebollado,* which was masterfully prepared by Miriam, Orlando's wife. We sat at the table and talked baseball, baseball and more baseball.

As I listened to endless stories, I saw in Orlando a man who was good, pure and simple. He was as human as the next guy, and human beings make mistakes. My hero—now turned friend—had made a few mistakes and paid dearly for them, more than anyone will ever know, but he had paid enough, and his legacy for his performance on the baseball field was long overdue.

Dinner was delicious, and the time came to say good-bye. Once more we walked past the wall of memories, and I stared like a little kid in front of a candy store. Orlando stood there pensively, and with a stroke of the chin, he turned to me.

"Yes, Carlos," said my hero, "it was all that, and then some. The smell of the grass, the crack of the bat, the chants of the fans. Every time I swung that bat, I did it for you and all those little boys who dreamed of being up there themselves one day. Perhaps you won't stand at home plate at the bottom of the ninth with the bases loaded and the game on the line . . ." He put his gigantic hands on my shoulders, looked into my eyes and went on, ". . . but you will have your own glory, and I hope I'm there to cheer you on."

Such words, coming from my hero. He admired the fact that I had come to Hollywood with nothing in order to pursue a writing career. He thought I had a great deal of courage. In a split second, I had become my hero's hero. Go figure.

I shook his powerful hand one last time.

"I'm proud of you, son," he said. "Don't give up on your dream." With that, I walked to my car, overwhelmed by a monumental feeling of hope. The void that was created back in 1975 had been filled.

My hero had regained his place in my personal hall of fame.

Carlos R. Bermúdez

[EDITORS' NOTE: *The veterans' committee finally inducted Orlando Cepeda into the Hall of Fame in 1999.*]

8

THE SPIRITUAL AND THE SUPERNATURAL/ *LO ESPIRITUAL Y LO REAL MÁGICO*

The spiritual is whatever allows us to notice the miraculous nature of life.

Aurora Levins Morales

NO RODEO®

NO RODEO © *Robert Berardi. Used by permission.*

Lavender Roses

"I can't get these lavender roses to grow," Papi complained to me one afternoon.

My father had been working all morning cultivating his rose garden, which in the bright light of this warm July day looked almost too lovely to be real.

"Don't worry about it, José," my mother advised him. "You already have so many beautiful shades of roses."

My mother worried about Papi's constant preoccupation with the perfection of things; my father's high blood pressure and fifty years of smoking his beloved hand-rolled Cuban tobacco gave her reason to be alarmed.

"I promised your mother lavender roses for her birthday," he explained to me. "I've been promising her for the last five years, but *aquí no brota nada . . . nada de nada . . .*"

My father was not a perfect man, but he was a man *de palabra*, a man who kept his promises. He had promised my mother lavender roses for her birthday, and Papi had little time left to work. He swore he would grow the lavender roses for my mother if it was the last thing he did.

Papi and Mami had come to this country from San Juan, Puerto Rico, in 1927. When Papi told my mother that he wanted to move to the United States, she put up quite a fight (family legend has it that she smashed all her wedding plates the night before they left Puerto Rico; she hides a smile when she hears this story but denies it and claims that the plates were stolen). But Mami eventually gave in to her husband's will, as women of her time were raised to do, and she reluctantly said good-bye to her life on the island.

In San Juan, my mother was an avid rose grower, and she was famous for her prized lavender roses, which everybody said were the prettiest in the region. One of the promises my father made to her before they left the island was that she would be able to have a rose garden in the United States. But for many years Papi's promise went unfulfilled. They spent the first thirty years in their new country in the frigid concrete of New York's inner city, and only when I got married and moved them to Southern California with me did they get a chance to have a garden. But after ten years of trying to reproduce her rose garden, my mother gave up on the lavender roses. Although all the conditions were right, she just couldn't get them to bloom. So my father, who had never been the slightest bit interested in gardening—or in roses for that matter, took it upon himself to make them grow. This was the fifth year that he worked in the yard, and even though he didn't like to admit it, he had come to love weeding, pruning bushes and cultivating the soil around the flowers. I think that working in the garden for my mother was one way that my otherwise cantankerous father could show his love for her.

Sadly, the growing season came and went that year, along with my mother's birthday, but the roses never bloomed. Months later, on a crisp winter morning, my father got up at his usual hour, brushed his teeth and washed his face. He sat down at the kitchen table, and my mother served him his customary huge bowl of oatmeal.

But as he raised the first spoonful to his lips, he turned to me and Mami, and, with a somewhat surprised look on his face, said, *"No me siento bien."* And with that brief announcement, "I don't feel well," he toppled to the floor.

Mami ran over to his crumpled body, and frantically tried to revive him. But it was no use. He was gone.

Mami spent the next few months grieving and getting her new life in order, sorting through Papi's things and distributing them among the family, answering sympathy cards, talking to relatives in Puerto Rico and Cuba who called with regularity to ask about her. She put the little house that they had shared for ten years up for sale, and made plans to come to live with us. The house sold rather quickly, and on the day of my mother's sixtieth birthday, the young couple who had bought the house stopped by to deliver some papers. When Mami answered the door, she was startled to see the young woman holding out a lavender rose. Mami thought it was a birthday present and was touched at the kind gesture of the young woman.

"Thank you so much!" Mami exclaimed. "You must have known it was my birthday!"

"I *didn't* know," answered the young woman. "I just wanted to bring you one of these lovely roses from your garden."

"From *my* garden?" Mami asked, with a look of disbelief.

"Yes," the young woman said, as she stepped aside and gestured toward the rose garden.

My mother looked out the front door and tears filled her eyes. In the middle of her garden bloomed the most spectacular field of lavender roses that she had ever seen.

"Ay, José, bendito . . ." Mami gasped, calling out my father's name as she wiped the tears from her eyes.

"They must be a birthday present from above," the young woman said.

My mother just smiled.

Caroline C. Sánchez

Vengo del Mar

My grandmother was born in 1880 in Santurce, Puerto Rico. She was the youngest of twelve siblings and the only girl. Her given name was Carolina del Carmen, but because of her extraordinary beauty, she was called *la bella*, the beautiful one, from the time she was a very small girl.

When my grandmother turned seventeen, her father died. Her mother, who was not in good health and was worried about her daughter's future, struck a deal with a Spanish merchant who frequented Puerto Rico on his business trips. The merchant, Benigno Saavedra, offered to help support my great-grandmother and her family if she would consent to let him marry *la bella*. She did.

Although no one really knows if my grandmother's feelings for my grandfather were inspired by love or obligation, she became his wife in 1897, and he made sure to always keep his promise to her family. My grandfather traveled a lot for business, and the story goes that when he used to come home from his trips out to sea, he would always sing this verse to my grandmother:

vengo yo del mar sólo para verte a ti
y darte un besito en tu boca de corí . . .

My grandfather's brother, Alejandro, was a jeweler living in Puerto Rico who made very good money for those times. In 1908, he was given a gold medal for being *el mejor orfebre de Puerto Rico,* the best jeweler in Puerto Rico. That same year, my grandfather died tragically in a train crash in Cuba, and my mother's family began to suffer economic hardship. According to my grandmother, Tío Alejandro had a wife named Isabel who was very vain and proud. She was also jealous of my grandmother, who at twenty-eight was more beautiful than ever and continued to turn heads wherever she went, no matter that she had five small children trailing behind her.

With her husband gone and her children in need, my grandmother went to Alejandro and Isabel to ask them for help. Although no one really understands why, they refused to help the family. They say that when my grandmother asked him for money to buy food to feed her children, Alejandro said that he couldn't help them out, blaming it on Isabel's expensive tastes and the money spent on fabrics, perfumes and other specialties shipped from Spain.

The family struggled on without his assistance. When my mother reached the age of twelve, she passed herself off as a teenager and got a job in a cigar factory. At the same time, my *tío* Luis got a job as a bookkeeper for a grocery firm in San Juan named *Cebollero.* Things improved quite a bit economically, and they managed to survive.

Time passed and when my mother turned eighteen, she was invited to a ball at *El Centro Español* in San Juan. Like her grandmother, my mother, also named Carolina del Carmen, was a dark-haired beauty who commanded everyone's attention when she walked into a room. It so happened that her *tío* Alejandro was also present at this ball, and when he saw my mother pass by as she danced with her partner, he smiled at her but then turned very pale—this gorgeous young woman he didn't know looked so much like his brother Benigno.

Alejandro approached my mother and asked her if she was Benigno's daughter, and she told him she was. He stammered for a second and then said, *"Nena, soy tu tío Alejandro . . . tu padre era mi hermano . . ."* My mother was courteous in her reply, but remembering the hunger they had suffered because of his selfishness and neglect, she remained aloof.

Many years later, my mother was living in the South Bronx in New York City. She lived in a high-rise building with a kitchen window that faced the back alley. These were the Depression years, and times were hard. Vendors, ragmen and handymen would come through the alley and shout up to the apartment windows, trying to sell their wares and services. Sometimes musicians would come by and play a tune or two, and people would throw a few coins to them from their windows.

This particular day around dusk, my mother heard accordion music coming up from the courtyard. She thought the tune sounded familiar, but it seemed to weave in and out of range. After a few minutes, she heard the same song again, this time louder, and she recognized it as the song that her father used to sing to *"la bella."* My mother thought that a strange coincidence. While she was trying to remember the words, she took a few pennies out of a jar and wrapped them in newspaper to throw them down to the musician. The music went on, but when she got to the window to throw the money down, the courtyard was empty. She pulled away from the window with a chill.

The next day she received a telegram from her sister Francisca in Puerto Rico telling her that Tío Alejandro was dead. My mother, already suspecting the answer, asked my *tía* Francisca when he had died. She told my mother that Alejandro had died the day before at sunset. As my mother listened to her sister's words, she leaned against the window and stared intensely into the empty courtyard.

"*Dios mío*," she whispered, "Alejandro has finally come to ask for forgiveness."

Susan Sánchez-Casal

Feliz Navidad

After eating *pernil, arroz con gandules, pasteles,* and desserts like flan and cake, *Feliz Navidad* and other Christmas songs resonated in the living room as my *tíos* and *tías* sat around singing while my cousins and I opened our gifts from under the tree. Around this time, my *tía* Magaly would disappear into her room and come back wearing her old clothes and accessories from the '70s, and she would put on a little show. She would dance and make us laugh with her songs and her jokes because seeing a smile on all of our faces was what she loved the most. It was her smile that brought us the most joy because we all knew that she was quietly suffering inside.

My *tía* was first diagnosed with breast cancer in 1989 and had her left breast removed. She recovered and regained her strength only to be told in 1997 that the cancer had returned and spread to her spinal cord. Again, my family and I watched her recover from her endless surgeries and nauseating chemotherapy treatments, all the while maintaining that beautiful smile on her face.

My family celebrated her health every day thereafter.

For every holiday, birthday, graduation or any small celebration, we gathered at her house to celebrate and feast as
if it were Christmas every day. She would decorate her
house and prepare everything with love because seeing
our family united was what kept her strong. She had left
the Dominican Republic with nothing but hopes and
dreams to create a better life for her family in the United
States. She studied accounting at night school and came
to run a successful, small cake business in her own home.
Her delicious "Dominican" cakes became famous in our
neighborhood for their incredibly unique decorations.

Tía Magaly was an inspiration for my family as we
watched her continue to work hard even though her body
was weak. Her health began deteriorating in 2001, and we
all worried that the cancer was attacking her body again. I
was to turn sixteen in December, and there had been
plans to throw a sweet sixteen party for me, but my mom
and my other aunts didn't want to because my *tía* was
constantly in and out of the hospital. I spoke to Tía
Magaly, and she made it clear that she wanted us to have
the party. In fact, she told me that she was looking forward to making decorations and baking the cake. Tía
Magaly had spoken, so it had to be done! A month before
my birthday, she and I planned the party. She made the
decorations, went shopping with me for my dress and
made the most amazing cake I have ever seen. I watched
in awe at how this family event gave her the strength and
courage to get up every day and do what she loved
most—supporting and celebrating her family. At my party,
she danced and laughed like someone who had never
been sick a day in her life.

A year later, on December 21, 2002, I embraced that
memory of her as I watched her leave this world behind.
The cancer had spread to her brain, and the tumors
made surgery impossible. My cousins, aunts, uncles and

grandmother all held each other as she passed away peacefully in her hospital bed. Christmas was only four days away, and we knew things would never be the same without her. Instead of preparing for our annual Christmas celebration, we made preparations for her funeral service. We spent Christmas Eve in the cemetery saying good-bye to Tía Magaly for the last time.

On Christmas day, we still gathered at her house, but there was no singing. There was no laughter, no dancing, no eating. Just tears and pain.

Her son could not bear to see our family like this, so he started singing, slowly at first, "*Feliz Navidad.*" Then, pushing back the tears and with more energy he sang, "*Feliz Navidad, Feliz Navidad, Prospero Año y Felicidad!*"

He told us that we had to stop crying and to start celebrating. He said we had to celebrate not because it was Christmas, but to celebrate my *tía*'s life, who she was and what she meant to our family. So we sang this song and many more because we realized that although she wasn't there in physical form, she was still there celebrating with us. Tía Magaly was still with us that Christmas day, in our hearts, in our souls, in our songs and, most important, in our family unity.

Adriana Rosales

On My Altar

Fall reminds me that time is always moving. It is the time of year when the warm Indian summer hardens into the chilly crunch of early winter. It is a time when change flutters all around us, as the tomatoes and basil in the garden make way for squash and figs. Fall gently nudges me to feel my own mortality, and in doing so, it pushes me to celebrate my life. Feeling the season turn reminds me to drink up, enjoy what is here, right now.

Mexicans have mastered the ability to squeeze the fullness of life from the cold reality of death. On November first, they celebrate Day of the Dead, lifting the delicate veil that separates the dead from the living. Graves are cleaned and adorned with flowers and candles. Altars are built, heavy with incense and *cempasúchitl,* the pungent marigold, the sweet acrid scents guiding the spirits back home. It is a scene awesome and bittersweet to observe, a day brimming with both life and death.

Day of the Dead honors those who have passed, but for me it also honors the passage of time itself. It demands that I pause, remember, grieve, celebrate, live fully. In savoring the past and grieving for that which is gone, I clear a path for my future.

Each year as October closes, I build my own altar. Last year as I scattered the orange petals across photos of my grandparents and a newspaper from September tenth, I was pregnant with my second child. This year, my family now complete, I balance my baby daughter in the crook of my arm as my son plays with a smiling sugar skull. I smooth the familiar embroidered cloth and acknowledge my once-young self, this body that will never again grow a child. I trim marigold stems, thinking back on life before my children came—driving home at sunrise, wandering through Oaxaca buying old silver, lazing in bed on a Sunday with my husband. Lighting the incense, I wonder about the future. Will my daughter be a musician? Will my son ride horses? Will I ever hold a grandbaby? I fill my altar with golden flowers, the keys to a business I once owned, a picture of my round, pregnant belly. These symbols of my own milestones brighten as I light the candles. I breathe in my past, hold it—then let it go.

With young children, there is no ignoring the passing of time. It saunters along as we buy new shoes (again!) and shake our heads at how those pants fit just fine last week. As my baby daughter sprouts into childhood, bittersweet pangs rumble as I pack away her now-too-small ruffley sundresses and doll-sized diapers. I mourn a little when my two-year-old son stops requesting a lullaby each night before bed. I pause for a moment, savoring the scene: my daughter crawling toward my son, who zooms his toy train past her. They both erupt in giggles. Then I taste future memories—watching my son fly away without wobbly training wheels, hunting for meteors on a dark night with my teenagers in the high Sierras, rejoicing as a mortarboard is flung into the air.

I watch as my memories play back, a kaleidoscope of

one thing becoming another. I entered adulthood on a Mexican adventure, which became a business in San Francisco selling folk art. I traded that business for motherhood and a home with a delicious garden in Berkeley. As my children grow, I find myself ripening into a writer. The cycle continues; endings become beginnings. And today, as I pull the last tomatoes from their sprawling gangly vine, I look both back and ahead, feeling the turn of the clock.

As the days grow shorter, I bow to the passage of time. I am grateful for the fall harvest: magnificent squashes, warm, spicy soups, sensuous persimmons, dripping with juice. Savoring the delicacies of this brief season, knowing that they are ripe only for the moment, makes them that much richer. I want to drink fully, open-throated. Winter approaches, the wheel keeps turning, my son learns to whistle, my daughter sleeps through the night. I find a gray hair and, smiling, set it aside for my altar next year.

Suzanne LaFetra

The White Butterfly

I come from a family of strong and confident Latino women. My grandmother greatly influenced my life with her common sense, humbleness and caring spirit.

Gloria Estefan

I was lucky: I got to take the afternoon city bus home from high school. Since both my parents worked and my mom's job was closer to my sister's grade school, they decided that I would take the public bus home from school every day.

The bus stop was smack dab right in front of my private, Catholic high school, so all of my affluent classmates could see us "bus riders" waiting for our slow transportation home. At around 2:45 every afternoon, the bus came by and picked up the waiting ragtag group of high-school students. The ride was usually a fun one, filled with lots of teenage chatter and gossip. As the bus dropped off each of my bus mates, I hoped the smelly homeless man or the crazy lady with the big hat wouldn't take the empty seat next to me. Otherwise, it would mean holding my breath or pretending to read one of my homework assignments for the rest of the ride to my stop.

I would reach up to ring the bus bell, letting the driver know my stop was coming, and the big smoggy monster of a bus would pass in front of my house and lurch its way to the bus stop that was only a half-block from my front doorstep. As soon as the bus passed my house, I could always see the small figure of my grandmother, Boya, as all her grandchildren called her instead of *abuela*, already standing at the steps leading from our front yard to the sidewalk. My grandmother had lived with us since I was about seven years old, which had been great until recently when I started feeling smothered and annoyed at what I had previously treasured as my beloved grandmother's attention and coddling.

When I would see her already waiting for me on the steps, I would automatically roll my eyes, frustrated that my seventy-something-year-old grandmother still treated me—a mature fifteen-year-old young woman—like a little kid who needed to be watched like a hawk. Ridiculous, I thought.

After giving her a hug and a kiss, I would tell her, in Spanish, "Boya, you don't have to wait out here for me, you know. It's only half a block. Nothing is going to happen to me. I can take care of myself."

She would shake her head and say, "You never know. There are lots of crazy people out there. Somebody might kidnap you."

I was always in awe at how paranoid she was. At my young age, I never imagined how someone could be that distrustful of everything. I just rolled my eyes (making sure she didn't see it for fear of getting the *chancla* thrown at me) and followed her into the house, hoping she had made one of my favorite dishes for dinner.

Some days, the bus would pass by, and I wouldn't see her in the front yard. I would get excited thinking that maybe she had got caught up watching her favorite *telenovela* and lost track of time, or maybe she had finally realized I was not a kid anymore and had given up babysitting me. As I jumped off the bus and onto the sidewalk, I would happily start my short path home. Before I could take even one step, there she would be, like clockwork, standing down the block, her small body somehow looking bigger on the sidewalk in front of my house—the sergeant standing guard. All I could do was give one of my big, annoyed-teenager sighs, roll my eyes and shake my head as I slowly made my way down that dangerous half a block.

Over the next seven years, my grandmother stood watch as my sister and I grew up and graduated from high school, then moved out of the house to go to college. She even saw me graduate from college, the first woman in our family to do so.

One month after my college graduation, my beautiful, tough, amazing *boya* lost her short battle against pancreatic cancer. Seeing her succumb to such a horrible illness was both heartbreaking and overwhelming.

As my family tried to heal the tremendous hole that her death left in all of us, I began thinking back to my bus trips home from school and her constant vigil over me. Every time I visited my parents on the weekends, I would think of my *boya* as I drove up to their house, always expecting to see her come down the steps to welcome me home. Of course, my guardian was no longer there, and I could only dream of those days of walking half a block to her smile, her hugs or even to her lectures.

One day, my cousin, Wendy, and I were leaving a restaurant, and I suddenly heard her say, "Hi, Boya." When I gave her a puzzled look, Wendy pointed to the white butterfly that was fluttering around us. "That's Boya," Wendy said. "Haven't you ever noticed that the white butterfly is always around, especially when you're thinking about her?"

I had not. Yet, after that day, I began seeing the white butterfly almost on a daily basis. No matter where I was— at work, at home, out shopping or running errands—the white butterfly was always nearby and would always make me stop and smile. I was comforted knowing that my *boya* had never left me—I just had not recognized her presence.

Even today, ten years after her death, the white butterfly still follows me wherever I wander. I see her everywhere I go, fluttering near me, watching over me as I continue my journey, making sure I always reach home safe and sound.

Gracias, Boya.

Jennifer Ramon-Dover

Abuela's Magic

My grandmother was one of the most influential people in my life. She moved in with us right after my grandfather died, and she lived with us from the time I was five years old. Every day when I got home from school, she was there to make my world magical. No matter what we were doing, she turned it into something bigger and brighter than it was.

Before my grandmother moved in with us, she lived in a little house in Wilmington, California. Behind her house was a shallow creek, dry usually, with a tiny wood bridge. When we visited, my grandmother would take my sister and me over that little bridge, which for anybody else was probably no big deal. But because there were no ordinary moments or events for my grandmother, she always got us ready for our walk by talking about our difficult "journey" over the bridge and about how we needed to pay close attention to every step we took. She praised us in advance and after our trip for our "courage" in walking over the dangerous deep creek, and she reminded us that by taking this daily journey we were preparing ourselves for life's bigger challenges.

My sister and I grew up with the impression that we were extraordinarily brave for performing this death-defying act; we felt proud of ourselves and confident. Years later as adults, we had the chance to revisit the "deep creek" and the bridge, and we were amazed to see that it was really just a small puddle covered by an ornamental bridge. My grandmother had created another world for us through her storytelling and her imagination, a world much more intriguing than anything our daily lives offered us.

My grandmother loved to tell me stories about growing up in Puerto Rico, stories about her brothers and sisters and her mother. To her, psychic experiences were just part of everyday life. When her brother Tito died in Puerto Rico, his shadow appeared to her in New York as she sat sipping coffee at the kitchen table. When her first great-grandson was born, she said an angel had appeared blowing a trumpet, saying that the baby was a boy. She wrote down the time, and it was just minutes after my nephew John was born. Just before my grandfather died, she and my mother had identical dreams about him.

So when my adored grandmother died four years ago, I thought that in some way I would "hear" from her, but I never did. I had been trying to have children and had become pregnant several times, but miscarried each time. I had been receiving fertility treatments, and two years after my grandmother's death I was in the process of taking treatment again. I came home from the doctor's office one day and took a nap. While I was sleeping, I heard the phone ring. When I didn't pick up the phone, the answering machine went on. It was my grandmother, and she was saying: *"Hola, Chinita!"* ("Chinita" was her nickname for me.) "I just called to tell you happy birthday; I love you."

When I got up I remembered the dream, and then I

thought how weird it was that my grandmother had mentioned my birthday because my birthday wasn't near. The following week I went to the doctor, and they told me that I was pregnant. I was so happy, I couldn't believe it. When I asked them my due date, they said October third.

October third is my birthday.

Michele Capriotti

Me and Don Paco

The best mirror is an old friend.

Latino Proverb

I woke up crying this morning. I realize the pattern now. I don't tell people how much I love them while I still can. That's the way it was with Don Paco, a chubby, balding, cuddly octogenarian who became my close friend and confidant. In the only photograph of us together, you can see how very dear he was to me. My eyes gleam as I cup my hands on his shoulder. Paco has a smug "she's-with-me; eat-your-heart-out" look on his impish face. It is one of my favorite photographs because I look so radiant. Paco and I seem to bask in each other's light.

It was Paco, not my father, who asked to meet my fiancé, Ed, to give him, as he expressed it, *"el A-OK"* to marry me. My father and I were estranged. He had been a good provider and a protective father. But as I grew older, I could no longer ignore his macho attitude toward my mother. When he cheated on my mother once too often, I finally and reluctantly drew the line and sided with her. I hadn't seen or spoken to him since their divorce over a decade before. So Paco's paternal interest in me was especially important at this turning point in my life.

Paco and I had lunch together once a month at his favorite restaurant, a Spanish *meson* in Puerto Rico, where all the waitstaff knew him and he was treated with grace. He always reminded me that it was our special time together, our own little secret. He'd say, charming *pícaro* that he was, that we needn't share what was said between us with anyone—not with Ed nor his wife, Martha, who had been my coworker for many years at an international cosmetics firm with field offices in Puerto Rico.

During our little lunches, Paco and I would sit with our heads together, and he'd softly tell me about his early life in Spain, his later migration to Cuba. How he fled to Puerto Rico after the Cuban revolution, leaving all of his possessions behind. He had to start his life over many times: a failed marriage, an unsuccessful business enterprise.

I sensed that he had displayed a very generous heart in each bad situation. He left everything to his first wife. In the collapse of his business, he had worried more about his employees than himself. But he had finally found the woman of his dreams in Martha. I shouldn't be jealous, he'd tease. He was certain that I had been his daughter or his wife in another lifetime.

He'd always bring a gift for me to remember him by— as if I could ever forget Paco—a Pierrot doll and later a smaller Pierrot who he said was its child . . . a Japanese tree ornament, intricately carved, yet so tiny and delicate . . . a row of little marble elephants holding tails . . . a small ceramic hearth for my kitchen, which, he told me, was always the heart of the home.

At our last precious luncheon together, he spent a lot of time just holding my hand. Paco shared how he had always hoped to take Martha to Spain to visit the important places of his childhood. He asked me to make sure that she traveled there, should anything happen to him.

When we parted, he accompanied me to my car, as he always did—elegant gentleman that he was. But there was something a little different that day. He seemed reluctant to let me leave and looked back sadly as I drove away. I wanted to stop and ask if anything was wrong, but I was late for my next business meeting across town, so I blew him a kiss and sped off. Shortly afterward, I traveled to my company's headquarters in New York City. The day I returned to Puerto Rico, I was brightly dressed and feeling on top of the world. Life held so much promise! I was met at the airport by another coworker, Aurea, who said that she had guessed somehow that I would be dressed in red because I was in love.

As she slowly drove me home, Aurea announced quietly that she had some bad news for me. I was singularly unprepared for what she was about to say. She explained that Paco had gone fishing over the weekend, and came home excited because he had caught his biggest fish ever and then let it go. Martha prepared one of his favorite Cuban dishes. He kissed her good night, told her how much he loved her and died peacefully in his sleep that evening, his hands folded under his head, like a gentle cherub.

As if that weren't enough for one small heart to bear, she added that on that same Sunday, my father had been rushed to the hospital. He had suffered a massive stroke. I knew immediately what I had to do. It was too late to be with Paco, but perhaps if I rushed to my father's bedside and held his hand, there was still time for us to make amends.

That was twelve years ago.

Today my father is still with me, and he knows that

whatever mistakes he may have made in the past, I'll always love him. There is no doubt in my mind that it was my angel Paco who, not wanting me to be without a father's love, brought us together again.

Marie Delgado Travis

Prayers, Potatoes and a Twister

"Tornados touched down near Dallas," the report said. Hearing this made me grateful to live in the western tip of the state, where the Franklin Mountains act as a buffer against such storms. Then a memory crept in from the back of my mind. I remembered the commotion that brought me outside one day, where I found Abuelita praying and watching a twister twirling in the distance. Abuelita's black hair was touched with silver, plaited in a long braid and wrapped into a bun. Her skin, the color of cinnamon, was wrinkled with time, and her brown eyes were intensely focused on the twister in the sky.

I was more interested in Abuelita's behavior than the funnel-shaped cloud in the distance. At eight, I was already accustomed to her ways. "*Jesús, María y José!*" she'd say at the clap of thunder and "*Jesús mil veces!*" when lightning followed. The beads in her pocket came out whenever she had spare time to pray the rosary. Never did she allow my chatter to interrupt the litany. I never asked about the motives for her invocations of God and his Holy Mother. I grew up in her faith, unquestioning.

I watched as she stood firmly facing the twisting clouds, holding a potato and a kitchen knife. She prayed fervently while keeping an eye on the approaching clouds. She held the potato up, sliced off a piece, and said, "*En el nombre del Padre, vete!*" ordering the tornado to depart in the name of the Father. "*Y del Hijo, no nos hagas daño,*" she said, and another slice fell to the ground as she invoked the Son's name, pleading that the storm do us no harm. "*Y el Espíritu Santo, vete!*" Her strong voice commanded the phenomenon to depart in the name of the Holy Spirit.

The richness of my heritage was learned at Abuelita's knee. Her devotion to the Catholic Church was colored by the culture of her native Mexico. "Nothing is possible without the will of God" was her constant refrain. I had seen her fix medicinal potions and teas from herbs, barks and even the weeds that grew in the field behind our school. She'd brew *istafiate* for stomachaches, *flor de saúco* for hacking coughs and colds, and had a plant in the kitchen that relieved the pain of all types of burns and helped clear my acne. Yes, my grandmother's remedies cured almost anything.

I watched while Abuelita sliced the potato, almost as if it were the twister in her hand. She seemed to be in a trance, oblivious to my presence. As the potato slices fell into the dust, I noticed the unusual form in the sky break up, just like the spud Abuelita was slicing. Abuelita continued pleading with the Holy Mother and all the saints to help her make the cloud disappear. I was enthralled by my grandmother's determination, her prayers and the tools she used. Soon the twister dissipated until it was nothing but a few dark clouds drifting in the sky.

Abuelita lowered her tired arms and said, "*Gracias a Dios, ya se fue.*" It was gone, thank God.

People gathered around us and stared, tracing a line of vision that went from the potato slices on the ground to the knife in Abuelita's hand. A woman threw her arms around my grandmother. *"Muchas gracias,"* she said with tears gathering in her eyes. Abuelita smiled as we turned and went inside.

I never questioned her actions with the potato, but I didn't have to. I know that my *abuelita* performed a miracle that day long ago.

Margarita B. Velez

NO RODEO®

NO RODEO © *Robert Berardi. Used by permission.*

NO RODEO, *Robert Berardi,* ©*2005, reprinted by permission of Robert Berardi.*

Faith of an Angel

Life lessons come in all forms. For me, inspiration came in the shape of a small, forty-pound, five-year-old cousin of mine. I'll be honest, Debra bugged me. I was about to enter my freshman year of high school, and the last thing a teenager wants is a little tag-along cousin. What I didn't realize was that although I felt like I was always the teacher and she was the pupil, roles can be reversed in a matter of seconds. We traded places one hot July afternoon when I discovered that, in the blink of an eye, happiness could be shattered.

We were all gathered at a friend's outdoor wedding reception. The decorations were simple yet elegant, and the setting sun illuminated the bride and groom's already glowing faces. *Comadres* traveled from table to table, catching up on the latest news, because when you come from a small town in South Texas, everyone is family. The children were running around, playing games of tag and greeting their extended family. The evening could not have been better. My friends and I gathered around and talked about our up-and-coming freshman year and all of the hot guys we would be meeting. After all, we were leaving behind the boys of junior high and looking for the "men" of high school. Debra wanted to join my friends and me, but what could a five-year-old contribute to our stimulating conversations?

I left the table where we were sitting, leaving behind my mother, Tía Jeri, Abuela and Debra. I walked inside the house and greeted everyone before making my way to the bathroom. The line wasn't long, thank God, because one body can take only so much punch! As I was washing my hands, there was a thud and the bathroom door came bursting open. It was an older cousin of mine, Sylvia. I will never forget the look of fear, helplessness and shock on her face. She immediately began opening cabinets in a mad dash to find towels. I figured that one of the kids had hurt themselves playing when she blurted out, "Cristina, there has been a terrible accident. Stay inside!"

What kind of accident? Who was involved? Was anyone hurt? Was it anyone I knew?

The questions flooded my mind. I gathered with my friends in the living room amidst the screams and cries of parents panicking to find their children and more towels. A woman approached and told us that a guest who was leaving the wedding had lost control of his car and plowed through the crowd. I couldn't believe it. *How could there be so much joy one minute and tragedy the next?*

Then I heard a voice calling my name. It was Paul, a student of my mother's. He told me that I needed to find my mother because she was looking for me. He then told me, "Debbie has been really hurt." My thoughts immediately went to the only "Debbie" I knew, my cousin Debra's babysitter. *Oh God,* I thought, *poor Debbie.*

I ran outside. Nothing could have prepared me for the war zone I saw. Bodies on the ground, tables and chairs overturned everywhere, and there, the cause of the destruction: a runaway sedan that had finally been stopped by the fence in front of the tennis courts.

I found my mother. She hugged me with tear-filled eyes and told me that we had to leave immediately—Debra was badly hurt! My heart dropped to my feet. Debra? So the girl who got hit by the car was not "Debbie" the babysitter but Debra, my five-year-old cousin. It was little Debra. I was in shock. My mother quickly drove our van around and laid down the backseat. *But where was Debra?* I saw two men running from the barn with a piece of board, perfectly Debra's size. I did not see my tiny cousin until she was hoisted onto the board and laid in the van. Her new white dress and shoes were torn and blood-stained, and on her left shoe was a tire mark, clear as day. We covered her with a blanket my mother kept in the van. It had a picture of *La Virgen* on it; how fitting, I thought. Debra never lost consciousness, but the trip seemed never-ending.

Just as my *tía* Jeri and I were about to lose it completely, Debra spoke in a quiet voice.

"Let us pray together," she said, and *she* led *us* in an Our Father and a Hail Mary. Here she was, a child, broken and bleeding, yet her spirit and faith never strayed. She was trying to comfort *us!* She asked if she was going to die and told us how much she loved us—it felt like she was saying good-bye.

Upon our arrival at the hospital, we were met by her brother, Jacob, and my *tía* Stella. I had never seen Jacob cry before. It terrified me! Debra immediately went into surgery, and we prayed for the best. Six hours later, Debra was brought to the recovery room. We were told that she had suffered extensive injuries and might never walk again. My mother entered the room and took Debra's tiny hand in hers. Debra awoke and asked my mother to lean in. In her ear, Debra whispered, "Tía Norma, I saw God with two angels." My mother broke down and held Debra close.

I learned more that summer in a matter of minutes than

I have in my whole life. I realized that I was so caught up in my "world" that I had not taken the time to see how precious my cousin was, and how lucky I was to be the object of her attention. I also learned from Debra to accept gracefully what life gives you, but to never give up, and to keep on loving and caring for those around you. Above all, I learned from Debra to hold tightly to my faith. Debra's example that day showed all of us that the size of one's heart and the depth of one's soul cannot be judged by age, but only by actions.

Thank you, Debra, for waking me up, and for sharing your lion's heart with us.

Cristina Cornejo

[EDITORS' NOTE: *Debra's recovery was long and painful, but, not surprisingly, she persevered. She not only learned to walk again, but also to dance the ballet folklorico!*]

Feeding the Soul

My parents are not educated. On my mother's side of the family, we are third-generation Texans. My father's parents were from Spain, and he was born in Mexico. Both my parents were very religious and active in the Catholic Church. We couldn't afford to go to Catholic school, but we went to daily Mass in the same way we brushed our teeth. In the evening, we would pray the rosary together as a family, and if our friends came around, Catholic or not, they too were included in our family rituals.

I recall one morning I overslept and was the only one in the family who missed Mass. It was a weekday, so I didn't think much of it. However, I knew my father would be waiting in his pickup that evening (as he was known to do for those of us who overslept in the morning). Since I knew I was the only one who hadn't gone, I didn't think my father would "bother;" but a few minutes before the evening Mass at our local church, I heard my father's knock on my door.

"Chela, didn't you oversleep this morning?" he asked.

"Yes," I replied, "but, Dad, I have a lot of homework, and I don't think I'll be going to Mass today."

I thought the issue was resolved (and *way too easily*) when my father responded compassionately, "Oh, I see. You have homework. Okay."

He started to walk away, and I thought, *Wow! That was easy.* I actually didn't think his response was too out-of-place. Since none of my siblings had ever challenged going to Mass on a daily basis, we really didn't know how he would react. *Hey,* I thought, *we really don't have to go.* I felt somewhat of a heroine, one who had rescued my other siblings from having to attend daily Mass.

But my father hadn't really left.

"So, you have a lot of homework?" he continued to ask.

"Yes," I justified, as I showed him my assignments.

"Okay," he replied, maintaining his interest. "I know now what you studied in school today, so I know you learned something, thus you've fed your mind. What did you have for lunch?"

I replied, telling him as much of the school menu as I recalled.

"That's wonderful!" he said. "I know you fed your mind because you have told me what you learned today at school. I know you fed your body, for you have given me the day's menu. Have you fed your soul today?"

That's all he had to say. I followed him to his pickup and attended Mass. But even more than that, I began to take seriously my father's lesson that I should spend as much time feeding my soul as the rest of me.

My father's lesson that day made me who I am. I went on to combine feeding my mind, body and soul by pursuing graduate degrees in theology, and to this day, I have always worked in ministry positions.

Thanks to my father, when I wake up in the morning, the first question I ask myself is: "How will you feed your soul today?"

Chela González

More Chicken Soup?

Many of the stories and poems you have read in this book were submitted by readers like you who had read earlier *Chicken Soup for the Soul* books. We publish at least five or six *Chicken Soup for the Soul* books every year. We invite you to contribute a story to one of these future volumes.

Stories may be up to twelve hundred words and must uplift or inspire. You may submit an original piece, something you have read or your favorite quotation on your refrigerator door.

To obtain a copy of our submission guidelines and a listing of upcoming *Chicken Soup* books, please write, fax or check our Web site.

Please send your submissions to:

Chicken Soup for the Soul
P.O. Box 30880, Santa Barbara, CA 93130
fax: 805-563-2945
Web site: *www.chickensoupforthesoul.com*

We will be sure that both you and the author are credited for your submission.

For information about speaking engagements, other books, audiotapes, workshops and training programs, please contact any of our authors directly.

Supporting Others

In the spirit of supporting others, a portion of the proceeds from *Chicken Soup for the Latino Soul* will be donated to the National Council of La Raza (NCLR).

Founded in 1968, NCLR began as a regional organization concerned primarily with providing grassroots support to Mexican-Americans in the Southwest. A private, nonprofit, nonpartisan organization established to reduce poverty and discrimination and improve life opportunities for Hispanic-Americans, NCLR is now the largest national constituency-based Hispanic organization and the leading voice in Washington, D.C., for the Hispanic community. Four major functions provide essential focus to the organization's work: capacity-building assistance; applied research, policy analysis and advocacy; public information efforts and special and international projects. These functions complement NCLR's work in five key strategic priorities: education, assets/investment, economic mobility, health and media/image/civil rights.

For more information, please contact:

National Council of La Raza
Headquarters Office
1126 16th Street, NW
Washington, DC 20036
202-776-1750
Web site: *www.nclr.org*
e-mail: *resources@nclr.org*

Who Is Jack Canfield?

Jack Canfield is one of America's leading experts in the development of human potential and personal effectiveness. He is both a dynamic, entertaining speaker and a highly sought-after trainer. Jack has a wonderful ability to inform and inspire audiences toward increased levels of self-esteem and peak performance.

He is the author and narrator of several bestselling audio- and videocassette programs, including *Self-Esteem and Peak Performance, How to Build High Self-Esteem, Self-Esteem in the Classroom* and *Chicken Soup for the Soul—Live.* He is regularly seen on television shows such as *Good Morning America, 20/20* and *NBC Nightly News.* Jack has co-authored numerous books, including the *Chicken Soup for the Soul* series, *Dare to Win* and *The Aladdin Factor* (all with Mark Victor Hansen), *100 Ways to Build Self-Concept in the Classroom* (with Harold C. Wells), *Heart at Work* (with Jacqueline Miller) and *The Power of Focus* (with Les Hewitt and Mark Victor Hansen).

Jack is a regularly featured speaker for professional associations, school districts, government agencies, churches, hospitals, sales organizations and corporations. His clients have included the American Dental Association, the American Management Association, AT&T, Campbell's Soup, Clairol, Domino's Pizza, GE, ITT, Hartford Insurance, Johnson & Johnson, the Million Dollar Roundtable, NCR, New England Telephone, Re/Max, Scott Paper, TRW and Virgin Records. Jack has taught on the faculty of Income Builders International, a school for entrepreneurs.

Jack conducts an annual seven-day Training of Trainers program in the areas of self-esteem and peak performance. It attracts entrepreneurs, educators, counselors, parenting trainers, corporate trainers, professional speakers, ministers and others interested in developing their speaking and seminar-leading skills.

For further information about Jack's books, tapes and training programs, or to schedule him for a presentation, please contact:

Self-Esteem Seminars
P.O. Box 30880
Santa Barbara, CA 93130
phone: 805-563-2935 • fax: 805-563-2945
Web site: *www.jackcanfield.com*

Who Is Mark Victor Hansen?

In the area of human potential, no one is more respected than Mark Victor Hansen. For more than thirty years, Mark has focused solely on helping people from all walks of life reshape their personal vision of what's possible. His powerful messages of possibility, opportunity and action have created powerful change in thousands of organizations and millions of individuals worldwide.

He is a sought-after keynote speaker, bestselling author and marketing maven. Mark's credentials include a lifetime of entrepreneurial success and an extensive academic background. He is a prolific writer with many bestselling books such as *The One Minute Millionaire, The Power of Focus, The Aladdin Factor* and *Dare to Win,* in addition to the *Chicken Soup for the Soul* series. Mark has had a profound influence through his library of audios, videos and articles in the areas of big thinking, sales achievement, wealth building, publishing success, and personal and professional development.

Mark is the founder of the MEGA Seminar Series. MEGA Book Marketing University and Building Your MEGA Speaking Empire are annual conferences where Mark coaches and teaches new and aspiring authors, speakers and experts on building lucrative publishing and speaking careers. Other MEGA events include MEGA Marketing Magic and My MEGA Life.

He has appeared on television (*Oprah, CNN* and *The Today Show*), in print (*Time, U.S. News & World Report, USA Today, New York Times* and *Entrepreneur*) and on countless radio interviews, assuring our planet's people that "You can easily create the life you deserve."

As a philanthropist and humanitarian, Mark works tirelessly for organizations such as Habitat for Humanity, American Red Cross, March of Dimes, Childhelp USA and many others. He is the recipient of numerous awards that honor his entrepreneurial spirit, philanthropic heart and business acumen. He is a lifetime member of the Horatio Alger Association of Distinguished Americans, an organization that honored Mark with the prestigious Horatio Alger Award for his extraordinary life achievements.

Mark Victor Hansen is an enthusiastic crusader of what's possible and is driven to make the world a better place.

Mark Victor Hansen & Associates, Inc.
P.O. Box 7665
Newport Beach, CA 92658
phone: 949-764-2640
fax: 949-722-6912
Visit Mark online at: *www.markvictorhansen.com*

Who Is Susan Sánchez-Casal?

Susan Sánchez-Casal holds a Ph.D. in Latin American literatures from the University of California. She is a tenured professor whose teaching and research expertise includes U.S. Latino studies, U.S. Latino literatures and women's studies. A published author of numerous essays on literary criticism and Latino studies, Susan is also the co-editor of an anthology of critical essays on creating racial and gender equality in teaching and learning in higher education. Susan is a dynamic, motivational and award-winning teacher whose talents for innovation in teaching methods and positive impact on students have distinguished her among her peers.

As an educator, Susan has devoted herself to promoting diversity and equal access in higher education. She is a dedicated mentor to the Latino/a student community on her campus and serves as faculty advisor to Latino/a student organizations. She is the founder and director of ICWES, an intercultural women's empowerment group that seeks to create intercultural cooperation among young women of diverse ethnic and racial backgrounds. Susan is also a member of the executive committee of the Future of Minority Studies (FMS) Summer Institute at Cornell University, a consortium of scholars and academic institutions with a primary interest in minority identity, education and social transformation.

In addition to her academic work, Susan is a powerful motivational speaker who addresses small and large audiences across the nation about Latino history, education, identity and women's empowerment. Susan was born and raised in Southern California and now lives in New York with her husband and family.

Please visit her Web site *www.latinosoul.com* for information on speaking engagements, book signings and Latino resources. For those interested in booking Susan as a speaker, please e-mail her at *susan@latinosoul.com.*

Contributors

Several of the stories in this book were taken from previously published sources, such as books, magazines and newspapers. These sources are acknowledged in the permissions section. If you would like to contact any of the contributors for information about their writing or would like to invite them to speak in your community, look for their contact information included in their biographies.

The remainder of the stories were submitted by readers of our previous *Chicken Soup for the Soul* books who responded to our requests for stories. We have also included information about them.

Maria Luisa Alaniz is professor and chair of the Social Science Department at San Jose State University. She received her B.A. and M.A. from San Jose State University and her Ed.S. and Ph.D. from Stanford University. Her current research, based in her hometown of Stockton, California, focuses on the effects of public policy on personal lives. Her hobbies are reading, hiking and travel.

Maya Alvarez-Galván received her B.A. in Spanish, and M.A. from California State University, Los Angeles. She completed her Ph.D. at USC. She teaches ESL at Mt. San Antonio College. She enjoys traveling with her husband. She is working on a novel focusing on educated Latina women. Contact her at *malvarez@mtsac.edu*.

A first-generation Mexican-American, **Irma Andrade** was born in Texas. She is the daughter of migrant workers who settled in southwestern lower Michigan in 1967. She enjoys writing personal essays and memoirs. In her spare time she enjoys traveling, mountain biking and training in the martial arts.

Ellen Batt is Associate Professor of Modern Foreign Languages and Education at Albertson College of Idaho. She teaches English as a Second Language, German, linguistics and courses for teacher certification in ESL, bilingual education and foreign-language education. She enjoys presenting her research on issues surrounding bilingualism and diversity.

Carlos R. Bermúdez, born and raised in Puerto Rico, graduated from La Salle University in Philadelphia with a B.A. in English and Communications. After writing for a number of television shows in Hollywood, most recently, he co-created and was executive producer of the hit comedy series *Los Beltrán,* produced by Columbia Tristar.

Juan Blea holds a Bachelor of Arts in Humanities from the College of Santa Fe. He works as a system analyst in Santa Fe and is working on completion of a Master of Science degree, specializing in Cognitive Science. He is an avid reader and has written two books, *Under the Same Sky* and *Butterfly Warrior.* He can be reached at *juanblea@sprintpcs.com.*

Michele Capriotti received her Bachelor of Arts from California State University Long Beach, and her Master of Arts from Azusa Pacific University in TESOL. She has been a teacher for twenty glorious years. She loves to travel and spend time with family.

Michele Carlo, a native New Yorker, a Nuyorican and a natural redhead, is a writer/performer whose work appears in New York City as a soloist, as comic character Carmen Mofongo and as a storyteller with The MOTH. Her novella about growing up as a redheaded Latina will be completed in 2005.

Angela Cervantes received her Bachelor of Arts in English from the University of Kansas. She credits her family and childhood in Kansas for most of her inspiration to write. Angela currently resides in Kansas City, Missouri, where she writes a monthly column for *KC Hispanic News,* sits on the board of The Writers' Place and pigs out on *queso fundido* every chance she gets.

Zulmara Cline is an inspirational writer for Latinas/os, publishing many articles dealing with voice, biculturalism and living in two worlds. As an associate professor at Cal State San Marcos, Dr. Cline is also a scholar practitioner, writing extensively in the areas of literacy, diversity and multicultural education. She lives in San Marcos with her family. She can be reached at *zcline@csusm.edu.*

Jose (Joe) Colón was born and raised in Brooklyn, New York, of Puerto Rican descent and is proud of his island heritage. He has been involved in the arts for more than twenty-four years, acting, singing and writing for mostly community events and projects. This will be his first foray into publishing, and he is thrilled to be published among other Latinos who are sharing their own stories of struggle, love, culture and transition.

Randy Cordova, a third-generation Mexican-American, lives in Phoenix, Arizona. He is a features reporter at *The Arizona Republic,* where he covers stories connected to the entertainment industry. He's a graduate of Arizona State University and a member of the Phoenix Film Critics Society and the National Association of Hispanic Journalists. He lives five minutes away from his brother. E-mail Randy at *rrc1230@aol.com*.

Cristina Cornejo received her Bachelor of Science from Texas A&M University in 2003. She currently works for a nonprofit organization specializing in the production of public service advertisements. Cristina is also working to attain her Master of Arts in Communication from Johns Hopkins University. Please e-mail her at *cristina_cornejo@hotmail.com*.

A former English and Women's Studies instructor, **Sylvia M. DeSantis** lives in Pennsylvania with her partner where she divides her time between administrating educational multimedia projects and writing fiction, poetry, and essays that complement her study of holistic healing. Her story was inspired by a true family portrait and is dedicated to both the immigrant women of the early twentieth century who worked hard in their selfless pursuit of the American dream, as well as to our autistic children who affect us in profound and precious ways. She may be reached at *wordsong@sylviamdesantis.com*.

Alejandro Díaz holds an M.F.A. in Film from the University of Miami and a communications degree from the University of Illinois, Chicago. He has written a number of scripts whose themes revolve around the vast Latino experience and is a published writer. Mr. Diaz directed the short film *Pan Dulce y Chocolate,* which was showcased in the following festivals: The 6th Annual Los Angeles Latino International Film Festival, CineSol Film Festival—TX, LEMI Emerging Filmmakers Mini-Fest—CA, San Antonio's CineFestival, and Tulipanes Latino Art and Film Festival—MI. Alejandro's main ambition is to continue writing and producing stories about people and topics that audiences have not been traditionally exposed to.

Johnny Diaz is a staff writer at the *Boston Globe* and was a reporter at the *Miami Herald* where he began writing at age sixteen. Johnny was born and reared in Miami Beach by Cuban exile parents. He visits them often for his mom's flan, his dad's *media noche* sandwiches and the warm weather. Pleas e-mail him at *johnnydiaz@aol.com*.

Maria Ercilla, born in Havana, immigrated to the U.S. at the age of four. Her life has been rich in both Cuban and American traditions, and it is this mix of cultures that has been a great source of inspiration for her writing. She graduated from UCLA with a B.A. in English and an M.A. in Education. She has been teaching Creative Writing and English Literature to high-school students for the past twenty years. She is presently teaching the handicapped. Her stories and poetry have appeared in *Calyx, Puerto del Sol, Amelia* and numerous other journals.

Her many awards include The International Hemingway Poetry Award (1997 and 1998) and the Allen Tate Memorial Award (1998). Her work just recently appeared in *So Luminous the Wildflowers,* an anthology of poetry by California writers. She is presently at work on her third novel, *The Year of the Bad Boy.* Her other interests are photography, collages and reading. Ms. Ercilla lives in Los Angeles, California, with her son and daughter.

Renee Fajardo found out early on that she really loved the art of story-telling. She began collecting and writing family stories for her children ten years ago. Today she is a writer and storyteller in Denver, Colorado, where she lives with her husband, seven children, two cats, a bird, a fish, a dog and a cactus.

Antonio Farias lives in New York, but pines for a place with warmer weather, preferably somewhere with a kiddie water park where he and his daughter, Lina, can pass the time chasing each other through water jets. He is currently working on a novel. You can reach him at *afarias@gmail.com.*

Roberto G. Fernández is a Cuban-American author. He teaches at Florida State University and has published the novels *Raining Backwards, Holy Radishes!* and *En La Ocha y La Doce.*

For thirty years, **Dahlma Llanos Figueroa** was an English and creative-writing teacher, as well as a high-school librarian in the New York City public schools. Her writing is based on her experience as a member of the Puerto Rican community in New York City and on the island. Dahlma is currently revising her novel, *Legacy,* and is working on a collection of short stories. Her work has been published in various literary journals.

Aurelio Deane Font recived his degree in bilingual education from Temple University in 1976. He has worked as a public school teacher, a musician and as a research assistant for the University of California, San Francisco. He can be e-mailed at *togerfont@aol.com.*

Elizabeth García teaches Latino Studies at Hunter College in New York City. She is the founder of two online sites, *www.latinopromo.com* and *www.latinafeminist.com.* She enjoys speaking to various audiences about her experiences as a Latina in the United States. Please e-mail her at *egarci@hunter.cuny.edu.*

Alvaro Garduño received his Bachelor of Arts in Chicano Studies with a minor in Creative Writing from the University of California, Berkeley in 2001. He works with International Scholars and their Health Insurance needs at UHS Tang Center. Alvaro enjoys spending time fixing his home. Please email him at: *alvaro_g14@hotmail.com*.

Rogelio R. Gómez received his Bachelor of Arts from The University of Texas at San Antonio in 1980, and his Master of Arts, 1990, from Southwest Texas State University at San Marcos, Texas. Roy enjoys riding his motorcycle, tattooing, jogging and playing the button accordion. He is completing his first novel.

Chela González has an undergraduate degree in psychology, and graduate and post-graduate degrees in theological studies. She has taught elementary to graduate students and has served as a Youth Minister, Catechetical Leader, Pastoral Associate and Permanent Deacon Formation Director. She is currently Archdiocesan Director of the Office of Catechesis in Santa Fe.

Linda M. González has been writing since the seventh grade. She received her B.A. from Stanford in English: Creative Writing and finally claims herself as a writer twenty years later. She is the mother of Gina and Teotli, her inspiration to create caminos of love and healing for this and future generations.

Religion and ritual have always been of interest to **Mónica González.** In the early '90s, she earned her B.A. in Religious Studies and M.A. in Theology. Since then she has worked as a campus minister and is currently developing a prayer book for young adults. Her e-mail is *livelongyprosper@yahoo.com*.

Cuban-born **Barbara Gutiérrez** lives in Miami where she has worked as a journalist in both print and television. For the past four years, she has worked in public and media relations. Barbara has always been interested in literature and belongs to a feminist women's book group. You can e-mail her at *gestela44@aol.com*.

Nancy Harless is a nurse practitioner now exercising her menopausal zest through travel, volunteering in various healthcare projects and writing about those experiences. Most of her writing is done in a towering maple tree, in the treehouse built specifically for that purpose by her husband, Norm. She is currently writing a book, *Womankind: Connection and Wisdom 'Round the World,* about strong, beautiful, courageous women who have illumined her journey. E-mail her at *nancyharless@hotmail.com*.

Patricia L. Herlevi Balquin was born of mixed heritage and considers herself a jane-of-many-trades. This fosters a sense of oneness with all races and species.

Cindy Jordan was born in Redondo Beach, California. Cindy wrote

Billboard's 1983 country song of the year, "Jose Cuervo, You Are a Friend of Mine."

Heather J. Kirk is a writer and photographer, and often combines both via digital artist. She published a book of poetry and can be reached at *HJKirk@juno.com*.

Suzanne LaFetra has contributed to numerous newspapers, magazines and literary journals. She lives in Northern California with her family, and is currently at work on a memoir. Contact her at *suzlafetra@yahoo.com*.

Yahaira Lawrence is a mother of two gorgeous children, Aislynn and Gabriel. She will be graduating from Pace University in Spring 2006 with two bachelor of art degrees in English and Applied Psychology. She is currently working on numerous writing projects and hopes to become a successful romance novelist.

Aurora Levins Morales is from Maricao, Puerto Rico, and lives in Berkeley, California, with her daughter, Alicia Raquel. She is a full-time writer and community historian, and the author of three books, and many poems, stories and essays.

Melody Delgado Lorbeer is a freelance writer living in the Jacksonville, Florida, area. She is a wife and mother of two, and enjoys reading and long walks on the beach. She is currently at work on a middle-grade children's novel. Please e-mail her at *cms6731@aol.com*.

Charles Arthur Mariano lives in Sacramento, California, born and raised in the Central Valley town of Merced, California. Charles currently works for the state government at a low-level position and writes in the basement of that building after hours.

Nilsa Mariano holds a Bachelor of Arts and Master of Arts from Binghamton University, New York. She teaches at a two-year college and does storytelling locally as well as for *Spoken Word*. She is published in several online literary 'zines.

Cynthia Leal Massey is the award-winning author of *Fire Lilies*, a historical novel of the Mexican revolution. Her second novel, *The Caballeros of Ruby, Texas*, is a 2003 WILLA Award finalist for Best Original Paperback. Massey is a magazine editor in San Antonio, Texas. Visit her Web site at *www.cynthialealmassey.com*.

Jacqueline Méndez is a former schoolteacher and is currently working on her writing on a full-time basis. She has a master's degree in education and a bachelor's degree in liberal arts. She has recently completed her first manuscript novel for young adults titled *Heart of the Jaguar.* You may e-mail her at *jmendez27@hotmail.com.*

Colin Mortensen-Sánchez is an award-winning writer and public speaker who attended UC Berkeley, appeared on MTV's *Real World,* and runs the popular Web site *www.colinsworld.com.* His authorial debut, *A New Ladies' Man: A Complete Guide to Getting, Pleasing, and Keeping the Girl,* hits bookshelves on August 2, 2005. Yippee!

Kathy Cano Murillo, the "Crafty Chica," is an artist, newspaper columnist and book author from Phoenix, Arizona. She is a pop-culture junkie addicted to glitter, reality TV, movies, music and quad mochas. See more of her work at *www.CraftyChica.com* or e-mail her at *kathymurillo@hotmail.com.*

Ruben Navarrette, Jr. received his Bachelor of Arts from the University of California, Berkeley in 1996. He works for the FOX television network in National Promotions working on such shows as *American Idol, The OC,* and the hit reality series *The Simple Life.*

Ruben G. Navarrette, Sr. a native of Central California, had a law-enforcement career that spanned from 1966 to 2003. He was a deputy constable for Fresno County, a police sergeant for the Sanger Police Department, a district attorney investigator in Fresno County and a Labor Standards Investigator for the State of California.

Marta Alicia Oppenheimer was born and raised in Puerto Rico. She received a bachelor's degree from Clark University and a master's degree from Pratt Institute of Art. She is currently a successful artist and, hopefully, a future author. She lives in Miami with her three wonderful dogs and her spoiled fat cat, Budweiser.

Norma Oquendo grew up in Connecticut, but currently resides in North Carolina where she works as an insurance manager. She has been writing poems since she was in elementary school. She recently published two books of poems and is currently working on her first novel. Please e-mail her at *spring049@yahoo.com.*

Johnny Ortez graduated from the University of Texas at Arlington with his Bachelor of Arts in Communications/Journalism. He has been a freelance writer for a variety of publications since 1996. Currently, Johnny lives in Los Angeles with his partner of two years, Kirkland Tibbels, and their red, short-hair, miniature dachshund, Rufus. Johnny works for Funny Boy Films, the nation's first gay and lesbian film studio. He is working on a novel and screenplay.

Salvador González Padilla received his Bachelor of Arts in Communications from the prestigious Loyola Marymount University, Los Angeles in 1995. Salvador currently divides his time between his three passions: teaching, acting and writing. A published poet, Salvador is currently working on his first novel. Please e-mail him at *api2010@post.com*.

Xiomara J. Pages is a freelance writer, journalist and motivational speaker. She is the author of four books and has given workshops in the United States, Europe and Latin America. She volunteers for the International RETT Syndrome Association in Maryland (an illness that her daughter Sandra suffers from). Xiomara is involved with parents of disabled children, the elderly, domestic violence and women's issues. She supports all the arts in her community. Please e-mail her at *PortaCu@aol.com* or *www.xiomarapages.com*.

Steve Peralta is a freelance writer and media consultant. He received his B.A. degree in English from the University of Colorado at Denver in 2000 and currently lives in San Antonio with his two sons, Stevie and Benjamin.

Lauren Pérez is twenty-one, a Nuyorican amateur writer from the Bronx with a B.A. in Forensic Psychology from John Jay College. She is blessed to have her mother, Barbara, Uncle Ivan, friend Mary Jane Torres, and Heriberta Figueroa, her *abuelita*, who unconditionally encourage her creativity. *Siempre Pa'lante!* E-mail Lauren at *perez_lauren@msn.com*.

Mary Helen Ponce is the author of *Hoyt Street, An Autobiography*. She holds a Ph.D. from the University of New Mexico and has been published in France, Germany, Mexico and Spain. She is currently at work on an eighteenth century historical novel. She can be reached at *mhpon@aol.com*.

Jennifer Ramon-Dover lives in Los Angeles, California, where she's a marketing manager with a major motion-picture studio. She thanks her husband, James, her Mexican mother, Ana Maria, her Peruvian father, Simon, and especially her late Mexican grandmother, Julia Escobedo, for always inspiring her to keep reaching for her dreams.

Regina (Reggie) Ramos is a Chicana who loves to travel, eat and laugh. She lives in California and remains active with her family, friends, Trenzudas and community. Ultimately, Reggie wants to obtain a master's degree and teaching credentials.

Anjela Villarreal Ratliff graduated with a B.A. from San Jose State University in California. Her work has been published in various publications, including *Cantos al Sexto Sol: An Anthology of Aztlanahuac Writing* and *The Mesquite Review*. Anjela grew up in Southern California, but now lives in Austin, Texas.

Esther Bonilla Read taught school for many years. She has always written in her spare time. Esther currently teaches part-time for Texas A & M University in Corpus Christi, Texas. She and her husband enjoy traveling, gardening, reading, attending movies, and visiting their four children and four grandchildren.

Rick Rivera, the son of illiterate farm workers, started college when he was thirty while working full-time in a factory. He received his M.A. in English from Sonoma State University and has published two novels, *A Fabricated Mexican* and *Stars Always Shine*. Rivera is a college English instructor in California.

Liza M. Rodriguez was born and raised in Puerto Rico. She is a wife, mother and educator. She has developed community-based education programs and city-wide initiatives in Philadelphia. She is currently pursuing her doctorate degree in Urban Education at Temple University.

Sylvia Rosa-Casanova, daughter of two Puerto Rican immigrants, was born and raised in New York City. She is the author of *Mama Provi* and *The Pot of Rice*, a picture book based loosely on her childhood memories. Sylvia lives in Congers, New York, with her husband and two sons.

Adriana Rosales is currently a student at Rutgers University majoring in English and education. She enjoys reading and writing poetry. As an English teacher, she hopes to inspire individuals to be creative and thoughtful because she believes knowledge has the power to change the world and people's lives.

Mónica García Sáenz is a native of Kansas City, Missouri, whose roots grow deep in Chihuahua, Mexico, where she spent her childhood summers. She feels blessed to be 100 percent bilingual and bicultural. She now lives in South Florida and is a mother of three and loves reading, writing and cooking authentic Mexican food. She currently has a few books in the "making." Please e-mail her at *monica_garcia_saenz@hotmail.com*.

María Luisa Salcines was born in Guantánamo, Cuba, and immigrated to the United States in 1963. Maria is a certified parent educator for The International Network for Children and Families. She is the author of *Little Things Remembered*, a collection of stories about life, parenting and cultural identity. For workshops and author visits, she can be reached at 956-631-7667 or e-mail her at *MLSalcines@aol.com*.

Caroline C. Sánchez comes from a long line of Spanish and Puerto Rican storytellers whose rich imaginations played an important part in her daily life. Caroline enjoys music, the arts and reading. She has many hobbies, among them, growing roses.

Melissa Annette Santiago is a language arts teacher at Pembroke Pines Charter High School in Pembroke Pines, Florida. She received her B.A. in English Literature from Florida International University in 2003, and is currently pursuing her M.A. in English Literature.

Raised in the nation's poorest congressional district, **Deborah Rosado Shaw's** strategies for success formed a bridge from a tough inner city beginning to award-winning entrepreneur and advisor to Fortune 500 CEO's. As founder of Umbrellas Plus, LLC. and Dream BIG Enterprises, Deborah has designed, negotiated and closed multi-million dollar deals. The critically acclaimed author of *Dream BIG!* is a graduate of Barnard College and lives with her three sons.

Robert Suarez received his degree in Computer Information Systems from Calumet College of St. Joseph in 2003. He is fifty-four years old, married and works as an Industrial Fabricator in the Chicago South Suburban area. Robert enjoys a passion for Cubs baseball, genealogy and operating an Internet bookstore. Although he does not intend to pursue writing as a hobby, he is eagerly waiting to pen his memoirs, tentatively titled, *Cubs Win . . . I Lived to See the Cubs Win!* Unfortunately, his memoirs may have to be written by his descendents.

Marie Delgado Travis is very proud of her Nuyorican roots. She writes poetry and prose in Spanish and English. She worked in marketing/ advertising on behalf of top international companies for over twenty years. Marie is married to Edmunds, a retired attorney. They divide their time between homes in Houston, Texas, and Isla Verde, Puerto Rico. Contact Marie at *marilutravis@aol.com.*

Olga Valle-Herr earned her Bachelor of Social Work, with honors, from the University of Texas-Pan American. Since her retirement, she takes creative writing classes. She is working on her first collection of poems for a book. She loves reading, writing and time with family. She welcomes e-mail at *poetaglo@aol.com.*

Margarita Velez is a writer from El Paso, Texas. Her work has been published in the *Southwest Woman, Deming Headlight* and the *El Paso Herald Post.* The *El Paso Times* published her weekly column. Velez has just completed a novel. Please contact her at *mbvelez@elp.rr.com.*

C. M. Zapata has a forthcoming memoir, *Magic Mountain*, with Avalon Publishing and has work in *Under the Fifth Sun: Latino Literature from California* (Heyday Books). She has been published in the Hispanic Link News Service, *Newsweek* and other international publications, sharing her son's courage and raising awareness about the rare genetic disorder, Fibrodysplasia Ossificans Progressiva (FOP). FOP turns muscle into bone with tumor-like swellings, and is usually heralded by malformed large toes missing a joint. For information about FOP, go to *www.IFOPA.org.*

Chicken Soup African American Soul
Chicken Soup African American Woman's Soul
Chicken Soup Breast Cancer Survivor's Soul
Chicken Soup Bride's Soul
Chicken Soup Caregiver's Soul
Chicken Soup Cat Lover's Soul
Chicken Soup Christian Family Soul
Chicken Soup College Soul
Chicken Soup Couple's Soul
Chicken Soup Dieter's Soul
Chicken Soup Dog Lover's Soul
Chicken Soup Entrepreneur's Soul
Chicken Soup Expectant Mother's Soul
Chicken Soup Father's Soul
Chicken Soup Fisherman's Soul
Chicken Soup Girlfriend's Soul
Chicken Soup Golden Soul
Chicken Soup Golfer's Soul, Vol. I, II
Chicken Soup Horse Lover's Soul, Vol. I, II
Chicken Soup Inspire a Woman's Soul
Chicken Soup Kid's Soul, Vol. I, II
Chicken Soup Mother's Soul, Vol. I, II
Chicken Soup Parent's Soul
Chicken Soup Pet Lover's Soul
Chicken Soup Preteen Soul, Vol. I, II
Chicken Soup Scrapbooker's Soul
Chicken Soup Sister's Soul, Vol. I, II
Chicken Soup Shopper's Soul
Chicken Soup Soul, Vol. I-VI
Chicken Soup at Work
Chicken Soup Sports Fan's Soul
Chicken Soup Teenage Soul, Vol. I-IV
Chicken Soup Woman's Soul, Vol. I, II

To order direct: Telephone (800) 441-5569 • www.hcibooks.com
Prices do not include shipping and handling. Your response code is CCS.